KUNG FU:
THE LEGEND CONTINUES

by

MICHAEL SLOAN

 BearManor
Media

Orlando, Florida

Published in the USA by
BearManor Media
1317 Edgewater Dr. #110
Orlando, FL 32804
www.BearManorMedia.com

Softcover Edition
ISBN: 978-1-62933-830-9

Printed in the United States of America

Table of Contents

Chapter One
DAVID CARRADINE

WHEN I FIRST MET DAVID CARRADINE it was like meeting a force of nature. And a *dangerous* one at that! He was charming, mercurial, volatile, passionate, willful, spiteful, endearing and, above all things, a wonderful actor. When I first met him, he was wearing a jeans shirt unbuttoned to the waist, designer jeans and cowboy boots. He wore a silver belt buckle. He had several tattoos on his body including a serpent snake that wound around onto his back. When I first met with him about *Kung Fu: The Legend Continues*, David was quietly spoken, reflective and introspective. But you could see that there was a fiery volcano waiting to be unleashed at the slightest provocation. I had been warned that David Carradine would be a handful to deal with---and he *was*! But, as it turned not, *not* with me. I think he sensed that I had a good handle on what the show should be. I was reminded of a line out of *Gunfight at the OK Corral*, a movie made in 1957, where Wyatt Earp and Doc Holiday were together in a barber shop. Doc tells the Marshal that he *"liked his cut"*, meaning his demeanor. I think David Carradine *"liked my cut"*. For some reason he had confidence in my ability to put together a great TV series for him. I do not know what he based that on, except his own instincts. We formed a bond that, for better or for worse, stayed the course that transcended the show. We shot 88 episodes of the TV series over four years. Some of them were wonderful. After I started working on the TV series, I did not have much time to deal with the "David Carradine" craziness, which could be pretty crazy. I was concentrated on the scripts for the episodes, most of which I wrote over the four years.

1

I went to the set a lot, but really just to touch base and make sure nothing had gone out of hand. David could be mercurial and perverse, but I had this saving grace during our relationship. He *loved* the scripts on *Kung Fu: The Legend Continues*! I wrote about 50 of the 88 episodes personally, and that was my salvation. As long as I was writing terrific scripts for the show, I could stay out of his line of fire.

In his signature role as Kwai Chang Caine, David had a soft-spoken way of speaking which was slightly stilted, at times confrontational and always direct. He could assume the Kwai Chang Caine accent easily as if it was part of his own speech-pattern. Which it was *not*. When he became Kwai Chang Caine, there was no mistaking when he was in the role. Then he could lose it just as quickly as David Carradine. I remember a classic time where I was on the set of the show. David was telling a story about a young woman he had been introduced to whom he was not overly fond. The director called for action just as David was hitting his stride. He paused in his character of Kwai Chang Caine, said in his soft-spoken line: "*I do not know.*" As soon as the director said the word "cut", David went back into his story of this dreadful actress he had encountered without a pause. He could turn the Caine inflections on and off at will. That always made me laugh.

When David Carradine was given a star on the *Hollywood Walk of Fame*, I was asked if I would present it to him. I considered it an honor. We had finished shooting the TV show at this point, but I turned up on the *Hollywood Walk of Fame*. David was there and so was Chris Potter, his co-star. They had gotten close over the years of *Kung Fu: The Legend Continues*. I stood up to the microphone. There were a lot of people there, fans and friends. David's brother Robert Carradine was there as well. I told the gathered crowd that we had a pet name for David. The crew called him "*Sparky*". Over the walkie-talkies we could hear the First A.D. saying to one of the drivers: "Okay, let's get Sparky traveling." A minute later, I could hear: "We need Sparky on the set!" Another pause. Then I would hear the First A.D. saying: "Has anybody here *seen Sparky?*" That generated a lot of laughter from the onlookers, particularly from Robert Carradine. I looked over at David who was smiling broadly. When he stepped up to receive his "Star", which Chris Potter gave to him, he was genuinely touched about the affection from his friends and family around him. I never forgot that moment.

Gregg Mayday was the executive at Warner Bros of *Kung Fu: The Legend Continues*. He was a great guy, very personable, very knowledgeable and a terrific boss. He held a meeting at Warner Bros Studios for a kind of "meet-and-greet" for David Carradine to get to know the Warner Bros executives. Gregg Mayday had hired a Supervising

Producer to join my staff named Maurice Hurley. Maury had a terrific sense of humor, was a very good writer and I liked him immediately. Toward the end of the First Season of the show things got tough between us and at the end of that 1ˢᵗ Season Gregg Mayday had let him know that he was going to hire a new Supervisor Producer. I had been sorry to see Maury go, but we had a lot of laughs on the show. This was back in the early days. Gregg Mayday had asked for this meeting and David Carradine was there. David was dressed in his usual attire, a silk shirt unbuttoned to his navel, myriad necklaces and rings, designer jeans and cowboy boots. He had brought his wife Gail with him.

I had met Gail Jensen a few years prior to this meeting before she had become Mrs. David Carradine. She had been David Summerville's girlfriend, a singer who had been in the *Four Preps* 50's pop group—which included Glen Larson. At that time, Glen Larson was a major force at Universal Studios and had long ago bid farewell to the 50's pop scene. But he had been talked into making a kind of comeback to the pop scene by Tom Moffit, a rock promoter in the Hawaiian Islands. Glen, along with the other *Four Preps*---Bruce Belland, David Summerville and Ed Cobb---was going to play the Hawaiian Amphitheater for one performance only. The group got together for moral support. Bruce Belland was a riot. David Summerville's girlfriend at that time was this *same* Gail Jenson before she hooked up with David Carradine. Gail was a very sweet, promiscuous honey, who even had a romantic encounter with me, even though she was spoken for.

Lap Dissolve---as the television executives would say---and there she was with David Carradine at this conference table meeting at Warner Bros. Gail wore a long fur coat which was open right down to her naval! She was wearing jeans and no shoes. David Carradine and Gail entered the conference room. It was pretty crowded at this point with Warner Bros brass. Gail took one look at Carradine, clutched his arm and said: "Oh, look who's here, David! It is Michael!" Where she proceeded to kiss me on the lips and hugged me. When we broke the embrace, I glanced over at David, but he was smiling and seemed to be enjoying this "reunion" immensely. Gail sat at the head of the conference table and David sat beside her. Gregg Mayday entered the fray, said hi to everyone assembled and they all found their seats. But it was a little difficult for the Warner Bros executives to know where to *look*! Every time Gail leaned over the table, with her fur coat open to her naval, her breasts were exposed to all. She seemed to be oblivious to the effect she was having on the Warner Bros executives. I glanced over at David who had a big grin on his face. He winked at me. The meeting went on for some time, with Gregg Mayday talking about *Kung Fu: The Legend Continues* and their plans for its initial launch. I had written the 2-hour Pilot script. I caught Gregg Mayday's eye and he seemed to be having a good time. I know I *was*! And David Carradine was having a *grand* time!

We had brought a wonderful Casting Director on board for *Kung Fu: The Legend Continues* named Susan Forrest. She was charming, savvy, forthright and knew all the actors on the Toronto scene, which was where the TV series would be shot. That included the players at the *Stratford Festival Theatre*. We would use a number of them during the course of the series. Susan Forrest was just a delight to know and to work with.

Chris Potter auditioned for us for the role of "Peter" on *Kung Fu: The Legend Continues*. He gave a terrific audition and seemed to be a really good guy. Chris let me know that he *really* wanted to get this role! In the end, it came down to Chris Potter and another contender for the part. Maurice Hurley was leaning toward the other actor who had auditioned for the role, but I was leaning toward Chris. It came down to Gregg Mayday to cast the deciding vote. He chose Chris Potter… and the rest is TV series history!

Tragedy finally took its toll on David Carradine. He died in his hotel room in Central Bangkok. It was ruled a suicide, or misadventure, which involved autoerotic asphyxiation, although there were continued reports that David had been murdered. None of these allegations were ever proven. But I felt that I had lost a dear friend in David Carradine.

I remembered a time when I was sitting in an outdoor café with some friends. I had not seen David enter, but suddenly there he was sitting beside me. He just gave me a kiss on the forehead and moved into the bar of the restaurant. No words were spoken between us. We had a kind of shorthand that I thought was, in a word, *mystical*!

I never forgot that moment with the free-spirited and mercurial David Carradine.

It turned to be a defining moment for me and plunged me into the most rewarding experience I ever had during in my television career.

Here were some of the most memorable episodes for me on the Kung Fu show.

4

Chapter Two

BLACK WIDOW

THIS EPISODE OF *KUNG FU: THE LEGEND CONTINUES* featured the skills and the considerable acting ability that Scott Wentworth (aka Kermit Griffin) brought to his role. He soon became an integral part of the ensemble cast and a fan favorite. There were dark overtones to his Kermit character which could be mysterious and lethal. Which made him that much more believable. When he headlined an episode, it was an event. Scott Wentworth, in my mind, and in the audience's mind, was a true original!

But I digress from our plot!

Kermit Griffin was a dangerous one-time mercenary who had fought other people's wars. He had been Paul Blaisdell's friend, possibly his *only* friend, when he joined the 101st Precinct squad. He could be cordial and friendly, but beneath the surface the Precinct gang had tried in vain the find a handle that would define him. Mostly they left Kermit alone. So it was extraordinary to see Kermit enter the precinct in a very good mood. In fact, his mood was positively jocular! He bounded into the precinct house with a smile on his face. He greeted Detective Jody Powell with: "Good looking today, Detective Powell" and Detective Mary Margaret Skalany with: "You, too, Mary Margaret!"

He paused beside Peter Caine's desk, leaned in conspiratorially to him and said: "How goes the battle of Jordan?"

In the show, Peter had been dating an undercover cop assigned to the 101st Precinct named Jordan McGuire, aka Kristin Lehman. The actress had appeared in six episodes and was a real find for our *Kung Fu: The Legend Continues* show. She went on from there to a slew of stellar starring roles including: *Poltergeist: The Legacy, Judging Amy, The Killing, The Outer Limits, Motive* and *Altered Carbon*.

When Kermit pivoted to his office, still beaming, Peter looked at the other detectives at the 101st Precinct who exchanged glances. Mary Margaret Skalany looked at Kermit's office, where she could see him behind his inevitable computer, and said: "He's *sick!*" Detective Jody Powell shook her head emphatically. "He's *in love!*"

Captain Karen Simms emerged from her office and dumped some files onto Peter Caine's desk. She was a new Detective at the 101st Precinct, forthright and savvy. We will come to her later in another episode. She asked who they were talking about. Peter said the rumor was that Kermit had a new ladylove! Captain Simms was seriously alarmed. Mainly because she harbored some romantic thoughts about Kermit herself!

"That's ridiculous!" she said. "When have you *ever* heard Kermit talking about another woman except his sister Marilyn? Kermit with a girlfriend! Now I've heard everything!"

Captain Simms returned to her office and slammed the door. Peter glanced at the other detectives and said wryly: "Me thinks the lady doth protest too much!"

The thought that Kermit, the ultimate loner, would be smitten with a member of the opposite sex was unthinkable. But there was no other explanation for his good-natured behavior. Peter's attention turned back to Jordan McGuire. Their relationship had had its share of ups and downs. Right now they were going through a rough patch. That was the intriguing premise for this episode of *Kung Fu: The Legend Continues*. The director was T.J. Scott, a terrific director who brought his own sense of style to the show. His first sequence was shot in the Chinatown streets. It was a very long continuous take on a *Steady-Cam* following David Carradine as Kwai Chang Caine and Peter Caine as his son. The take must have lasted four minutes, which was very unusual for the show, but it was a style that T.J. Scott used to perfection. Peter was telling his father the gossip from the 101st Precinct and about Kermit Griffin's uncharacteristically jovial moods. Caine looked at his son askance.

"You are taking lessons in romance from *Kermit the Frog?*"

Peter laughed, but he had to admit that it was very strange behavior for Kermit to be so wantonly out-of-control. Then Caine's attention had been diverted. He glanced over at a good-looking, somewhat intense man who was watching father and son from across the Chinatown street. There was a smile on his lips, but it did not reach his eyes.

They were glacial. Caine knew at once he was looking at a formidable foe. Peter asked him if he knew the man standing on the Chinatown street.

Caine said: 'I do, and yet, I do *not*.' Peter remarked that he loved Caine's obscure riddles and drove away. The Satanic young man, whose name was *John Latrodect*, gave Caine an ironic wave. The throng of people in the Chinatown street obscured him for a moment. When Caine looked back, Latrodect had gone.

The encounter had brought a *sense memory* back to Caine. In the temple he had been attacked by assassins in black who had dragged a thick netting around his head, incapacitating him. The memory was brief but disturbing to Caine. He knew that this sadistic killer would bring grief to the Chinatown community.

Back at the 101st Precinct we were introduced to Peter's new girlfriend, Jordan MaGuire. She was a sassy, take-no-prisoners kind of a girl who was working undercover at the 101st Precinct. When we first see her, Detective Roger Chin reacted to her striking persona. He said: "Who is *that*!" Sergeant Broderick glanced over. "Detective Jordan Maguire, on loan from vice. She'll break both of your arms if she catches you looking at her!" Detective Chin said ironically: "Will I need them *today*?" Sergeant Broderick gave him a wry look.

Peter Caine was concerned that Jordan McGuire was going undercover to try and nail a serial killer. Peter did not think she had the right "bait" for this potential killer.

Jordan leaned into him. "You're thinking of handing this case over to an Officer in Traffic Control? I am the right build and the right age. Not to mention the right curves. You don't run my life!" But then Jordan added, mischievously: "But I *do* like sleeping with you!"

Peter grabbed her arm. "Can you say that a little louder?" he muttered. "So the rest of the precinct can hear it?"

Jordan grinned. "You think it's a secret?"

She gave Peter a major kiss on the lips and moved away. Kermit came up beside Peter and put an arm around his shoulders. "It is tough at the beginning of a new relationship. The moods, the subtleties of emotion. You will learn how to read the lady."

Peter glanced at him, irritated. "Maybe I should have asked an expert like *you*!"

Kermit just smiled and walked away.

Later, we saw that Caine had been cornered in one of the Chinatown streets by assassins. He fought off them off, but there were too many of them. They threw a constricting net around his head and shoulders. Eventually Caine found himself trapped in a cellar underground. The director T.J. Scott's handling of this scene was masterful. The "Spiderman" came out of the shadows to confront Caine with sinister menace.

"You are Caine," he said. "I am John Latrodect."

Caine said: "What is it you want to talk to me about?"

"You are revered member throughout the Chinatown community. 'Go to Chinatown. Talk to Caine. He will help you.' I represent some wealthy businessmen."

"You represent creatures of the night who do your bidding at the least provocation," Caine spit out. "I have not forgotten the torture your sect put me through at the temple."

"What sect would that be, sir?" Latrodect asked him, matter-of-factly.

"The sect," Caine said, "of the Black Widow Spider!"

Latrodect shrugged. "I understand they are quite prevalent in the Western States, but I would be rather surprised to find any of them in a large Mid-West city such as this one."

"What is it you seek from me?" Caine demanded.

"People in Chinatown heed your advice and counsel," Latrodect said. "You are, after all, a *Shambala Master*. You will persuade your friends the inevitably of my…"

Caine interrupted: "Your *infestation*?"

Latrodect smiled. "That is not the word I would have used, but that will suffice. You are getting weak, Caine. I have introduced a poison in your system. It is getting stronger. We did not give you lethal dose, of course, just enough to take the edge of hostility. You are an apothecary in the China community, is that not correct?"

Caine was way ahead of him. "You wish me to administer those who would be afflicted with this insidious plague?"

"A little Earl Grey with some harmless properties that you will mix in," Latrodect said.

"So you can press your spider's venom into my herbs," Caine retorted. "So you can control their minds!"

Latrodect shrugged. "No violence, no disturbances, no one gets hurt."

"And your businessmen take over Chinatown," Caine realized.

"What's your answer, Caine?"

Caine said: "I will not help the cause of darkness. Pestilence can be destroyed."

Latrodect laughed. "What are you going to do? Give out cans of Raid to all of the shopkeepers in Chinatown?" The odious *Spiderman* leaned over Caine. "Why don't you join us?"

Caine shook his head. "I cannot."

Latrodect rose and sighed. "I am saddened to hear that. I will destroy you and all of others around you. Your chi is strong." He shrugged. "But we are *many*."

Latrodect walked away through the overlapping shadows. "See you, Caine."

And he left Caine in darkness.

The way T.J. Scott used shadows and bars of darkness to set up this pivotal scene in the show was wonderful. I knew that David Carradine appreciated his handling of this crucial confrontation.

Caine escaped the thugs who had been guarding him in the underground cellar. A big celebration was happening in the Chinatown community. The streets were jammed with people. Kermit arrived with Emma Bartlett, his "new squeeze" as Strenlich described her, into the party atmosphere. Kermit introduced her to the Precinct gang. He guided Emma to Lo Si, saying he relished the name of *The Ancient*.

"That is because I am so old!" he said. He kissed Emma's hand. "If only I was a hundred years younger!" Then he used his signature expression: "Bloody marvelous!"

It was when Emma was introduced to Kwai Chang Caine that her expression had changed. She was suddenly cold and dispassionate. She asked him: "What do you see, Caine?"

Caine said: "Colors can blind, sound deafens, beauty beguiles the senses. The enemy of stillness is desire. Eliminate desire and the truth becomes clear again."

"That's very beautiful," Emma said. Then she laughed. "Now if I only understood what it *meant*!" She was looking mischievously at Kermit. He took her arm and they walked on through the boisterous Chinatown crowd. Emma turned back as Caine watched her. She opened her mouth and exposed her tongue which had a Black Widow Spider wrapped around it. No one but Caine had seen this transformation. Then Emma took Kermit's arm again as they mingled with the Chinatown crowd.

Meantime, the Mayor of the city was showing her new guests the wonders of Chinatown. This role was played Katherine Trowell, a terrific actress who had played on five of the *Kung Fu: The Legend Continues* episodes. In the end there were about 50 auxiliary characters on the show by the time series had finished its run.

John Latrodect had an entourage of his Hong Kong business partners with him in Chinatown. He spotted Kwai Chang Caine at the party scene and was not at all surprised he had escaped from his henchmen. He just shrugged.

"There would be another time," the *Spiderman* vowed.

The verbal exchange between Caine and Emma had been noted by Kermit. He moved away from Emma, promising to be right back, and caught up with Caine amid the festivities. He was terse. He said: "Mind telling me what was going on between you and Emma?"

"She is not what she seems," Caine responded.

"I'm a loner, Caine, just like you," Kermit said. "Maybe both of us have been alone too long."

"She will use that vulnerability against you," Caine promised him. "She will strike when your back is turned."

"Why would she do that?" Kermit demanded. "Is she some kind of agent from my mercenary past with Blaisdell? I have respected and admired you, Caine, and I reserve those emotions for very few people. So now every beautiful woman I meet is a *potential spy*? You know, the CIA could use you," he added, sarcastically.

Peter came up to them, trying to defuse the situation. Kermit just turned away from him. "Just mind your own business, Peter," he said shortly.

Kermit moved back into the crowd and rejoined Emma. Peter moved over to Caine. He was aware that there had been heated words between Caine and Kermit, but he had not offered an explanation. "Kermit is a friend to both of us," Peter reminded him "But he can be a dangerous enemy. Don't underestimate him."

"I will not," Caine promised.

Peter let it go. He was aware that his father had once been kidnapped by this evil sect in Chinatown. He recognized a bodyguard in Latrodect's entourage who had tried to kidnap Peter when he had been a boy at the temple. Caine followed his gaze and nodded.

"Yes," he said. "Black Widow Spiders. A sect older than the Sing Wah."

"What do they want?" Peter asked him.

"My soul," Caine said darkly.

Later that afternoon, John Latrodect kidnapped the Ancient. He was hiding him in an underground cellar, a place that was crawling with venomous spiders! The following night, in a frightening sequence, Peter and Jordan Maquire were sleeping together in Peter's apartment. Peter suddenly awakened to find a large Black Widow Spider crawling along Jordan's bare back. He roused her and whispered to her not to move a muscle. He rolled up a piece of paper and coaxed the spider to crawl onto it, while Jordan held her breath. Then he set fire to the rolled-up newspaper and tossed it into a wastebasket. Jordon jumped up and collapsed in Peter's arms, shaking with fear. He comforted her. She asked where the spider had come from. "I felt that thing on my skin and…" Jordan shuddered.

Peter told her that he had first come across this evil when he had been a boy at the temple. Jordan looked at him. "*What* temple?"

Peter said: "I guess there's a lot about me I haven't shared with you."

But Jordan did not question him further. She just hugged him more tightly.

In the precinct the next morning Peter caught up with Kermit. "There was a Black Widow Spider in my room last night," he said.

Kermit was still irritated with Peter. "Call pest control!"

"They got to the Ancient," Peter said, reacting to Kermit's hostility. "They got to *me*. This is a dangerous sect. They are trying to destroy my father and anyone close to him."

Kermit tried to brush Peter off, quoting a line from Shakespeare about "venom" from Antony and Cleopatra. Now Peter was very frustrated. "I'm trying to save your life, Kermit!" he said.

Kermit threw Peter back into a wall, his arm at Peter's throat. Around them, all activity in the precinct ceased. No one there had *ever* seen Kermit this angry. "My life belongs to me," he said. "I will protect it in my own way! You take care, if you'll forgive the expression, of your own affairs and I will take of mine!"

Kermit let Peter go, moved to his office and he slammed the door. Detective Mary Margaret Skalany looked at Peter. "What was that all about?"

Peter returned to his desk a bit shaken. "Just seeing if Kermit's mercenary reactions were still working," he said, ironically.

John Latrosect sought out Caine in the Chinatown square. He sat at a table calmly drinking tea. Caine sat down beside him. His mood was almost murderous. "There would be no redemption for you if you hurt the Ancient," Caine told him.

Latrosect said: "If you leave Chinatown, we will spare the old man."

The *Spiderman* stood off from the table, having finished his tea and moved away. This time it was Caine who was visibly shaken.

That night Kermit was in his apartment fixing dinner for himself and Emma Bartlett. She was in a playful mood. She had donned Kermit's dark glasses. He smiled at her. But Kermit had been a mercenary and he was always on his guard. He stood at his sink as Emma came up behind him. She had surreptitiously taken out a syringe from her pocket and was going to inject him with it. Kermit glanced down and saw her reflection in a kettle beside him.

"Kiss of the Spider Woman," he murmured.

He backhanded her, sending Emma to the floor. When he whirled around, she was gone. Kermit picked up his dark glasses that she had discarded and quickly left his apartment.

Kermit found Peter at Caine's apartment in Chinatown. He was standing beside the glass doors that opened onto the balcony. Kermit said: "You were right about Emma. She came at me with a loaded syringe!"

"Full of poisonous venom?" Peter asked.

"Oh, yeah," Kermit said.

Peter turned to Kermit. "I put a bug on Emma's sleeve when she came to see you at the precinct."

Kermit nodded. "I saw you do it."

Peter was amazed. "You knew?"

Kermit said: "A little voice talking to me from my subconscious. Sorry about this morning. We will go after her. I'll use the *Kermitmobile*."

The "*Kermitmobile*" was a souped-up convertible in a bright shade of green that belonged to Kermit. Peter and Kermit tracked the bug that Peter had planted and found John Latrodect's underground lair in Chinatown. They descended into the cellars looking for the Ancient. Then Kermit took a wrong turning in the maze of cellars and disappeared.

Peter came upon the Ancient. He said: "Peter! Do not come any closer! You will break my concentration!"

Peter saw there were hundreds of spiders crawling on the Ancient's body.

Peter carefully freed the Ancient. He kicked away the murderous spiders. Lo Si moved away. Peter had no idea where Kermit had been taken. But he *did* have had an old score to settle with one of Latrodect's bodyguards from the temple. The thug attacked Peter in the cellars. Peter came back with four major Kung Fu moves to turn the table on his assailant. He knocked him to the ground, unconscious. At the same time, the Ancient took care of another of Latrodect's bodyguards.

Caine had made his way into the cellars beneath the streets of Chinatown. More shadows dissected it. Caine was going to confront John Latrodect and finish off the *Spider Man* once and for all. Latrodect had ordered his men to kill Emma for her failure to kill Kermit. Kermit was a prisoner in the underground cellar which was permeated with shadows. He grabbed the poisonous netting that cocooned him, but she could tear it away.

He was trapped!

In the meantime, Emma had managed to escape her bonds. She was free, but she was not going to leave Kermit to his fate. She ran into the cellar and pulled apart the sticky netting that covered his face and body. But having saved his life, when Kermit looked again, she had disappeared once more.

In the underground cellars, Caine was ready for his deadly confrontation with the *Spider Man*. Latrodect came at Caine with a sword. The fight was fierce, as all the fights were in this episode under T.J. Scott's adroit direction. In the end, Caine prevailed. He disarmed Latrodect and threw him down to the ground. But when he looked down at his body, he saw it had *shriveled up* and had become a Black Widow Spider.

It scuttled away from Caine and was gone.

Caine did not believe he had seen the last of the Black Widow Spiders.

When the Tag Scene was played out, the precinct was quiet. Most of the detectives had already left, leaving just Sergeant Broderick at his reception counter. Kermit emerged from his office at the same time as Captain Simms emerged from hers. Kermit asked the Captain for a drink. She was somewhat ironic. She would not want to tear him away from his new lady friend Emma Bartlett! Kermit just said that they had parted ways.

"She had a poisonous personality," he said sardonically and left it at that.

Kermit and Captain Simms, arm-in-arm, headed to Delancey's Bar and Restaurant to join the rest of the Precinct gang.

Chapter Three
QUAKE

KWAI CHANG CAINE COULD FEEL A SENSE of impending disaster. He was a Shambala Master and the feelings of imminent danger assailed him. He was just puttering around his balcony when the warning came to him. He looked down at the Chinatown street which he could see was bustling with life. He saw the Ancient in the melee of the marketplace, stopping to converse with friends and acquaintances with a mixture of humor and self-effacing humility. The old man did not look up to see Kwai Chang Caine standing on his far-off balcony above the lives of the people.

Caine descended down to the street of his apartment building and entered into the melee. He knew of a phone kiosk in the street from which he could make a call. He dialed the Seismology Department at the University. A lovely actress named Elizabeth Lennie played our Seismologist technician who answered Caine's call. Her name was McMasters. She was really outstanding in a small role which lent color and gravitas to the scene.

She asked Caine who he was. He just said: "I am Caine." He told her that an earthquake would strike the city at exactly 11:15 AM. One of her colleagues, Scott Kavanaugh, passed by and said: "First bedbug of the day!" Caine told Professor McMasters that he was a priest in Chinatown. There was something chilling about Caine's warning. Professor McMasters asked what evidence that he was he basing his information on. Caine told her he felt the earth tremble. Scott Kavanaugh was ironic. "Does the earth move for priests?" Dr. McMasters just told Caine they were checking it out. Caine told

15

the Seismologist that people needed to be evacuated from the market square.

"I can't do that," Professor McMasters said, "without proof of some scientific data."

Caine hung up the phone. Dr. McMasters looked the dead receiver with some concern.

She had believed this Shaolin priest.

Meanwhile, at the 101st, the Precinct gang was getting together for a surprise birthday cake and card for Chief of Detectives Frank Strenlich. Detective Blake was the main instigator for getting the cake ready and a huge card signed by all of the 101st Detectives. Detective Jody Powell was there as well as Detective Mary Margaret Skalany and Sergeant Broderick. The Precinct gang had all signed the huge birthday card, then they tried to find a place to hide it. Chief of Detectives Strenlich arrived at that moment. Blake got the card out of the way fast. Skalany handed him a cup of coffee. "Here you are, Chief! Just the way you like it. Hot and strong." Strenlich was immediately wary. "What's going on?"

The Precinct gang assured him that everything was in order.

Detective Kermit Griffin was late for a meeting with Captain Karen Simms at the Town Hall. Simms was impatient to get this show on the road, but Kermit was stalling. He was on his computer as usual and looked up as Captain Simms stood in his doorway.

"There is a German U-Boat at the bottom of the sea if I can just crack this code," Kermit told her.

Captain Simms was in no mood for Kermit today. The Mayor was waiting for them. Reluctantly Kermit closed his computer and followed his Captain out of his office. The relationship between Captain Karen Simms and Kermit Griffin was an edgy one. Karen knew that Paul Blaisdell had hired Kermit, a one-time mercenary, to join the 101st Precinct, ostensibly as a computer programmer. Blaisdell and Kermit went back to the days when Paul Blaisdell *himself* had been a mercenary. Captain Simms tolerated Griffin's iconic behavior out of loyalty to Blaisdell. She could feel the violence that simmered beneath of surface of Kermit's persona. And, if the truth were told, there was something charismatic about Kermit that attracted her.

That relationship between the one-time mercenary Kermit Griffin and Captain Karen Simms got tested in this episode. Scott Wentworth, the actor playing Kermit Griffin, had quickly become a favorite with the Kung Fu fans. I remember there was a time on a *Kung Fu: The Legend Continues* episode when Scott was living in New York City. The show was in hiatus. He was walking down Fifth Avenue. A truck pulled into the curb. The driver rolled his window down as Scott was passing and shouted: "Hey, Kermit! Did you kill anyone today?" At one point in the television series Scott Wentworth was getting as much fan mail as David Carradine or Chris Potter.

We followed Kermit and Captain Simms to the City Hall buildings. Captain Simms was attempting to crack Kermit's façade. She knew Kermit had been a mercenary. Kermit responded that he did not allow people to get to know him.

"If you listened very closely you could almost hear their lives crashing," Kermit said. "I suggest you read my file, Captain. I do not allow people to get to know me better."

"*I'd* like to get to know you better," Captain Simms said.

Kermit looked at her and shook his head. "No, you wouldn't," he said, softly.

The elevator doors opened at that moment. A sleazy attorney whom Karen Simms knew slightly, Maurice Snyder, moved into the elevator. It was clear that Captain Simms detested this guy. Also a very pregnant secretary named Jennifer Morgan clambered aboard the elevator. She had a very sunny disposition with an infectious laugh.

Peter Caine and Detective Jody Powell rousted a felon in Chinatown whom they had been chasing down for a while. His name was Danny Paulsen, who was being played by Robert Carradine, David Caradine's brother. He turned in an arrogant, understated performance which was chilling. Paulsen vowed to Peter that he would *never* get him back to the 101st Precinct. That his lethal confederates would come for him! Little did Peter Caine realize at the time that the earthquake that was about hit the city made his words prophetic.

Danny Paulsen had been sleeping with a young woman in his apartment in Chinatown. Her name was Kyra. She was played by a wonderful Canadian actress named Cristina Cox. She was discovered in bed with Paulsen when Peter and Jody rousted them. Peter told Kyra to get dressed. She would have to go with them. Kyra was frightened and disoriented. She protested that she did not know Paulsen at all. He had picked her up and took her with him to his apartment for a one-night stand. Detective Jody Powell nodded.

"Yeah, yeah," Jody said. "I have heard it all before."

Paulsen shrugged for Peter's benefit. He told the cops that Kyra "liked the candy", which did not sit well with Jody at all.

Back at the 101st, the precinct was eerily quiet. Strenlich entered and looked around. "Where the hell is everybody? Did crime stop? Did I *miss it*?" Then the Precinct gang wheeled out the huge cake out from its hiding place. They wished Strenlich a *Happy*

Birthday! We noted that there were 50 candles on the cake. Strenlich was embarrassed. He said: "Why are there 50 candles on the cake? I'm only 43!"

Blake muttered: "Oops!"

Strenlich made to blow out the candles.

The elevator at the City Hall was slowly ascending. Jennifer Morgan, our very pregnant office worker, looked at Kermit and grinned. "I love your dark glasses! They make you look like Jack Nicholson!"

Kermit smiled. "At least you didn't say *Kermit the Frog!*"

Jennifer's infectious laugh bubbled up from her.

Maurice Snyder said snidely: "I never heard of anyone wearing dark glasses *inside.* Poor eyesight?"

Kermit let that one go. "It's for people who grate on my corneas!"

Snyder's expression was smug. Captain Karen Simms just shook her head. She really loathed this attorney, but Kermit seemed to be unfazed.

The clock tower in Chinatown hit the quarter hour.

And the earthquake struck with unrelenting force!

People were thrown to the ground with the ferocity of the tumbler. Geysers exploded from the cement. The Chinatown market was devastated. Buildings collapsed or were partially destroyed. The shaking continued for several seconds.

At the precinct house, Chief Strenlich had just leaned down to blow out the candles on his birthday cake. He stumbled and actually fell into the cake! Windows and glass partitions blew out, showering jagged daggers through the precinct house. Detectives, patrolmen and visitors were thrown to the ground. A large filing cabinet crashed down, pinning Mary Margaret Skalany to the floor. She was trapped under it, but no one at first heard her cries for help.

Outside in the Chinatown street, Kwai Chang Caine was helping people get back onto their feet. He found the Ancient trapped under the rubble. A heavy weight had come crashing down across his legs. Caine tried to lift the crushing weight from old man's body.

The elevator in the City Hall had plummeted down with the passengers trapped inside. Kermit grabbed Captain Simms hand. "Haberdashery, shoes, ladies' lingerie, umbrellas, E-tickets!" Then the elevator came to a screeching halt. Of course Maurice Snyder was the one who panicked.

"What happened?" he demanded.

Kermit said: "The emergency brake came on."

He found a pencil flashlight in his suit pocket. Captain Simms was beside him. He said: "Boy scouts and old mercenaries are always prepared!"

In the wrecked Precinct house, Sergeant Broderick was getting people outside. Chief Strenlich was back on his feet helping him. Detective Blake was on his hands and knees searching for his glasses which had fallen somewhere in the debris.

No one saw Detective Skalany trapped beneath the filing cabinet.

Outside in the Chinatown street, Caine realized that the Ancient was trapped by a jagged spar of wood. Caine continued to throw debris away to one side.

Outside Danny Paulsen's apartment a car had crashed. Peter and Jody tried to free a family trapped inside, but the car door had been wedged shut. At this moment Paulsen took off, using the trauma to his advantage. Kyra slammed a trash-can lid against his head, sending him down to the ground. Jody ran through the chaos and dragged Paulsen to his feet, putting the cuffs on him. She looked at Kyra and nodded.

"We owe you one!" she said.

Peter was trying to get the car door in the street opened, but it would not budge. Simultaneously, Caine had moved more of the rubble away from the Ancient's body, but the old man was still trapped in the rubble.

Lo Si shook his head. "It is no use, Kwai Chang Caine," he said, hoarsely. "Leave me! Tend to others!"

Caine knew that Peter was somewhere in the Chinatown streets. He reached up his arms. "You have my strength, my son!" he said. "*Use it*!"

Peter took hold of the buckled car door of the mangled vehicle. Caine lifted the spar of wood off the Ancient's legs. At the same time, Peter wrenched the car door off its hinges and threw it to one side. He reached into the car, helping the family trapped there to get out. They had not run more than a few feet with Peter when the car exploded in a fiery ball of flames.

Caine, at the Ancient's side, lifted Lo Si as if he weighed a feather. Paramedics, who had arrived on the street, put the old man onto a gurney. Caine instructed the EMT's: "Strap him in if you have to!"

Lo Si murmured: "I heard that!"

In the wrecked Precinct, Sergeant Broadhurst was helping more people to get outside. He sniffed the air. "Escaping gas! Everybody out!" Most of the people who had been in the Precinct were now out. Detective Blake was still feeling around for his fallen glasses which he finally found. He put them back on.

A news team pulled up into the ravaged streets and Sandra Mason got out. The actress who portrayed the role was named Catherine Blythe. She had a recurring role on *Kung Fu: The Legend Continues*. It was these characters who added authenticity to the episodes. Sandra Mason was broadcasting from the quake area, telling people to stay home if they could. Looters could be seen around her in the streets of Chinatown.

In the trapped elevator, Kermit tried to bypass a panel in the elevator. Maurice Snyder was still panicking. "You should leave that alone!"

Kermit muttered: "Instructions and following orders were never my long suit."

But it was clear to him that the passengers trapped inside the elevator compartment needed a way to escape. Kermit removed a hatch in the roof of the elevator. Using Captain Simms, with Snyder's help, he crawled up out onto the top of the elevator shaft. He realized there was a bypass switch that he needed to reach, but it too far for him to reach it as yet.

At the precinct house, Detective Blake, having found his glasses, heard a soft cry for help. He looked around the rubble and found the source. Mary Margaret Skalany was trapped by the large filing cabinet. She was conscious, but barely. Blake knelt down toward her. More gas was escaping from the ruptured street. An aftershock rocked the streets. More glass exploded from the windows in the Precinct. Blake was thrown halfway across the room, lying in shards of fragmented glass.

Kwai Chang Caine was searching for Peter. He came across a pool hall, but he did not find him there. A laid-back guy named Jason Quirk was shooting pool without seeming to care what was happening outside in the aftermath of the quake. He was about twenty years old with long, unkempt hair, wearing jeans with a baseball cap turned around. Caine told him there was looting out in the streets. Quirk shrugged. That was no concern of his. He just came in here to shoot pool!

Two of the pool players attacked Caine who dealt with them handily. Jason Quirk seemed to be impressed. "You've got a lot of nerve for an old man," he said. "I like that." Caine said: "It is not a question of nerve. It was a question of *hope*."

To make his point, Caine took the pool cue and pocketed *all of the balls lying on the pool table.* Quirk had listened to Caine's words. They made sense to him. If these looters were out in the streets, he would do something about it.

Caine had noted a young girl standing apart from the pool tables. Gently he asked her how old she was. She told him that she was seventeen. There was a fragility to her that resonated with Caine. We used David Carradine's real-life daughter in this scene, Kansas Carradine, a first-time actress. Caine had seen that she was troubled. He told her: "Come to Chinatown. Ask for Caine. I will help you."

The girl nodded and thanked him. Quirk took her hand and propelled her from the pool hall.

In the City Hall, Captain Simms had joined Kermit at the top of the elevator. He told her: "I put together a skyscraper once. On the computer, of course." He tried to reach a panel that might have opened the elevator doors above them. Captain Simms held onto him.

Below in the elevator Maurice Snyder was pacing restlessly. He looked at Jennifer. "You know," the attorney said, "if you lose your baby, you can sue the city." Jennifer stated to cry uncontrollably. "Stop that!" Snyder demanded. "Does my pacing bother you? I am a little agitated! Any more of these aftershocks and it will be bye-bye Baby!"

Jennifer cried some more. "Will you stop that!"

Kermit jumped down from the roof of the elevator and slammed Snyder back against the wall. His face was right next to him. "If she wants to cry, you will let her," Kermit said. "Or I will break your fingers! Do we understand each other, Counselor?"

Snyder just nodded, severely intimidated by Kermit. Almost reluctantly Kermit let him go. He let Snyder raise him back up to the open elevator hatch. Kermit tried again to release the box fuse, but he could still not reach it, even with Karen Simms holding onto him.

Captain Strenlich went back into the wrecked Precinct where Blake was getting to his feet. Strenlich heard Mary Margaret Skalany's soft cries. He staggered to where the filing cabinet rested on her legs. He hurled the filing cabinet to one side and lifted Skalany onto his shoulders in a fireman's lift. He and Blake escaped from the escaping gas outside into the street.

Caine finally found Peter in a restaurant which was closed right now. They embraced each other. The building had been hit by the quake. Terry, our stalwart bartender, another regular in the *Kung Fu: The Legend Continues* family, was in the restaurant. Caine remembered a scene from his temple days where he and Peter had been fighting off looters at the temple. But this was not the time for Caine to mention it.

Detective Jody Powell had been hurt in the street fight and Peter tended to a wound on her face. Gingerly he cleaned it up. Jody said that she thought she had lost Peter to Rebecca (but that was another story for later). There were some tender moments between Jody and Peter. Peter said he did not realize that she cared so much.

Jody asked him: "How could you? You have your on-and-off relationship with

Kelly (who was a detective also in the 101ˢᵗ Precinct who was not in this episode). And you have your relationship with your father." This was difficult for Jody to say. "Maybe if he looked closer, you would see a partner who truly worried about you, who cared about you, and someone who could love you."

Jody moved away from Peter at this point. He looked after her, realizing that the feelings she had expressed were very heartfelt. And, perhaps, he felt them too.

Meanwhile, Danny Paulsen told Peter that he was expecting to be rescued from the streets by several of his thugs. Peter would never get him back to the Precinct alive! Outside, Paulsen's ride had finally arrived. Six men get out the car. More aftershocks rocked the streets. Jody hauled Paulsen to one side with Kyra. Caine and Peter looked at each other as the men approached them.

"They don't look like they will negotiate?" Peter commented, wryly.

Caine shook his head. "They will not."

"Then we go to Plan A?" Peter said.

"What is Plan A?" Caine asked.

"We beat the beat the hell out of them!"

"Ah!" Caine said.

A major martial arts fight ensued with Caine and Peter using fast, lightning moves on the street thugs. Eventually they clambered back into their car and took off.

In City Hall, on top of the elevator car, Kermit used his dark sunglasses to finally trip the breaker. The elevator on the next floor opened. Anxious onlookers were crowded into the ajar elevator doors. Kermit handed Captain Simms up into their arms. Then he reached down and grabbed a very pregnant Jennifer and handed her up to the waiting rescuers. Maurice Snyder climbed onto the top of the elevator and was grabbed too. Then it was Kermit's turn. But another aftershock shook the foundation of the City Hall. It almost rocked Kermit off his feet. The elevator dropped a little way, and then stopped again. Captain Simms leaned down for Kermit while four or five men held onto her legs.

"Take my hand!" she told him, urgently.

The elevator was about to plummet down the elevator shaft.

"That is an order, dammit!" Captain Simms said. "Take my hand!"

Kermit took her hand and was hauled up out of the elevator.

That was it for the elevator. It tore loose and plummeted down the shaft to the floors below with a resounding crash. Kermit was helped back to his feet.

Outside the Precinct building, Detective Blake was shaky, but he was okay. He had a blanket wrapped around him. Skalany made her way through the debris outside to thank Captain Strenlich who was still helping people. He told her she should not be thanking him. It was *Detective Blake* who had come back for her. Skalany found Blake among some survivors and thanked him. Blake just shook his head.

"I couldn't have left you in there," he said, his tone subdued.

"You could have, but you *didn't*," Skalany said. "And I'll never forget it."

She kissed him on the cheek.

There were firemen and rescue personnel in the lobby at City Hall. Paramedics were taking Jennifer out of the building on a gurney because her baby was coming. Maurice Snyder took Kermit's arm.

"You could have left me to climb out of that elevator and be last one out," he said, which was as close to an apology that Snyder would ever get.

"The thought did cross my mind," Kermit admitted.

"I'm trying to say something meaningful here," Snyder said with an edge. "It doesn't happen often. You want to work with me here?"

"Be a little kinder when you're questioning someone on the witness stand," Kermit advised him, and moved away.

Snyder was besieged by people in the lobby who wanted to meet the "hero" from the elevator! Captain Simms moved over to Kermit. They still had to give a deposition to the District Attorney.

"Can we get an office on the ground floor?" Kermit asked, wryly.

Captain Simms smiled, but she was looking at him with newfound respect. "Did you save many lives when you worked as a mercenary for Blaisdell?"

"Took too many of them," Kermit said. He shrugged. "Saved a few."

"I think of you as an unlikely hero," Captain Simms said.

"Most heroes are."

"I don't think that anymore," Karen Simms said quietly.

Kermit smiled at her as they walked across the City Hall lobby.

In the Tag scene of the episode in Delancey's Bar and Restaurant, Captain Simms told Kermit that Jennifer had had a baby boy named Dylan. Kermit raised his glass in a toast. "To Dylan!"

They clinked glasses.

Peter found Jody to make sure she was all right after their wild day out in the streets. She was embarrassed. She told Peter to forget everything she said to him about loving him during the earthquake. She had been delirious. Then Jody moved quickly away. Peter was not buying it. He knew there had been a lot of truth to what she had said to him when he and Jody had bonded. But what to do about it? Peter would need to reassess his feelings about Detective Jody Powell! He moved over to Caine, telling him that he would be reporting to the 9th Precinct while the 101st Precinct was being repaired. He told his father they had come a long way together.

Caine smiled. "The journey of 1000 miles, or *a few blocks*, begins with a single step."

"I couldn't have walked those blocks with you, Pop," Peter said.

"Our steps will always be entwined," Caine said. "They will continue to cross until we have reached our destination."

"And where is that?" Peter asked him.

Caine shrugged, but Peter was way ahead of him. He spoke in the cadence of Caine: "*We do not know!*"

Caine just smiled again.

On a television set in the corner of the Sports Bar, Terry, our ubiquitous bartender, had turned up the sound a little louder. Sandra Mason was concluding her news broadcast.

"The city had been saved from destruction by a Shaolin priest," she said. "If Kwai Chang Caine has any words for us, please be sure to pass them along." She glanced at Caine with heartfelt thanks. Caine gave her one his small formal bows. She signed off with: "This is Sandra Mason for Channel Three News."

Chapter Four
DEMONS

KERMIT GRIFFIN WAS NOT THE KIND of person who sought out anyone's help. He had been a mercenary, now assigned to the 101st Precinct. He was a loner who relied on his own instincts to get him out of any situation that he found challenging. But this time it was about his family. His sister Marilyn and her two children were being threatened. This episode was directed by Jon Cassar, a wonderful director who would direct many episodes of *Kung Fu: The Legend Continues*. I first got to know him when my wife Melissa Anderson was filming the *Alfred Hitchcock Presents* episode called: "*Murder in Mind*." The plot called for Melissa to go up and down stairs in her house with Jon Cassar operating a *Steadi-Cam* camera. He followed Melissa everywhere with the camera, with no linking shots, just the *Steadi-Cam* at his side. It made for a unique episode. I remembered Jon and I hired him to direct some of the *Kung Fu: The Legend Continues* episodes. He was masterful, a great guy and went on to direct many other shows, including the great show "*24*" for Fox for which he won two Emmy's. He was just a delight to work with and be around. Another show he directed for me was called "*Gunfighters*", which was our only western episode on the show, but I will get to that in another chapter. I believe Demons was the first episode that Jon Cassar directed for *Kung Fu: The Legend Continues*, to which he brought tremendous style and chutzpah.

Kermit had come to see Kwai Chang Caine in Chinatown. Caine was surprised to see him. "You seldom leave the Precinct, Kermit," he said. "I feel privileged."

They were having tea together in Caine's fourth-floor apartment at night. Kermit shrugged and his mood was subdued. "Ask for Caine. He will help you."

"You've never asked for my help," Caine said. "You are not a man who asks for assistance."

Kermit explained that he had come to talk to Caine about his sister Marilyn. Her husband had passed away. She was starting a new life with her two children.

And she was scared to death.

Kermit shook his head in frustration. "I deal with computers, with facts and data, with bullets and tangible evidence. I don't deal with the Dark Forces."

Caine cocked his head to one side. "With Demons?"

"That's *exactly* the word that Marilyn used on the phone last night," Kermit said. "She was fighting Demons and she was terrified."

"Where is this battle taking place?" Caine asked him.

"At a house called the Gables," Kermit said. "It is two hours from here in the country. She moved there with the kids about a month ago."

"Does this house have a history?" Caine asked.

In true Kermit fashion, he said: "Oh, yeah." Then he said: "I want to show you something."

Kermit took out a tarnished locket from his pocket and set it down onto the table. He told Caine that Marilyn had found this locket two nights ago. Caine picked up the locket, staring at it.

"Where did she find it?" he asked.

"Around her *throat*," Kermit said. "Like someone had put it there."

Caine weighed the locket in the palm of his hand. "Very old. I feel pain here. And grief."

Kermit explained that his sister was having a dinner party that weekend and he wanted to invite Caine to it. Caine promised he would be there.

At that very moment, Peter Caine was in the Precinct working late. The phone on his desk rang and he picked it up. Marilyn's emotional voice came through on the line. She was traumatized and almost incoherent. "Put me through to Kermit Griffin!"

"He's not here now," Peter said. "Can I take a message?"

"This is his sister Marilyn. They are *here*!" She was trying to hold back her tears. "From out of the darkness!"

Peter was at a loss to follow her. "Who's here? Who's coming out of the darkness?"

"The Demons!" Marilyn said. "They're---"

But she could get no further. The sound of maniacal laughter echoed over the phone. In her living room in the Gables, Marilyn looked down at the phone receiver.

Blood seeped out of the phone!

Marilyn dropped the phone, horrified, and screamed.

The next day at the 101st Precinct, Peter was at his desk. The door to Captain Simms' office opened and the newest member of the Precinct squad was introduced. He was a redheaded, brash Police Officer with a pleasant face and a disarming manner. He introduced himself as *Thomas Jefferson Kincaid* – Do not call me *"T.J."*! He started handing out cards to all of the Precinct gang.

"If you ever need back-up, I am your man!" T.J said. "I also deal with antiques, rare coins and real estate."

He handed a card to Mary Margaret Skalany, who was ironic. "I'll treasure it."

Peter Caine moved over to Chief of Detectives Strenlich. The Chief was chagrined. He nodded at T.J. "He just transferred from the 54th."

The door to Captain Simms opened again and a heavyset, good-looking man emerged. Peter's back was to him. Peter was just shaking his head. "Bribery, forgery? Spats at garden parties? What idiot would transfer him to a Fort Apache precinct in Chinatown?"

Police Commission Kincaid, standing behind Peter, said wryly: "The idiot who fathered him!"

Peter's horrified expression registered on his face. He turned and murmured: "My apologies, Commissioner!"

Chief Strenlich suppressed a smile. Kincaid moved further into the bullpen. He said: "No one likes the boss's kid on their team. But give him a chance. He might surprise you."

With that the Commissioner strode out of the room. T.J. came right over, shaking hands with Chief Strenlich. "*Thomas Jefferson Kincaid*! Don't call me *T.J.*!" He grabbed Peter's hand. "You must be Peter Caine! I thought you'd be larger than life after all of your press coverage."

"Well, don't believe everything Sandra Mason says on the Channel Three News," Peter muttered. "I can get you set up at a desk beside Skalany."

"Day or night," T.J. said. "I'm your back-up!"

"I'll sleep a lot better now," Peter murmured, but T.J. was oblivious to his sarcasm.

When I created the "new kid on the block" role for T.J. Kincaid, I cast an actor and a very good friend of mine named Sandey Grinn. He was just what the role called for – brash, funny, with a good heart, even though he was subject to a lot of ribbing being the Commissioner's son. He became a fan favorite on the show, even though he did not shoot many episodes. I was glad to have given him a chance to shine.

That night at Chandler's Bar and Restaurant, which was the usual hangout for the cops at the 101st Precinct, the place was packed. T.J. was playing piano with an enthusiastic crowd around him. At the bar were Detective Blake, Chief Strenlich, Detective Jody Powell and Kermit. Peter Caine arrived and ordered a beer. Jody thought T.J. was playing a pretty hot piano! Peter nodded. "Not too bad!" Jody said she was going to check T.J. out and moved to the piano. Peter had not seen Kermit for a while and asked him where he had been?

"I've been checking out a little town called Brazelton," Kermit said. "Population 1200, if you don't count the ghosts. It's where my sister lives now."

Peter nodded. "She sounded pretty desperate to get hold of you. She called the Precinct."

T.J. turned from the piano to the raucous crowd. "Can I get some back-up here?"

Blake threw up his hands. "Not me!"

Jody moved over to Peter and dragged him from the bar to the piano. Peter did an improvised duet with T.J. At the back of Chandler's, Kwai Chang Caine entered the place, watching Peter playing with T.J. with a smile on his face. T.J. led Peter into a chorus.

At the piano:

T.J.: "You're just a regular Joe…"

Peter: "But the P.R. here is minimal…"

T.J.: "That's no way to live…"

Peter: "But don't tell that to a criminal!"

The crowd was loving it! T.J. came up with another impromptu verse for Peter…

Peter: "They say I'm a hotshot cop, but my partners sometimes bore me."

Kermit, Blake and Strenlich agreed loudly.

Peter: "If I can't solve a crime, my Pop will do it for me!"

There was more applause from the lively crowd.

At the back of the room, Caine suddenly staggered. He took out the locket that Kermit had given him. He clutched it in his hand, feeling the dark forces gathering around him. He saw hideous gargoyles perched on a roof of a house. He heard the cries of Demons. He witnessed a young girl at the top of a staircase dropping a large ball down the stairs. She cried out: "Help me!" There were more images: A man and a younger man struggling with a gun. A distraught young woman. The younger man was shot and collapsed to the floor. Caine held onto some stacked chairs while the menacing images flooded his mind.

Peter was greeted by Detective Blake, Chief Strenlich and Kermit, congratulating him for his impromptu duet with T.J. Then he spotted Caine and moved over to him. Caine had recovered from the memories that had crowded into his mind. He was unnerved by them. He slipped the locket back into his pocket and took Peter's arm.

"We must talk," was all he said.

Caine and Peter walked through a park at night. Peter was shaking his head. "I can't believe you're seriously considering becoming a ghostbuster!"

"Evil can manifest itself in many ways," Caine reminded him. "You remember the Dark Warrior who was released from the urn in 'Shambala'."

Peter said: "Pop, that was an old house. The stairs creaked and the old pipes rattled. Imagination takes over."

Caine shrugged. "I can go alone."

"And miss the chance of going to a haunted house over a weekend with you?" Peter said, ironically. "No way! Besides, Kermit's sister *did* sound a little terrified on the phone."

Caine suddenly put his hand onto Peter's chest.

"What is it?" Peter asked.

Caine looked out into the dark park. "We are being surrounded."

Caine and Peter fought off several attackers who came out the darkness at them. This was a brilliant fight sequence that Jon Cassar had staged because it was filled with shapes and eerie images. The audience never got a real glimpse of these attackers. Jon Cassar just left it to their imagination. At the critical moment, T.J. came to the rescue, firing his gun into the air. The attackers dispersed. Peter thanked him and he went after them, but they were only shapes and shadows again. Peter thought they might have been dealing with Sing Wah or Bon Bon Hai (villains from another episode), but Caine says that they were not.

He did not know if they were even *human*.

"Pick me up tomorrow morning," Caine said. Then, as an afterthought, he added: "Not too early!"

That morning at the Precinct, T.J. shared a memory with Peter. He knew that he had brushed against dark forces last night. T.J. put some silver bullets on Peter's desk, telling him that only silver bullets could kill a Demon.

Peter was ironic. "Should I wear a mask?" he asked.

T.J. ignored that remark. He took out a small vial from an envelope. "Holy Water," he said.

"Do you also have some garlic and carry a cross?" Peter was not buying this *ghostbuster* act for a minute! T.J. confessed that he lost a friend, a young woman to the Dark Forces. Until the time he could step through the mists and rescue her again, he would wait and watch. His sincerity resonated with Peter.

At Caine's apartment, the Ancient was very concerned about his friend Kwai Chang Caine. He knew that Caine could not fight these Demons alone. Caine told him not to worry about him.

Caine and Peter arrived at the Gables in the country and were greeted by Kermit. They were also watched by two intruders. One of them was a young man named Tom Fleming who had just arrived there. The other man was older; a killer named Matt Larchmont. The attackers in the park had not succeeded in stopping Caine and Peter from coming to the Gables. "They are not leaving," Fleming said.

Larchmont lowered a set of binoculars. "So we'll have to stop them ourselves," he said, softly.

Inside the Gables, Kermit and Peter entered the kitchen, but Caine lingered in the hallway. He had heard soft *voices muttering*, rising in cadence. A young girl, maybe sixteen, walked down the staircase. She was outgoing, beautiful, somehow elfin.

"I'm Mitch," she said. "Is that a dumb name for a girl?"

"Not to me," Caine said.

"You must be Caine," she said. "Kermit talked about you. I am to show you to your room." Then she stopped on the stairs and looked back at him. "Wow! How about that! They are frightened of you. The voices have all stopped."

"You can hear them?" Caine asked, surprised.

"Sometimes," Mitch said. "She is so sad. So very sad."

Caine did not know who Mitch was referring to, but he felt the dark forces that gathered around them.

In the kitchen, Kermit introduced Peter to his sister Marilyn. She dismissed her anxiety about living in this old house. "I'm sure you don't believe in walls that contract and phones that bleed!"

Peter smiled. "My father is a better listener to stories like that."

Marilyn introduced her son Jason to Peter. Jason's attitude was dismissive. His mother told him dinner was at eight. He barely acknowledged her. Marilyn told Peter that Jason was having a lot of trouble coming to terms with the passing of his father.

"Kermit was mysterious about why he had invited you and Caine to come to the Gables," she said. "But then again…" Marilyn just shrugged. "You know Kermit!"

"Not really," Peter murmured. He glanced over at Kermit who was sampling stuff on the stove. "Does *anyone*?"

Marilyn said she would show Peter up to his room. Kermit came over and put his arm around Peter's shoulders. "She's a very special person," Kermit said of his sister. Peter nodded his agreement. "If you touch her," Kermit said, "I will have to terminate your existence."

Kermit moved away and Peter sighed.

It was going to be a very long weekend!

Mitch led Caine up a big staircase in the house. She said that she sometimes saw Rachel, who was trapped here in the house, as a gauzy, unreal figure at the top of the stairs in her white party dress. Mitch said she was a *ghost*, albeit not a not a *malevolent one*.

"The light shone through her," Mitch said. "The Demons could move things." Then she was suddenly a kid again, no mention of a traumatic incident. "What to see my room?"

Caine just nodded and followed the young girl to her room.

A Civil War battle was displayed on a huge table with small figures, all of them brightly painted in great detail. Mitch said that sometimes her Civil War toy soldiers did nothing!

She picked up a toy soldier from the battlefield. "July 21st, 1861," she said. "First Battle of Bull Run. General McAllister's Union troops were here." The young girl pointed to a place on the makeshift battlefront. "The Confederates fall back to Henry House Hill. Generals Johnson and Jackson make their stand." Mitch moved a Union soldier who was in the wrong place and picked it up. "This is my friend, Caine. Can I show him our battle?"

Caine stared down at the table as the Civil War toy soldiers came to life! There were drummers on the battlefield, buglers, canons being fired, sabers held high, hand-to-hand combat from some of the troops. Smoke rolled across the table. The sounds of the Civil War battle echoed to Caine. This sequence was very cleverly choreographed by Jon Cassar with stop-motion photography. In the end, one of the toy pieces leapt up from the battlefield and a startled Caine caught it in his hand. Mitch had been leaning down across the table. She straightened.

"Cool, huh?"

Caine nodded, amazed. "*Very* cool!"

Peter was on his way to a guest room in the house when he heard a child's soft sobbing. It was eerie and plaintive. Peter pulled his gun and climbed the staircase up to an attic room. It was filled with the usual junk found in an attic. There was a tall, standing wardrobe prominent in the room. Peter opened it, not sure what he might find, but it was just some knickknacks and clothing. Peter closed the wardrobe door, still hearing the eerie sounds of the child's sobs. Finally another sound turned him around. It was only Jason, Marilyn's son, fetching him to come to dinner.

"I heard the sound of sobbing coming from the attic," Peter said.

Jason could have cared less. "Mitch must have the television blasting again!"

Peter followed Jason down the staircase. He was adamant. "I heard sobbing coming from this attic!"

"It's just the wind," Jason told him. "The roof leaks like a Swiss cheese. The house is falling apart."

"But it is home, right?" Peter said.

Jason shrugged again. "I eat and sleep here. That's it!"

Peter reached out and stopped the boy on the staircase. "I had an attitude like that when I lived here at the orphanage," he confessed. "Until I realized that there were people who cared about me."

Jason was dismissive. "Yeah, right," he said.

He went on down the stairs. Peter shook his head. He thought he was going to have a lot of trouble trying to reach to this teenager. He was determined to find a way to give Jason some self-esteem. He would talk to his father. He always had the right answer.

That night at dinner the Real Estate Agent for the house, an attractive, garrulous woman named Helen Addams, was regaling them with stories about the Gables. None of the people in the town would come anywhere near the place! It was haunted and cursed. Sometimes there was a "stench of Hell" that emitted from it.

Jason nodded. "That is my favorite!" he said with heavy sarcasm.

Caine asked what *did* happen in this house. Helen Addams told them there was a family living here at the Gables, a mother and father and their daughter. The realtor continued in a hushed, theatrical voice. "One night the husband went berserk, beat his wife and their daughter to death and shot himself."

Peter was not buying it. There would have been police reports and microfilm evidence.

"It was all hushed up," Helen said. "It had kept everyone in the town away from this place." Then she launched to peals of irreverent laughter. "Sometimes the house *did* have a stench from Hell. But nothing frightens our Marilyn," Helen said, breezily.

"But a house like this would require a staff," Peter said.

"The only staff I have ever seen is the new chef," Helen said. "I have to thank Kermit for that!"

Kermit looked blankly at her. "Thank *me?*"

The Ancient made an appearance in the dining room wearing an apron and a chef's hat. He poured soup for all of them. "Wonton soup with a touch of ginger," he said. He went around the table. Caine said sotto voce to the Ancient: "What are you doing here?"

The Ancient, also sotto voce, answered: "Protecting you!"

Kermit looked over at Marilyn. "I found him in Chinatown! He caters all my parties!"

"As if you have parties that need to be catered!" Marilyn scoffed. She rose from the table. "I must huddle with my culinary accomplice about the main course!"

Marilyn exited the dining room with the Ancient. "Marilyn made a rock bottom offer on the house," Helen Addams said. "And hey, Presto! Gables had a new family! The place has so much atmosphere! Don't you just love it?"

At that moment Marilyn screamed from the kitchen. The table emptied. Caine ran into the kitchen to see Marilyn cowering in a corner. Pots and pans were being hurled around the kitchen. Knives flew from their racks. The Ancient fought off the missiles with his hands. Caine caught some of the sharp kitchen knives that came flying at him and threw them to the floor. He finally raised his hands above his head.

"You will desist!" he shouted. "*Now!*"

Immediately all the pots and pans and kitchen items dropped to the floor, including the lethal knives. Kermit went over to Marilyn and took her into his arms.

"All over now," he said.

Helen Addams was seriously rattled. Kermit offered to take her home. The realtor could not leave quickly enough. Peter talked quietly to Marilyn in the kitchen as they picked up the knives and the pots and pans. "If these Demons are real," he asked her, "why are they trying to run you out?"

"In the village," Marilyn said, "they say it's because I look so much like her. The woman who had been murdered by her husband in this house. It's said her spirit walks the corridors of the Gables, raging."

Up in his room, Peter heard more of the soft sobbing from within the house. He took out the silver bullets and holy water from his bag. "These had better work, T.J.," he muttered. He ascended the stairs to the attic. He found some discarded dolls with blood on them. Outside the Gables, at one of the windows, Peter found some wires and an amp. He pulled them out.

Caine found the Ancient in the kitchen. The old man said that there were powerful forces at work here. "We are not here to stop them," Caine said. "But to find their rage."

Peter re-entered the Gables. He looked down from his bedroom on the second floor and saw someone on the grounds in the shadows. He climbed down on one of the gabled roofs, then jumped onto the ground.

One of the hideous gargoyles came crashing down on top of him, almost killing him.

Up in the attic, Caine came upon Mitch. She was wearing a beautiful white dress, rocking back and forth on a rocking horse. She was wearing very pale make-up and looked fragile and a little disoriented.

"Mitch!" Caine asked her. "What are you doing up here?"

"I come here when I can't sleep," Mitch said. "This was *her* room. She is so sad. She does not want him to hurt Mommy anymore." She looked at Caine thoughtfully. "Maybe you can help them?" She indicated the large wardrobe at one of the walls. "She lives in the closet with her Mom and her Dad."

Caine followed her gaze. "She lives *in a closet?*"

"I'll show you," Mitch offered.

She jumped off the rocking horse and ran to the free-standing wardrobe. She opened it. There were no clothes hanging there or odd knickknacks. But there *were* stairs leading down to some kind of a hallway. Mitch shook her head.

"I've never seen those stairs before! Could that be because of you?"

Caine said: "It could be. Wait here."

Mitch said: "Be careful!"

Caine descended down the short flight of wooden stairs. Mitch closed the wardrobe door behind him.

Outside, on the grounds of the estate, Peter found more wires and a heavy magnet. "Nice trick," he said, realizing that this was the way the knives and the pots and pans had been hurled around the kitchen. He raised a trapdoor down to a cellar and immediately slammed it shut again. "The stench from Hell!"

At that moment Peter was attacked by four thugs. Our director Jon Cassar staged another great fight here where Peter took care of the intruders.

Inside the house, we were back in time to the 1980's. Caine descended the main staircase of the house. He was listening to an old re-run of *The Dukes of Hazard* on a television. The narrator was saying: "*One* Duke... *two* Dukes... *three* Dukes... *four* Dukes! It's enough to drive Boss Hogg *wild*!" Caine entered the living room. It was decorated for the late eighties. He found the beach ball which Mitch had dropped down the stairs. Then he heard an altercation from the kitchen. A husband was slapping his wife around. He was angrily accusing his wife of having an affair. Caine quickly entered the kitchen and intervened. He raised his voice. "Enough, Senator!" he shouted.

Caine realized this was the couple who had lived in the Gables many years before. He pulled Rachel away from her husband who had moved back into the living room. Rachel turned to Caine.

"My husband has fits of temper," she said. "I am afraid this old house would be become our grave!"

Caine noted the jade necklace she was wearing around her neck. It was the *same* *one* that Kermit had given to him. Caine looked around them. "What is the date?" he asked, suddenly.

Rachel said, surprised: "15th of November."

"And the year?"

"1982."

Caine nodded.

The house was suddenly making sense to him.

In the kitchen of the Gables, in real time, the Ancient got a visit from Peter. "I have been hearing sobbing all over the house," Peter said. He produced the small tape recorder he had found on the grounds. "A neat little trick! Where is my father?"

"He said that he went upstairs into the attic!" the Ancient said. "You must be careful!"

At that moment, Caine walked into the kitchen, but he was not really there. He was in the past in 1982. He and Peter merely passed each other as if neither of them realized the other was there.

In the living room of the Gables, still in the past, Caine confronted the husband, Jack Hamilton. Hamilton was subdued. He stared down at the floor. "I never meant to hit her!"

"You have the power of life and death in your hands," Caine told him. "You must use it wisely."

Hamilton nodded. "I am sorry."

"You are sorry *tonight*," Caine said. "Will you be sorry when a final blow kills your wife or your daughter? A father must not instill fear. He must bind his family together."

Hamilton nodded, contrite. "I don't know who you are, but can we talk some more?"

"Talk to your wife," Caine said. "Make her believe she doesn't need protection from you."

Hamilton nodded again and moved past Caine into the kitchen. "And yet," Caine said, softly, looking around him. "All of you have a right to be afraid. But of what?"

Peter moved into the attic room on the third floor and saw Mitch on her rocking horse in her pale make-up and her white dress. She told Peter that his father and disappeared and she pointed. "In there!"

"It is just a closet," Peter said.

Nevertheless, he moved to the wardrobe door and threw it open. There were no clothes in closet, but he saw stairs leading down. Mitch jumped off the rocking horse and moved beside Peter. "Sometimes it is just a closet," she said. "I wouldn't go down there if I were you. You are not special. The Demons will get you!"

Peter put the vial of holy water over his head. "I'll take my chances. Stay here!"

Peter walked down the staircase that led down to the ground floor. He entered the living room. The Dukes of Hazard was still playing on the television. He picked up a couple of 8-tracks from a shelf.

"The Dukes of Hazard?" he said. "Eight track cassettes? What the hell was going on here?"

Caine moved over to him. "It is a different time." he said, simply. "A different dimension. But the same place."

Caine handed Peter a diary from a table. He noted the date. "November 15th." And then he looked closer. "1982?"

"Twelve years ago," Caine said. "Jack Hamilton lived here in the Gables with his family. Now vengeful ghosts walk these rooms angry with their pain, unable to be set free."

"How could this be 1982, Pop?" Peter said. "That's crazy! It is a scam! There was blood on some of the dolls I found in the attic. It was fresh. I have a tape recording of a little girl sobbing in my coat pocket. It can be turned on and off by remote control. I found a heavy magnet on the windowsill outside."

Caine nodded, but he appeared distracted. "That was how those knives in the kitchen were thrown around."

"Exactly!" Peter said. "I just fought off some intruders who want Marilyn and her family out of this house. If we *are* somewhere in the past, then we'd better get back to the present fast!"

Caine shook his head. "The answer is in the past. I can feel it."

They moved out of the living room to see Matt Larchmont coming down the staircase with a gun in his hand. Caine and Peter followed him and saw him grappling with the gun with Jack Hamilton. Then Matt Larchmont killed Hamilton. Peter tried to get off a shot, but nothing happened. Caine shook his head. "There's nothing you can do," he said. "This all happened in the past!"

Kermit returned to the Gables, having escorted Helen Addams to her house a few miles away. He was immediately knocked out by Tom Fleming. He had a couple of his mercenaries with him. He glanced over at the Gables. "Let's get the girl!"

They left Kermit lying on the ground.

Caine and Peter returned to the hallway beside the main staircase. Caine said: "They are dead. The wife and daughter in one of the bedrooms. The husband in the dining room. Murdered by the intruders. Killed by a man named Matt Larchmont."

"How do you know that?"

"I have seen him in my mind."

"But he's no longer here!" Peter said.

"He will be! That is why the Demons have gathered from the past. We must hurry!"

Peter turned away from Caine. "This way, Pop!"

Peter moved to a door beside the staircase. Caine tried to grab him. "Peter, NO!"

Peter opened the door and suddenly found himself in a vortex of wind that was sucking him through the doorway. Ethereal Demons with clawing fingers reached out for Peter. Caine grabbed his son, trying to pull him back from the abyss.

"You have opened the tunnel!" Caine cried. "The one that brought the Demons to this place!"

Peter unhooked the holy water from his neck and threw it at the Demons. White light surged through the opening where the Demons were clawing at Peter to take him through the open doorway.

"They are still coming!" Caine shouted. "We must close the door!"

Peter grabbed hold of the door, trying to shut it. Caine had hold of his shoulders. Peter fought against the power of the skeletal fingers of the Demons.

"Close it!" Caine shouted.

Finally Peter got the door slammed shut. He collapsed against it. "The doorway to Hell!" he gasped.

Caine propelled him away to the foot of the staircase.

Marilyn entered the kitchen, pulling her robe around her. The Ancient was sitting in an easy chair. She told him she could not sleep. The old man was concerned.

"You must go back to your room!" he told her. But it was too late! Marilyn was grabbed by Matt Larchmont and Tom Fleming. Lo Si tried to intervene, but Larchmont knocked him down to the floor. Marilyn was distraught.

"What do you want?" she demanded.

"Just what belongs to us," Larchmont said, whispering in her ear. "Too bad you don't scare so easily. I needed the house empty." To Tom Fleming he said: "Get the keys to the cellar."

Larchmont dragged Marilyn away.

Caine and Peter made it back up the phantom staircase to the wardrobe door in the attic room and shut it behind them. Mitch was still on her rocking horse. She looked surprised to see them.

"Wow!" she said. "You made it back! I thought the monsters had got you both."

"That makes two of us," Peter murmured.

Jason entered the attic. "What's going on?"

"We've got intruders on the grounds," Peter told him. "They may be already here in the house. Take care of your sister."

Caine and Peter moved out of the attic and down the stairs.

Caine said: "These intruders were led by the same man who murdered the Hamilton family twelve years ago."

Kermit had got to his feet on the grounds of the Gables. He entered the house from the hallway. He drew his distinctive gun with its laser sight attached and started down a long corridor. He heard the sound of Marilyn being dragged down to the basement. Kermit headed for another staircase, but frightening voices were taunting him. Wispy fingers clawed at him in the corridor as the Demons surrounded him. Finally Kermit broke free of their demonic embraces, getting to the far end of the corridor. He leaned against the wall, striving for breath. More hands reached out for him from out of the wall. They were strangling him! He clawed at their grasping fingers until he broke away. When Kermit turned back to the wall, the Demons had gone. Kermit was rattled, but he moved on down another staircase that led to the basement.

Marilyn was trapped in the basement with Matt Larchmont. Tom Fleming and his two accomplices were smashing out a wall.

Marilyn was terrified.

Larchmont was ironic. "I know you have questions for me," he said. "I robbed a Citizen's Bank in Clareville. I would have got out of the country if I had not broken down outside the Gables. I buried the money in the basement. When I got back I could not find it. Everything had changed."

Unseen by the intruders, Kermit had entered the basement area and crouched down in front of some stacked boxes. Larchmont continued to harass Marilyn, but she had put it altogether.

"The Hamilton family was living here in 1982," Marilyn said, realizing that Larchmont must have killed them. The killer nodded, enjoying the game he was playing with her. "Yeah, they were. They saw me bury the money." He sighed, as if in regret. "I wish now I'd kept them alive."

"That's why the Demons are here," Marilyn said.

Larchmont knelt beside her, very close and intimating. He was laughed softly. "Demons? There are no Demons in this house, honey! Just the ones I conjured up."

Tom Fleming turned triumphantly and raised a suitcase that he had pulled out of the wall. Larchmont looked up, his eyes shining. "You found it?"

Fleming opened the suitcase, revealing stacks of old money.

Then Caine was in the basement!

He kicked the suitcase out of Fleming's hands, sending him to the floor. Kermit fired at one of the intruders. Peter took care of the two other accomplices with several martial arts moves. Matt Larchmont grabbed Marilyn and dragged her out of the basement. All of the fights in this episode were very carefully orchestrated by our wonderful Director, Jon Cassar.

Matt Larchmont got into the hallway, dragging Marilyn with him. Caine grabbed him and threw him in front of the stairs. Larchmont turned and raised his gun at Caine and Marilyn. There was nowhere for them to go. Larchmont had them cold. Then the door into the hallway opened. More Demons spewed out into the corridor, their sinewy fingers reaching out for Larchmont's throat. He was encircled by them. He started screaming. He was dragged through the open doorway. The door was closed by the Demons. Mitch, Jason and the Ancient walked down the main staircase. Mitch looked around, as if a little stunned. She could not hear any voices now.

"They're all gone," she said, softly.

Outside the Gables the next morning, Kermit thanked Caine who bowed to him. Then he walked to his car where Peter was waiting. Caine said: "The Hamilton family are at peace now. There is no reason for the Demons to return."

The Ancient got into Kermit's green *Kermitmobile*. "Nifty car!"

Kermit smiled and pulled away. Caine and Peter did the same. Marilyn moved inside the Gables with her son, Jason.

In the attic, Mitch was standing framed in front of the window in her white dress. She made a sepulchral, eerie figure.

Back at the 101st Precinct, it was business as usual. Mary Margaret Skalany came over to Peter's desk. "Good weekend?"

Peter smiled. "The best!"

Peter rolled over to T.J.'s desk and handed him the rest of the silver bullets. T.J. looked at him. "Did they come in handy?"

Peter smiled again. "As Kermit would say: 'Oh, yeah!'"

Chapter Five

SUNDAY
AT THE HOTEL
WITH GEORGE

THIS WAS AN OUTSTANDING EPISODE of *Kung Fu: The Legend Continues* with a special place in my heart. It was shot at the Sutton Place Hotel in Toronto where I spent most of the four years on the show. It starred, of course, David Carradine as Kwai Chang Caine and Chris Potter as his son Peter. A wedding reception on the 30th Floor of the hotel was being held for Captain Paul Blaisdell and his daughter Carolyn. Peter was dressed in a tux and Caine was wearing a satin white shirt and a casual Kung Fu broidered jacket.

Some of my favorite actors in the world were in this episode. Geordie Johnson is one of my best friends. He starred in the TV series *Dracula: The Series* which was shot in Luxembourg. I directed an episode of that show. Geordie gave a wonderful performance in this TV series as *Count Dracula*, complete with a slight *Dracula accent*. When it came time for me to cast the leading villain in *Sunday at the Hotel with George*, I wrote the episode especially for him. I also cast him in a sequel episode which was entitled: *Sunday at the Museum with George*, where he played the same debonair, icy antihero.

This episode of *Kung Fu: The Legend Continues* starred an old friend of mine for many years, Simon Williams. He was playing Alan Carstairs, the catering manager

41

of the Sutton Place Hotel. Simon added his considerable skills as an actor to the role with his usual panache and style. The episode also starred Bernard Behrens, who had also starred in *Dracula: The Series* with Geordie Johnson. So it was a reunion of sorts for these two actors.

My friend, the wonderful Robert Lansing, played Captain Paul Blaisdell, which he played for two years on the show. This episode had many of the regulars in the supporting cast of *Kung Fu: The Legend Continues*, including Chief of Detectives Frank Strenlich, Janet-Laine Green playing Blaisdell's blind wife Annie and Nathaniel Moreau playing Young Peter in the *Flashback Temple sequences*. Blaisdell's daughters were in the episode in recurring roles, played by Kim Nettle as Blaisdell's daughter Carolyn and Jhene Erwin as Blaisdell's daughter Kelly. There was a brief appearance by Matt Trueman in the wedding reception scenes who had played a bartender in several episodes.

A new character named Tyler Smith was introduced during Sunday at the Hotel with George. She was played by Maria Schaffel who portrayed Peter's love interest in this episode, although she did not come back for later episodes. She was a terrific singer and sang briefly in the episode with a haunting voice. I was really chuffed—as we would say in England---to be able to assemble this great cast for this special episode of *Kung Fu: The Legend Continues*. I thought it worked out very well.

At the beginning of the episode, Captain Paul Blaisdell emerged from a police bus with Annie, his wife, who was blind. He was dressed in a tux. Annie had a lovely sequined dress for the occasion. Not far behind them we noted Kwai Caine and Peter Caine stepping off the bus. They were all going to a wedding reception at the Sutton Place Hotel for Blaisdell's older daughter, Carolyn.

At the back of the hotel we were introduced to "*George*", a sophisticated, urbane killer, dressed entirely in black with a slight a *Dracula accent*. The truck behind him at the loading bay at the hotel said: *Harlequin Renovations*. One of George's men, a mercenary named Tom Vallance, who was played by David Nerman with frightening menace, passed him. David was terrific in the episode. He had a simmering rage that threatened to explode at any moment.

Alan Carstairs, the Catering Manager for the Sutton Place Hotel, walked over to George who was busy consulting a small notebook in his hand. Carstairs was somewhat officious and fussy, but nevertheless charming. He called out: "Mr. Malkovich!", but George barely looked up.

"I am Alan Carstairs, assistant manager of administration." After getting no response from George, Carstairs glanced over at the lettering at the side of the truck. "You *are* with *Harlequin Renovations*, isn't that right, Mr. Malkovich?"

Finally George turned to him. His manner was friendly, but a little reserved. "George Malkovich, yes, that's right."

Feeling somewhat flustered, Carstairs did his best to carry on. He looked at the truck that George's men were unloading. "I see you've come loaded for bear!"

"Always," George said, ironically.

George and Carstairs moved toward the back of the hotel. George said: "I understand that the admin floor has been completely cleared?"

"Oh, yes," Carstairs assured him.

"Splendid. Perhaps we can look at the lobby. I understand it is beautiful. Is the hotel very full?"

"It's our quiet time of the year," Carstairs said, "but it should pick up when the summer kicks in and the film festival is over." George did not respond. Carstairs cleared his throat. "And, of course, it *is* Sunday."

That appeared to amuse George. He said, with a flourish: "Sunday at the Hotel with George!"

"Yes, quite right," Carstairs muttered, more to himself.

George and Carstairs entered the hotel from a side entrance. The lobby, with its marble floors and myriad mirrors was, indeed, very beautiful. Carstairs said: "My office is up on the second floor if you need anything else." A dapper, attractive man in his forties passed them. Carstairs acknowledged him. "Hi, Mr. Gerhardt." He lowered his voice, as if conspiratorially. "Hans Gerhardt, Manager of the hotel."

Hans Gerhardt was in fact the *real* manager of the Sutton Place Hotel! He was a charming hotelier who became a very good friend of mine during the years we shot *Kung Fu: The Legend Continues*. I stayed in a suite at the Sutton Place Hotel for the whole four years of the show, for no charge, thanks to the generosity of Hans Gerhart. A very good guy who has been a terrific friend of mine ever since.

Paul Blaisdell stood in the lobby of the hotel with his wife Annie, who was wearing large, stylish dark glasses. The bride, Carolyn, looking fabulous, stood nearby with other members of the wedding party. Hans Gerhardt moved over to Blaisdell and Annie and shook their hands.

"Mr. Blaisdell, Hans Gerhardt. Allow me to welcome you to the Sutton Place Hotel."

"I'm sorry for the short notice," Blaisdell said.

"No problem," Gerhardt said. "It's a pleasure to see you here."

Behind them, Carstairs indicated the wedding party. "Wedding reception in the rooftop ballroom."

But George was not listening. He looked at the wedding party as if he were calculating its odds. His very silence was intimidating. Carstairs carried on blithely. "I'll see if I can get your men into the freight elevator and up to the 30th floor."

"Do that," George murmured.

Carstairs moved away. George retreated to a deserted corridor in the hotel where he discreetly loaded a gun. He rode up to the 27th floor where there was a hive of activity with George's men preparing to work on the renovations on the floor. George was joined once more by Alan Carstairs.

"Your work will finish in this office here," he said.

George indicated more office space. "And through there?"

"Our safe deposit boxes and the vault," Carstairs said.

George feigned surprise. "Not down in the lobby?"

Carstairs preened a little bit. "No, that's for casual guests. Those are for our... ah..."

"Special guests?" George asked. "The ones who stay for months. The ones with *real valuables* to protect."

"Quite so," Carstairs said.

George indicated one of the doors in front of the offices. "I hope that door is locked. Not all of my men are saints."

Carstairs led George over to it. "Locked, sealed and impenetrable. And if anyone did get in there, we have a time lock with a complicated computer fail-safe mechanism."

George smiled tolerantly. "Of course you do."

George hustled Carstairs out of the suite offices. "If you need any further assistance?"

"If you want these renovations in one afternoon, we can't be tripping over hotel staff."

"All sorted," Carstairs assured him. "I've set up a temporary office down in the lobby and the 30th floor is off-limits for the day."

"How can you be sure of that?" George asked him.

"We'll program the elevators to bypass the floor."

George smiled. "Perfect."

He and Carstairs moved out into the corridor and the elevator doors opened. Carstairs turned back. "Well, good luck!"

George smiled again, but there was no humor in it. "Thank you so much."

The elevator door closed. George went back into the site of the offices. One of his mercenaries, a man named Gantry, dragged a weary, frightened man over to where George was waiting for him. He was in his middle forties. He had long since been beaten down into submission. We can see that George and the man, whose name was Andrei, had a long history together. Gantry indicated the man.

"He tried to escape twice! I thought you boys went way back!"

Andrei took a stance against George, but his defiance had a hollow ring to it. "I will not do this!"

George's voice was chiding. "Andrei! Consequences! That's how men like us have lived our lives."

"You cannot threaten me," Andrei said. "I am dying."

George seemed surprised by the revelation. "Of what?"

"None of your business!"

"Do try to make it through the afternoon," George murmured. He put a friendly arm around Andrei's shoulders. "I'm helping you. Your wife and family will be on a 747 out of St. Petersburg, aren't you glad they changed it to from Leningrad? A peasant's name. Your family will be together tomorrow afternoon for dinner at the Vladivostok Restaurant. Rather authentic cuisine I'm told."

"Your contacts are gone," Andrei said, bitterly. "The KGB is finished!"

"Shadow Men!" George said, and his voice now had a more sinister tone to it. "We are everywhere. Isn't that right, Mr. Becker?"

The mercenary called Becker said: "That's a fact, George."

George gripped Andrei's arm, his voice a silky whisper. "Cut a spy and fifteen more run out of his pores. Make him bleed and that blood breeds rats. I can wipe your family out with one phone call or introduce them to the wonders of the American nightmare. Your choice."

George nodded at Becker who propelled Andrei down the corridor.

Downstairs in the lobby, Alan Carstairs was giving instructions on his cell phone. "Jack, this Alan Carstairs. Seal off Floor 27, would you?"

In the elevator, Peter rode up toward the 30th floor with some of the guests, including the two bridesmaids, aged six, who were mischievously trying to push elevator buttons. Peter had just threatened to arrest them!

In the offices on the 27th Floor, George's men were putting together AK47s. George roughly pulled Vallance to him. "Keep the firepower out of sight! If everything goes to plan we wouldn't have to fire a single shot!"

In the elevator, the doors opened on the 27th floor. More buttons pressed by the two little girls amid much giggling. George's men turned, like deer caught in headlights, putting their weapons behind them. Peter grinned and shrugged. "We're stopping at every floor!"

George's face was expressionless. One of the kids fired at him as if her finger was a trigger. "Get your hands up! This a bust!"

George raised his hands in mock surrender. "Are you going to arrest *all* of us?"

The guests in the elevator laughed and so did the mercenaries.

Peter said: "I'm sorry about this!" To the little girls, he said: "You're going to be punished for this!"

But as Peter looked back at George, something was bothering him. The stillness and the muted atmosphere of these mercenaries had registered with Peter, although he did not think much more about it at the time. The elevator doors finally closed again.

George's men continued loading their weapons. Tom Vallance shrugged it off. "They saw nothing."

George moved over to him and his voice was deadly. "You are standing in front of polished gilt marble, a reflective surface. He won't be sure of the shape of the weapons, but he'll be thinking about it."

"Who? Some guy in an elevator?" Vallance said. "Who cares!"

"He's a Police Officer," George said, forcefully. "He's off-duty. I know about this cop. He is never off-duty." He raised his voice to the other men. "Get out of the overalls and splash on some aftershave. We're going to crash the party."

"Are you nuts?" Vallance asked.

George grabbed him and held him in a vice-like grip. He lowered his voice to a harsh rasp. "Don't *ever* ask me that!" He released Vallance and turned to the others. "Take out all of the elevators but one. Secure the stairs."

George's mercenaries did exactly that. They opened the elevators at another floor and eased down a hose which started a flood of water. They used walkie-talkies to communicate with George. One of them, Callahan, said into his walkie: "Secure on the 30th floor."

In one of the offices on the 27th floor, Andrei sat at a desk in front of a computer. He was guarded by another of George's men. Andrei worked on the blueprints on the computer screen that would eventually grant George's mercenaries access to the vault room.

Upstairs on the 30th floor, the wedding party was in full swing. Caine looked around, seeming to enjoy the camaraderie and high spirits he observed. Paul Blaisdell, looking elegant in his tux, moved over to where Caine was standing.

"I wanted to thank you for blessing my daughter's marriage," he said. "It meant a lot to Peter to have you there. He's gotten very close to my family in the past few years."

"It is he who is fortunate," Caine said.

"I want you to know that there is no one happier in this room that Peter has found his real father."

"The generosity of your spirit does you great honor," Caine said.

Blaisdell smiled. "There's no generosity about it! I have been holding a tiger by the tail since he was fifteen years old. How is he handling the reunion?"

Caine took a deep breath before replying. "He has much anger, doubt, fears."

"How are *you* handing it?" Blaisdell asked him.

Caine thought about that. "Rage, pleasure, hope." He gave one his signature shrugs. "I am dealing with it as best that I can."

Annie Blaisdell moved over to them and took Caine's hands in hers. "Your benediction was beautiful."

Caine smiled at her. "A simple prayer."

"I am so happy you're with our family today," she said. "Stepmothers and lost fathers have to stick together!"

"You have not always been blind?" Caine asked her.

"That's right," Annie said. "A nurse turned up the oxygen a tad too high when I was three months old in hospital with whooping cough. But I am disappointed. Most people who meet me don't know I am blind at all."

"I can see beyond the eyes," Caine said. "At sometimes an unfortunate gift. You do not use a cane?"

Annie released Caine's hands and took Blaisdell's hand in her own. She smiled at him. "*He's* my cane. And you know what they say about the other senses intensifying? Well, I can hear soda being splashed into a highball glass from fifty yards!"

Caine laughed at that.

Alan Carstairs moved over to them. "Anything you want, let me know." He addressed them as if they were co-conspirators. "Double duty today. The catering manager is off sick. Touch of food poisoning. I'd stick clear of the flaming rum trifle," he added, wryly.

He moved on through the crowd. Up on the raised dais, Chief of Detectives Frank Strenlich had picked up the microphone. "May I introduce the bride and groom, Mr. and Mrs. Todd and Carolyn McCall."

Carolyn and her husband came over to the raised dais.

Strenlich said: "The father of the bride and the mother of the groom please step forward.

Peter was standing with his girlfriend Tyler Smith, a beautiful, fiery girl. They had a kind of abrasive, combative relationship. Peter indicated the bride. "She looks beautiful."

Tyler was ironic. "Is this a pitch?"

"No, just a hell of an idea!" Peter said.

"First we'd have to be in love."

Peter considered. "We've done that."

"Then we would have to sleep together again," Tyler said.

"We can do that," Peter said.

"And one of us can't be crazy," Tyler added.

Peter grinned. "Now you got me!"

Blaisdell had been summoned by Strenlich, which left Annie beside Caine. She nodded at Peter who had just parted from Tyler. "He told me he never knew his mother."

Caine shook his head. "No."

We went to a *Flashback Sequence* of the episode. Caine and Young Peter were sitting surrounded by myriad candles. Caine was holding a small photograph of Peter's mother in his hands.

Young Peter said: "Tell me again about my mother."

Cain shrugged. "She was very beautiful. She always wore a yellow flower in her hair."

"Ping Hi said she looked like a movie star."

Caine smiled at that. "She did."

"Which one?" Young Peter asked.

"Rhonda Fleming?" Caine said.

Young Peter looked at his father blankly. "*Who?*"

Caine smiled. "Watch the late show. It was her soul that radiated most of her beauty."

He turned the photo over. On the back of it was written: To My Own True Love.

"Why did she have to die?" Young Peter asked him.

"I cannot answer that," Caine said, quietly. "To return to the roots is to return to one's destiny."

"Will I ever have a new mother?" Young Peter asked.

Caine shrugged. "Perhaps, my son. One day." Then he added again: "Perhaps."

We returned to Caine standing with Anne Blaisdell in the Sutton Place ballroom. He said: "Peter always carried her picture with him."

"He still does," Annie said. "In his wallet."

"But now it is *your* image he carries in his heart," Caine said.

Annie gave Caine's arm a squeeze. "I think I'm going to like you a lot!"

Strenlich moved over to Peter in the ballroom. Tyler Smith had just left him. The Chief of Detectives indicated the place where she has disappeared. "Is she thawing out?"

"Yeah," Peter said, wryly. "Like the iceberg that hit the Titanic!"

Strenlich glanced around the room. "Look at this spread! When I got married it was in Vegas with a casino dealer as a witness, the guy who married Elvis hauled out of bed and a handful of rice."

"I wish I could have been there," Peter murmured.

"Now I have got the mortgage, the kids, and the tag team of orthodontists to support. Who knew?" Strenlich looked over at Blaisdell who was dancing with his daughter Carolyn. "He's kind of a mystery, the old man. Never talks about his life before the police force. I hear whispers about the CIA and the killing of a top terrorist leader in Nambia. You remember when he disappeared a couple of years ago during Desert Storm?" He lowered his voice conspiratorially. "Advising Schwarzkopf! I swear to God, that's what I heard."

But Peter was not listening any longer. He had spied some of George's mercenaries moving through the ballroom wearing street clothes. George was dressed in his usual dark colors. He helped himself to a glass of champagne from one of the waitresses. Alan Carstairs hustled over to him. George smiled at him welcomingly. "Carstairs! You certainly know how to throw a party!"

"A private party!" Carstairs said, highly agitated. "If you want to take a coffee break, there's a machine on the Admin floor. I have donuts and sandwiches ordered."

"How thoughtful," George murmured.

"Listen to me, Mr. Malkovich, may I remind you this is a private party! You are not invited. You are a decorator here!"

One of George's men grabbed Carstairs and hustled him away. "What are you doing?" he asked, indignantly.

Then the crowd swallowed him and the mercenary up.

Further down the ballroom, Peter turned his attention back to Chief Strenlich. "Mystery is part of the Blaisdell family," he said. "Excuse me, sir."

Peter moved over to where George was standing sipping his glass of champagne. There was an edge to Peter's voice. "When you decide to crash a party, you really go for it."

George looked him wryly. "Are you going to arrest me?"

"I left my handcuffs at home."

George indicated the groom who was dancing with Carolyn Blaisdell.

"Let's hope *he* hasn't!"

Up at the bar, Caine had noted the exchange between Peter and George. He also noted the other mercenaries moving through the ballroom. George turned his attention back to Peter, his manner relaxed and insouciant. "Here's the deal. We are going to spend Saturday afternoon here at the Sutton Place Hotel. You are going to enjoy a lovely wedding reception. We're robbing the hotel."

"You've got a lot of nerve telling me that," Peter said.

George's attitude shifted suddenly. He looked Peter in the eyes. "You don't know what nerve *is*."

Alan Carstairs walked up to the raised dais to the microphone. "Ladies and gentlemen, an announcement that shouldn't cause any alarm. Elevators will be out of action for a couple of hours. A bit of flooding; a burst water main. But they will be operational long before you want to leave such a beautiful reception. And now it is my pleasure to introduce you, from the *Agrippa Club*, Tyler Smith!"

Tyler took Carstairs place at the microphone and launched into a kick-ass song.

George's attention was still fixed on Peter. "You will also find that the phones have been temporarily disconnected," he said. "So no one calls for help."

Peter said: "So, I'm supposed to sit here while there's a robbery in progress three floors below?"

George shrugged. "Unless you have a fortune in diamonds in one of those safe deposit boxes, I wouldn't give it another thought."

"What if I *do* give it another thought," Peter said, evenly. "And maybe share that thought with others?"

"We did bring more than paint rollers and carpet tacks with us," George admitted. "At the first hint of betrayal we will come up here with AK47's and hose the room. A great many people will die. Do not be a hero," George said. "They don't die young. They die stupid."

George left Peter abruptly. Peter made his way to the bar where Caine was waiting for him. "We got trouble," he said.

"Yes," Caine said, quietly. "I know."

In one of the ladies' bathrooms on the 30th floor, Kelly Blaisdell had just put on some make-up. The door opened behind her and Tom Vallance entered. He stifled her scream.

"Come on, baby, come with us!"

He manhandled Kelly through the doorway.

Back in the main ballroom, George helped himself to some hors d'oeuvres from another waitress and wandered over to the bar where Caine and Peter stood. "Excellent hors d'oeuvres," he said. "In particular the salmon roll. We took out a little insurance in case you became restless. Your bridesmaid will be returned without harm in two hours and the bride will be an old married lady by that time. Enjoy!"

George moved away.

Caine said: "We must act."

Peter shook his head. "We can do nothing! He's holding all the cards."

"His eyes are dead," Caine said. "Like Tan's."

Tan was a vicious foe who Caine had faced, but we will return to him in a later episode.

"He sleeps without dreaming," Caine said in an undertone. "He breathes through his heels. He has no dread of death. This man has no passion. He has no lust for life. His word cannot be trusted."

Meanwhile, in a different part of the ballroom, George had cornered Alan Carstairs, forcing him back against one of the gilt mirrors. George held him there effortlessly. "One elevator is working," he said. "I sent it down to the lobby. It will bring no one past the 30th floor."

"You would need an elevator bypass to accomplish that," Carstairs said.

"I have friends in low places," George said, dryly. "You are going to keep this reception running smoothly and efficiently. One false move and my men will open fire into the crowd. Do you understand?"

Carstairs swallowed and nodded. "Perfectly."

George adjusted Carstairs' tie, then reached into his suit pocket and removed his cell phone. He smiled at the assistant manager encouragingly. "Carry on."

Tom Vallance entered the suites of rooms that George had commandeered in the hotel. He threw Kelly down onto an ornate chair. She whirled to him defiantly. Her lip was bleeding. "Do you know who my father is? He's a Police Officer!"

Vallance gripped her shoulders. "Mine, too! Only he is dead. His face was blown away by a half-crazy junkie for the change in his pocket." Vallance leaned down very close to Kelly. His voice had taken on a manic tone. "Let's hope that doesn't happen to your Daddy."

George stood right behind him. "It won't," he said, smoothly. "Because he won't be down here. Keep her quiet; keep her comfortable and no more rough stuff."

Vallance straightened. He was at the boiling point with George. "She wouldn't come down the stairs!"

"Neither would I," George said reasonably. He wiped the blood off Kelly's lip with a silk handkerchief. "This ordeal will be over in a short time," he told her, "and then you may return to your party."

Kelly looked up at him, grateful for his intervention, but scared what was going to happen next. George turned back and the mercenary retreated a little. George did not say anything more to him. He exited the room and went to find out how his other mercenaries were doing. They were cutting through panels in the hotel corridor with blow torches.

"How goes it?"

One of the men removed the helmet that protected him. "Slow. There's more than three sealed panels here."

"I don't care if there are *ten*," George said, curtly. "Cut through them!"

He walked down the corridor into the empty suite of offices where Andrei was working on his computer. More diagrams and schematics revolved on the screen. The sick man was hunched over his work, his fingers flying over the keys.

"We're got to get into that vault, Andrei!" Georg said, impatiently. "Come on, you know the alarm systems backwards."

"I can't think!" Andrei muttered. "I can't work it out!"

George leaned a little closer. "The contents of just one of those safe deposit boxes will ensure that you and your family will spend the rest of your days in comfort. How about Orlando in Florida? Disney World down the street, McDonald's at the corner, what more could you want?"

"Why should I believe you?" Andrei asked, bleakly.

"I gave you my word," George said, more quietly.

"How many innocent people will die?" Andrei retorted. "What are you after? Coin collections? Stocks, bonds, cash, a Contessa's jewels? A small black book where numbered Swiss bank accounts are listed along with the names of Nazi traitors? Tell me it's something provocative!"

"Just get me there," George said, curtly. "Time is running out. That's a good boy."

George left him. Andrei continued assaulting the computer keys with a vengeance, but his entire demeanor was beaten down.

In the hotel ballroom the wedding party was still going strong. Carolyn moved over to her father who was talking to the groom. She shook her head. "I can't find Kelly!"

Blaisdell was not alarmed. He glanced at the groom and smiled. "She's cruising."

Carolyn dropped the earrings that Kelly had been wearing into the palm of Blaisdell's hand. "I found these on the floor of the bathroom."

Blaisdell looked at the expensive earrings. "She probably didn't even know she dropped them. I'll find her." He indicated the groom. "You two mingle and entertain. That's an order."

Carolyn and the groom back moved into the crowd. Blaisdell looked down again at the earrings in his hand. His cop instincts had kicked in big time.

Something was defiantly wrong.

Caine stood up at the bar where Terry, our bartender, had just handed him a green cocktail. Caine was surreptitiously watching one of George's mercenaries moving through the crowd. He picked up the fluted glass and knocked it back. He looked at it appraisingly.

"What do you think of it?" Terry asked.

"Quite a kick," Caine said. "What do you call it?"

"It's called a grasshopper."

Caine reacted. "A *grasshopper*?"

In the original Kung Fu TV series, the name "*Grasshopper*" had a special meaning for Kwai Chang Caine. He had been called *Grasshopper* by the priests at the temple.

This was a gentle nudge for the series.

Alan Carstairs found Peter in the kitchen where more food was being prepared for the 30th floor. He was looking for something. "Guests aren't allowed in the kitchen!" Carstairs said. "What are you doing?"

"My knife wasn't sharp enough to cut the salmon roll," Peter murmured, still searching.

"Now look here…" Carstairs began.

Peter took out his badge from the pocket. "I am a cop. I know what is going down. Just keep cool, keep the food coming, keep the party humming."

Carstairs was somewhat nonplussed but took it in his stride. "I'll do my best. What are you going to do?"

Peter found a very sharp stiletto knife which he slipped down to his ankle and pulled his sock over it. "Damned if I know," he said.

In the ballroom, Annie Blaisdell joined Caine at the bar. Her voice was subdued, her manner quiet. "Something's wrong. I can feel it."

Caine shook his head. "No, I am uncomfortable at these occasions."

Blaisdell joined them. He looked at Annie. "Have you seen Kelly?"

"No, I haven't." Annie smiled at Caine. "Does that seem a weird question to a blind chick?"

"Not to me," Caine said.

"What's that in your hand, Paul?" she asked him. "Are those Kelly's earrings?"

Blaisdell was constantly amazed at his wife's perception. "How did you know that?"

"I can smell her perfume," Annie said. "It came off her fingers when she put them on."

"She dropped them," Blaisdell said. "I'm going to take a walk around the room. Maybe Master Caine will take you to your seat, all right?"

Blaisdell moved into the crowd. Annie smiled again at Caine. "I didn't know you were a *Master*?"

"A priest," Caine corrected her. "Not a master."

He escorted Annie back to her seat at one of the tables. "There *is* something wrong," she said. "I can feel it."

"Yes, there is," Caine said. "But I will fix it."

Caine moved away. Immediately Frank Strenlich knelt beside Annie, smiling, somewhat hammered. "Great party, isn't it?"

Annie smiled tolerantly and patted his head. "Yes, Frank."

Caine caught up with Peter and moved to one side with him. "If the elevators aren't functioning," he said, "there are always the stairs."

"Do you think we should check them out?"

"It would be logical."

Peter laughed. "You sound just like Spock."

Caine frowned. "*Who?*"

Peter shook his head. "I've got to get you into the 20th Century. Here is the deal. Today, you're my partner."

"I would be honored," Caine said.

"Okay," Peter said.

They moved to a door leading out to the staircase. Once on the staircase, they pulled up. Two of George's men were sitting on the stairs holding M16 rifles. Peter nodded at them.

"Hi, guys," he murmured.

He and Caine had no choice but to go back the way they came. There was no way for them to get past George's mercenaries. They moved back into the ballroom. Peter tried the exit door there, but it was locked. He shook his head in frustration.

"We're stranded," he said. "I don't see a way out of this, Pop. Unless your Shaolin skills include climbing down the outside of a building. And I know, don't call you 'Pop'!"

Peter turned around and suddenly realized that Caine was gone. He had approached one of George's mercenaries and rendered him unconscious. He gave Peter an 'a-okay' sign. Caine found another one of George's men standing at the bar. The man tried to pull a gun on him. Caine sent him down to the ground and then leant down over him, as if concerned.

"Sir, are you all right?"

Caine hit him in the chest with a quick kung fu jab and he passed out. Alan Carstairs moved over to where Caine stood over the unconscious thug, raising his voice. "Nothing to worry about, ladies and gentlemen. A little too much of the grape, that's all."

Caine and Carstairs carried the thug between them. They dropped him onto the carpet at the back of the ballroom. Peter took out another of George's men, but the last mercenary threw him down to the floor. Caine sighed, leaving Carstairs to hold up the other fallen thug. Caine dealt with the third mercenary, then he hauled Peter up to his feet. He was a little dazed, but he was all right. Caine tossed the fallen M16 rifle at Carstairs who deftly caught it.

"Gosh!"

Peter and Alan Carstairs tied up the fallen thugs.

"This would be awfully exciting if it wasn't so damn terrifying," Carstairs said, getting back to his feet.

"Can your staff be trusted to keep our little secret?" Peter asked.

Carstairs smiled. "Of course! They are in my cricket team!"

"I don't suppose you have a window-washing team outside the ballroom?" Peter asked him.

"That would be handy, wouldn't it?" Carstairs said. "I'm afraid not."

Caine said: "There is another way down."

Caine and Peter left Carstairs and made their way back toward the bar. Blaisdell moved over to them. "Want to tell me what is going on?" he asked them, sotto voce.

"Robbery in progress," Peter said. "You see that big guy over there? And the other guy at the head table?"

"Yeah, I saw them," Blaisdell said.

"There are only three of them now," Caine said.

"Administration is housed on the 30th floor," Peter said. "Men on the stairs."

"If you've taken out three of them," Blaisdell said, "you've got their guns."

"Kelly is a hostage," Peter told him.

Blaisdell was shocked. "Kelly!"

"One shot goes down those stairs, they'll cut her throat," Peter said. "We'll find her. We've got a chance to get below the 30th floor."

"Okay," Blaisdell said. "We'll take the other three out." He glanced around them. "We should break this up. This might be a time for you to laugh at my bad jokes."

Caine and Peter faked laughter about something Blaisdell had said. Peter moved away. Blaisdell looked over at Caine and put a restraining hand on his arm. "This is police business. You don't have to go with him."

"But I do," Caine said, softly. "He is my son."

Caine and Peter found their way across one of the roofs of the Sutton Place Hotel and entered through another doorway. They moved to the elevators on that floor and forced open the elevator doors.

The elevator was a long way down.

Peter blanched, staring into the abyss. Obviously, he was frightened of heights. He shook his head. "I can't do this!"

"Yes, you can," Caine said.

We go into another *Flashback Sequence*. Caine, in his saffron robes, stood at the bottom of a wooden staircase. Young Peter stood above him on the first-floor landing, but he had not yet climbed over to leap down. There were pebbles in a symmetrical pattern on the ground around Caine. He put arms to catch the Young Peter.

"You must land without disturbing the pebbles," he said.

Young Peter shook his head. "I can't! I'm afraid!"

"Great fear is accepting the unknown," Caine called up to him. "Small fears eat at the heart. You must learn to overcome them. They will devour reason."

"I get dizzy," Young Peter said. "I'm not a bird! I can't soar like one!"

"Yes, you can," Caine insisted. "I will catch you to break your fall. Trust me."

The *Flashback Sequence* ended. Now we were back with Caine and Peter at the mouth of the open elevator. Peter shook his head. "I can't! I can't jump down!"

"Trust me," Caine said again. "I will catch you. I will break your fall."

Peter said: "Even Butch and Sundance had a river to jump into!"

"Think of not disturbing the pebbles," Caine said.

"You're going to have to come up with better imagery than that!" he said.

"Think of the hostages they are holding," Caine said.

Peter nodded. "Okay, that's better imagery!"

"Here we go," Caine said.

He steeled himself, then leaped at the elevator cables and caught them. When Caine looked up, it was no longer Peter standing there in the abyss, but *the Young Peter* who looked down at him. Caine held onto the elevator cables, looking up at the memory of his young son.

"Jump!" Caine said. "Trust me!"

In his mind, Caine could see the *Young Peter* jumping down to the ground in the temple and catching him when he stepped onto the pebbles.

Then it was Peter who was standing above him.

"Jump!" Caine said again. "Do not let your fears haunt you. They are small and of no consequence."

Peter gathered his courage in hand and jumped down onto the elevator cables. His hands slipped and he fell. Caine caught him at the last moment, grabbing hold of his wrists. Peter struggled, dangling on the elevator cables. He tried to get his feet entwined in them.

"Grab my hand!" Caine shouted down.

Peter took hold of the elevator cables and slowly pulled himself up.

In the hotel suite that George had commandeered, Kelly Blaisdell was watching Tom Vallance as he played with a switchblade knife, throwing it around in his hands. She was frightened, but defiant. Vallance was in his own world.

"George used to be the best," he commented. "A lean, mean machine. Cut a man's throat and play chess over the phone with the Romanian champion. Mysterious, that was our Georgie. We all thought he was born in Transylvania. We really did."

"Where was he born?" Kelly asked.

"Baltimore," Vallance said, ironically. "He's butter now. It may be time for him to retire." The mercenary leaned down close to Kelly. She slapped his face. Vallance grinned at her. "Sassy! I like that! I like that a lot! We have time!"

The mercenary moved away from the bed. Kelly cowered away from him, her breathing shallow.

George's mercenaries were still working on punching a way through the wall outside the vault. George walked back into the back offices to see Andrei. Andrei did not even look at him.

"If I cut the wrong wire, the alarm will go off whether I open the door or not," he said.

"Cut the right one," George said, patiently.

Andrei turned to look at him. "All of my family, my wife, my children, my grandfather, *everyone*. That is our understanding. They all come here."

"I told you," George said, softly. "You have my word."

Andrei punched a key on the computer. The screen lit up. Andrei sat back, as if drained. But George was jubilant. He walked down from the offices and right from there into the vault room of the hotel. He used his walkie-talking to contact his mercenaries.

"Becker?"

In the ballroom, beside some of the reception guests, Becker brought up his walkie. "Stage three secure, George."

One of the other mercenaries caught Becker's arm, their voices drowned out in the overall ambiance of the party. "You didn't tell him that we're missing three men?"

"And have George go ballistic?" Becker said. "We'll take care of it up here ourselves. Now find them!"

The two mercenaries split up. But Blaisdell had overheard their conversation.

In the elevator shaft, Caine and Peter precariously climbed down the elevator cables.

Meanwhile, in the hotel suite, one of George's mercenaries grabbed his arm. "You better come quick!"

Alarmed, George ran with him to the empty office where Andrei has been working. He was slumped in his chair. George grabbed stricken man's arm.

"What is it, Andrei?"

"My pills," he gasped. "I need my pills! A prescription. Hurry!"

George reached into Andrei's pocket, pulled out a rumpled prescription and moved quickly from the office. Down in the suite offices where Kelly was being held hostage, Tom Vallance continued to pace restlessly. Finally Kelly said: "I need to go to the bathroom."

"Can't you wait?" Vallance asked her.

"No!"

Vallance leaned over Kelly, then grabbed her to kiss her. She struggled in his arms. George entered the suite behind them. "That will be enough, Vallance!" The mercenary pulled himself away from Kelly, startled at hearing George's voice. George stared at him with malice dripping in his tone. He leaned down and gently pulled up the strap of Kelly's evening gown where Vallance had tried to paw her. "Let the young lady have what she requested."

Kelly jumped up and another of George's men led her out of the suite. George turned with deadly calm to Vallance and handed him Andrei's prescription. "Get this filled in the pharmacy in the lobby."

"It's *Sunday*," Vallance retorted. "They're closed."

"I need those safe deposit boxes open and that won't happen if Andrei has a heart attack," George said, reasonably. "Talk to Hans Gerhardt, the manager, tell him it's an emergency." George's voice suddenly came aloud. "*Now!*"

Vallance left the suite.

In the elevator shaft, Caine and Peter laboriously pulled themselves down the elevator cables. Below them on the 27th floor, Vallance pressed the button for the elevator. In the elevator shaft the elevator started to rise. Caine leaped onto the other elevator cables. While Peter held on, Caine made a loop with the sash of his embroidered Kung Fu jacket.

"Grab the sash!" Caine called to him. Peter grabbed it. "Now swing!"

Peter swung over to the hanging elevator cables to join his father, his heart pounding. The elevator stopped.

"Here we go!" Caine said.

Below them, the elevator door opened at the 27th floor. Caine and Peter landed on the top of the elevator. Vallance entered the elevator and pressed the button for the lobby. The elevator doors slid shut and the elevator car started to descend.

Caine and Peter rode on the top of it.

In the hotel ballroom the reception party was still in full swing. Chief of Detectives Frank Strenlich was dancing with Carolyn, the bride. Blaisdell motioned for him to join him.

"You sure know how to throw a party, Captain!" he said.

"We have a problem," Blaisdell said, quietly.

Down in the lobby, the elevators opened and Vallance exited, looking around for the manager. The elevator closed behind him and proceeded to the next floor. Caine and Peter jumped down through the hatch into the elevator and forced the doors open at the mezzanine level. They moved into one of the offices where hotel staff was working. Peter flashed his wallet with his ID and badge to the secretary there.

"Police!" he said. "We need to use your computer system."

The secretary stood up. "What's the trouble?"

Peter took her chair at her desk and leafed through pages in a directory on the desk. "I need the codes for the security system. A woman's life is at stake."

The secretary shook her head. "I'm sorry, sir. I can't give out that information without Mr. Gerhardt's permission."

"It's a class one felony," Peter told her. "It's an emergency. Just give me the codes!"

Flustered, the secretary said: "70529."

Below in the lobby, Hans Gerhardt opened the pharmacy door for Tom Vallance. "Here we are, sir."

The real-life Hans Gerhardt was not an actor, but he rose to the occasion beautifully. I told him when we were shooting the episode that his performance was terrific!

Back up in the suite offices on the 27thfloor, Andrei was still in distress. But he hit some keys on the computer screen. "The safe deposit boxes are about to open, George," he said, hoarsely.

In the vault room, where George was waiting in the darkness, the safe deposit boxes opened all at once. There had to be *a hundred* of them. "That is a beautiful sound," George said.

In the hotel offices, Peter had accessed the computer program, bringing it up on the screen. He stabbed a few computer keys and the screen lit up like a Christmas tree.

"It's too late," Peter said. "They're in."

In the kitchen, Alan Carstairs hurried over to one of George's mercenaries. "Excuse me, sir, guests are not allowed in the kitchen."

The man turned to Carstairs. "Open this door!"

"I'm afraid I've given my keys away!"

The mercenary's voice hardened. "I said, *open this door!*"

He took out a gun from his jacket. Behind him, Blaisdell hit him with a small wooden shelf. Carstairs threw a punch at the mercenary. Blaisdell finished the man off with another smash with the shelf. Blaisdell caught his gun before the mercenary crumpled to the kitchen floor. Carstairs looked over at Blaisdell in triumph.

"Now that felt awfully good!" he said.

In one of the restrooms off the ballroom area, Strenlich came in to wash his hands while another of George's men glanced over at him.

"Swell party, isn't it?" Strenlich said, and nailed him. The mercenary collapsed to the bathroom floor.

In the corridor outside the elevators, Peter pressed the button for the elevator, checking one gun in his belt, then another. Caine stood beside him.

"They're going to the vault and the safe deposit boxes will be empty," Peter said. "They'll be out of here before we can make a phone call."

He offered Caine one of the guns, but he shook his head. "I cannot accept a weapon."

"Then you had better get out of here right now," Peter told him.

"Could I be considered back-up?" Caine asked.

Peter looked at him, then nodded. "All right! You and me! We will take them out one at a time."

The elevator door opened up and Peter entered it, followed by Caine.

In the vault room, George was emptying the safe deposit boxes while his men were doing the same. They were stuffing boxes of jewels and the bank notes and cramming them into bags.

One of them said: "I can't believe all of this stuff!"

At the 27th floor, the elevator door opened. Two more of George's mercenaries were guarding the corridor, but no one emerged from the elevator. The men moved forward to the open elevator door. Caine and Peter jumped down to take them out. Peter nailed one of them, but the second one knocked Peter down to the ground. Caine took him out and hauled Peter up onto his feet. He nodded, a little blearily.

"I know," Peter said. "Practice, practice."

Down in the main lobby, Tom Vallance emerged from the pharmacy with Hens Gerhardt. Vallance has a prescription in his hand. "Thanks."

"You're very welcome," Hans said.

Vallance proceeded over to the bank of elevators and pushed the button.

In the ballroom, Blaisdell and Strenlich sat down on either side of one of George's men. He reached into his pocket for his gun, but they disarmed him and sent him down to the floor.

In the vault room, George's mercenaries had just about finished putting the contents of the safe deposit boxes into their gym bags. George left them.

In the suite, Andrei was slumped at his chair in front of his computer. George entered. Andrei turned around him expectantly. "My pills."

George took out a gun from his coat and screwed a silencer onto it. His manner was cold and impersonal. "I don't think you'll be needing them now," he told him. "I'll say goodbye to your family."

Andrei looked at him contemptuously. "So this is what your word is worth."

"You betrayed me once," George said. "Now we are even."

Before George could fire, Caine came from behind him. With two punches he knocked George to the floor. Andrei looked up at Caine. "Don't kill him," he said, softly.

Caine nodded and moved out of the office.

In the lobby, Vallance was getting antsy for the elevator to arrive. "Come on! Come on!"

In the suite on the 27th Floor, one of the mercenaries grabbed Kelly. "I am not as patient as Mr. Vallance. Time for you to polish my shoes, darling!"

Kelly jumped up, but the thug grabbed her and threw her onto the bed. "Think of it as your wedding night!"

Peter stepped into the suite and put a gun to the man's head. "Stop right there!"

The thug's reactions were like lightning fast. He disarmed Peter, sending him down to the ground. Peter and the thug struggled. Peter tried to reach for his fallen gun, but he was too far away. He fought off the thug. "Kelly! Go!"

Kelly jumped to her feet and escaped from the hotel suite. In the lobby the elevator finally arrived. Vallance got into it and punched the button for the 27th floor.

In the hotel room, Peter reached down, pulled up his pant leg, grabbed the sharp stiletto blade he had concealed there and stabbed the thug. He collapsed. Peter crawled away and managed to get back to his feet, gasping for breath.

Outside the hotel room, Kelly ran down the corridor. The elevator door opened at the 27th floor and Kelly ran right to Tom Vallance. He grabbed her, grinning, and manhandled her forward. Peter came down the corridor, his gun aimed at Vallance. The mercenary turned Kelly around and put his gun at her head.

"I'll blow her away!" he shouted.

Peter turned his gun around and dropped it. At that moment Kelly bit Vallance's finger. He let go of her with a yelp and she flung herself away. Peter pulled a second gun from his coat and shot Vallance in the chest. The mercenary slid down to the floor, dead.

Caine slid a light fixture against the vault, trapping the rest of George's men inside. He moved back into the corridor, holding an arm around Andrei's shoulders, supporting him. He moved over to where Peter was comforting a teary Kelly. Peter looked up and offered his hand to Caine.

"Secure, partner?" Peter asked him.

Caine gripped his hand with his. "Secure!"

In the ballroom, Carolyn and her groom were about to cut the cake. Carolyn saw her sister and moved over to her. "Where have you been?" she demanded.

Kelly had dried her tears. She smiled a devil-care smile. "Oh, just having a grand old time."

They made their way to the cake. Caine and Peter came around the corner with Strenlich and moved over to where Blaisdell was standing. Peter's expression told the Captain all he needed to know. Blaisdell nodded gratefully to Caine and moved to Annie. Standing with them was one of the guests who was talking to Annie, both of them smiling. An eagle-eyed reader might recognize the guest as being *myself*! A little "Hitchcock" cameo!

In the ballroom, Tyler kissed Peter, which he had not been expecting, and walked away. Blaisdell called him over. "Peter! Come on! You're family!"

Caine moved over to his son. "For a man to have two families is riches beyond measure." He wiped off the lipstick from Tyler's kiss and shook his head. "You will never grow up."

Peter stepped into the wedding photo which being taken by the photographer with all of his family around the wedding cake.

"Okay everyone, look over here!"

Blaisdell found Caine at the back of the room and smiled at him. Caine bowed to him. The photographer took a picture of the family all gathered together. But when Peter looked back, Caine had gone.

Annie Blaisdell moved over to Peter's side. "I can see him, Peter," she said, softly. "He hasn't gone far."

Peter nodded and kissed Annie's forehead.

Chapter Six

DRAGON'S WING

MY FAVORITE EPISODE FOR *KUNG FU: THE LEGEND CONTINUES* was titled *Dragon's Wing*. It was a pastiche on "*The Magnificent Seven*" which was one of my favorite movies of all time. In the end, after the 88 episodes were finished, David Carradine told me that it was his favorite episode of the TV series as well.

The action started in the teaser. We established a *Flashback Sequence* in the temple. Students were being taught kung fu. A parade with colorful masks wove its way through the temple. Caine's son Peter, ten years old, was with him. Caine became very wary. He told Peter he needed to deal with what he called "bandits" in the temple. He told his son that the Dragon had a "*wing*".

"You can see it," Caine said. "Its head and its tail. Look at the tip of the Dragon's tail!"

Caine moved away from where Peter was standing so he could deal with two of the bandits. Old Ping Hi took out another two. Master Khan, a teacher at the temple, dealt with the rest of the marauders. They cleared out of the temple. Caine gave the Young Peter one of his signature shrugs. He told his son that these bandits would come again. But that he, Ping Hi and Master Kahn would be ready for them. Caine told old Ping Hi to take note of the Dragon's Wing. Young Peter asked if *he* could be the Dragon's Wing. Caine thought about that, then he nodded.

"When you are older and real danger arises again," he said.

Then we were out of the *Flashback Sequence* and back in *real time*.

The Dragon's Wing episode opened on a small, rural town. Three black SUVs were converging on the main street. They had struck the town before. People were clearing out of the way, slamming their doors. Shopkeepers closed up their stores. Restaurants were closing. There was a sense of terror that permeated the town. The black SUVs rolled into town like something out of a vision of Hell. There was virtually no one left on the streets. Black-suited mercenaries moved out of the vehicles, all of them armed with AK47 rifles and submachine guns. They were led by a charismatic, ironic man named David Macklin who was in his thirties. The mercenaries blew away jagged glass shards from the shop windows. They helped themselves to computers, camera equipment and other sundry merchandise.

Kyle Bettinger walked down the main street of the town with his girlfriend Jenny Quinn. He was laidback, in his mid-twenties. They had not yet seen the commotion that the marauders had created.

"Have a nice day," Kyle said.

Jenny kissed him. "Go to work!"

Then they became aware of the mercenaries who were shooting out the windows on more of the stores. A uniformed Police Officer, Deputy Sheriff Taggert, stood to one side. He said nonchalantly into his radio: "Got a situation here on Main Street. Disturbance. Request back-up."

It was clear to Kyle and Jenny that the Deputy Sheriff was obviously in no hurry to lend a hand. One of the mercenaries had knocked down a young man in the street. Kyle ran down the street to help him.

"Hey! Are you all right?"

The man nodded that he was okay. Kyle helped him up.

David Macklin made a signal to one of his mercenaries. The man grabbed Jenny. He manhandled her into one of the black SUVs. By that time Kyle had realized what was happening around him. Kyle tried to rescue Jenny, but Macklin knocked him down into the street. He lay there hurt, gasping for breath. Macklin climbed back into one of the SUVs which screeched away. The other mercenaries got back into the other two SUVs carrying their stolen merchandise. They roared down the suburban street. Kyle turned over, unable to get to reach Jenny who had been kidnapped.

We started the episode in a Dojo where Caine was teaching martial arts. He wore a silk shirt with the graphic of a fierce tiger on it. This was an outfit he wore in many of the episodes. The Dojo was filled with students grappling with each other, doing kung fu moves under Caine's watchful eye. Caine's son Peter was with him.

Kyle Bettinger entered the Dojo, looking around. Peter was delighted to see his old friend. "Kyle!" he exclaimed.

Caine followed Peter's gaze. "He is a friend of yours?"

"Yeah," Peter said. "We shared some smokes and broken dreams at the orphanage." By this time Kyle had reached Peter and Caine. "Hey!" Peter said. "Nice to see you again!" He turned to Caine. "I'm sorry. This is my father. This is Kyle Bettinger." Caine gave Kyle a small bow. Peter shook his head. "How did you find me here?"

"I have been keeping track," Kyle said. "I never figured you for a cop. But then again, I didn't figure I would become an architect." Caine went back to his teaching while Kyle took Peter off to one side. "I didn't come here for a reunion," he said in a hoarse voice filled with emotion. "I came here because I needed an honest cop!"

We went to Paul Blaisdell's office in the precinct. Peter was off duty, but he needed to talk to his Captain. He did not shut the office door, but their conversation was tense. He had brought Blaisdell up to speed on the situation.

Peter said: "Mansfield has a Sheriff's office which my friend Kyle says is about as crooked as Lombard Street and is probably being paid off by these marauders. The girl was taken in broad daylight. His fiancé says they grabbed her off the street. Some Deputy Sheriff just stood by and watched. That is still a Federal offence, isn't it?"

"The Feds have spent eighteen months looking for these guys," Blaisdell told him. "They can't find them. No one can." Blaisdell looked at Peter a little caustically. "Haven't you got enough crime right here in your own precinct?"

"You know, I got out of the orphanage and made something out of my life thanks to you," Peter said, quietly. "Kyle got out of that orphanage and made something of his life thanks to someone *like* you. Now the girl he loves has been kidnapped. He wants some answers. He wants to know what we are to going do and I have to come up with an answer for him."

Blaisdell sighed, nodding. He chose his next words carefully. "What I am going to tell you is off the record."

"Why?"

"Because what I am going to say is not official," Blaisdell said. "It makes me nervous saying it here in my office."

"Okay, let's talk about here in here," Peter said.

Blaisdell nodded. "All right."

The Captain got to his feet and closed the door to his office, shutting out the myriad conversations echoing around them. "These marauders are survivalists," he said. "They strike, then they disappear."

Peter was watching his Precinct boss carefully. "You seem to know a lot about this?"

"The FBI brought me in eight months ago," Blaisdell said. "These raiders torched the town."

Peter was amazed. "The FBI brought in a Police Captain?"

"I have a history, you know that. These marauders usually hit a town and then they move on," Blaisdell said. "But for some reason they seem to have an affinity for Mansfield. They have hit the place four times. I think they are coming back."

Peter just shook his head. "Why?"

"Because your friend's fiancée, Jenny Quinn," Blaisdell said, "also happens to be the Mayor's daughter." Peter groaned. "He is quite ready to pay for her return."

"How much?"

"Fifty thousand dollars is the usual acting price for a hostage," Blaisdell said. "In Jenny's case, it's a hundred."

"Okay," Peter said, "we will go in with a bunch of undercover men and make the exchange."

Blaisdell shook his head. "No! They will know! They will slit the girl's throat and throw her into the middle of the street." The Captain leaned closer to Peter. "But one small elite group might have a chance against them."

Peter reacted. "A commando unit?"

"Yeah, something like that. I know you are going to Mansfield no matter what I say to stop you. All right. Just take some back-up with you."

"Who do you have in mind?"

"John Steadman!" Blaisdell said. "He is a retired British spy. Forget the rakish attitude and the ironic wit. He is a very dangerous man. He is also a specialist."

"At what?" Peter asked.

"Demolition." Blaisdell sat back down at his desk. "You could also use a weapons man. I will see what I can do. Will your father go with you?"

Peter nodded. "I can ask him."

Peter returned to the Dojo where Caine was waiting for him. All of the students had left. Kyle hung back, allowing Peter to talk to his father. Caine lit some candles in the soft gloom of the room, feeling Peter's tension. Without turning around, he said: "You have a problem?"

"If we were in the days of my great grandfather," Peter said, "I would say that my friend's town had been overrun by bandits."

That gave Caine pause. "As in… *gunfighters?*"

"That's right," Peter said. "If you were up against these gunfighters, who have high-tech weapons and laser sights, who would you take with you?"

Caine finished lighting the candles. He turned to the Ancient who had emerged from the shadows behind him. Caine nodded at him. "Him."

"Only *him?*" Peter asked.

"If I have him," Caine said, "I do not need anyone else."

"No disrespect, Pop, but get real! These guys are killers."

Kyle moved forward, looking at the Ancient. "No disrespect, but they would break this old man like a matchstick!"

The Ancient picked Kyle up and deposited him on the ground. "So sorry!" he murmured. "Old man clumsy. Dangerous to have around!"

Kyle got back to his feet, a little contrite, as Caine smiled. He looked over at Peter. "You intend to face these men?"

"With or without you," Peter said.

"Why is it so important to you to be a hero to others?" Caine asked him.

"Because they have kidnapped a young girl," Peter said. "I am not about to sit by and let people suffer. I learned that from *you*."

"I do not want to fight," Caine said.

Kyle just turned away. "Thanks very much. I am out of here!"

"However," Caine said, "it does not mean I will not."

Peter turned to Kyle, nodding his head. "See? It only takes a minute!"

Caine turned back to the Ancient. "Just because I ask you, it does not mean you must come."

"It is because you asked," the Ancient murmured, "that I will come."

Caine gave him a small, kung fu bow. Peter took Caine's arm. "Father, we need a Dragons Wing here! We have part of it! And this time *I* will be the tip. Let us get the rest."

Caine, and Peter found John Steadman in a bar where he was in the process of pouring champagne into a tier of champagne glasses which were stacked one on top of the other. Kyle was with them. Steadman was in his fifties and wore the years well. His personality was droll and charming, but there was an edge of steel beneath the witty exterior. He was up to eight champagne glasses being precariously stacked. The atmosphere around the bar was lively, but no one was really paying any attention to Steadman's parlor trick. The ex-spy was engrossed in stacking the champagne glasses until they reached the level he wanted. Caine turned to Peter with a shrug.

"Captain Blaisdell *did* say he was larger than life."

"But he didn't say anything about his age," Peter muttered. "What is this, the geriatric A-Team?"

"The years a man wears brings him down or holds him up," Cane said, levelly.

Steadman had stacked the last glass at the top of the bar, so that the champagne flowed down into all of the other glasses. "Champagne for everyone!" he declared.

A gaunt man had detached himself from one of the tables where his girlfriend was waiting. His name was Bruce McFee who had several run-ins with Steadman. Before Caine, Peter or Kyle could move, McFee tapped the precarious stacked glasses over. They all toppled to the bar. They did not break because the glasses were plastic, but Steadman turned around. He looked at McFee with caustic eyes. He grabbed the older man's arm and held it in a rigid grip.

"That was rather bad form, old man," Steadman said, mildly.

"Take your hand off my arm!" McFee retorted. He pulled out of Steadman's grasp. "Stay out of my way. I have told you that before!"

"So you have," Steadman murmured.

"You want some pain?" McFee asked him. "You know where to find me."

The man moved back to his table having put Steadman in his place. His girlfriend, whose name was Cindy, said: "Did you really have to do that?"

McFee slapped her across the face. She cowered away from him. A small trickle had formed on her lips. Peter moved to Steadman's side. Steadman was staring at McFee with outrage. Peter followed his gaze.

"That guy is a jerk," Peter said.

Steadman turned to Peter, noting Caine and Kyle behind him. "So ill-mannered!" the ex-spy said. "In the time of *Camelot, King Alfred* I mean, not the Kennedy era, one received a slap in the face!" Steadman slapped his own face with a black glove to make his point. "Charming custom! Pity they lost it!"

Peter cleared his throat. "I am Peter Caine. This is my father and my friend Kyle. Paul Blaisdell told me you might help us rid a small town of some locusts."

"Did he now?" Steadman said. "What a stimulating imagination. Excuse me."

Steadman moved to McFee's table and sat down at it. "May I join you?"

Caine and Peter watched from the bar. Kyle looked unconvinced. Gently Steadman wiped the smear of blood from Cindy's lips. His attention was centered on McFee, who was looking warily at him, ready for anything.

"You wanted to talk about pain," Steadman said. "It is a fascinating subject. The Marquis de Sade made a career out of it. A tricky one to understand."

"I warned you, Steadman," McFee began.

"Yes, when was that?" Steadman said, as if remembering an incident from some time ago. "In Bulgaria in the riots, or in Vienna? You were going to assassinate that charming concert pianist who wanted to defect to the west. Let us try an experiment, shall we?" Suddenly Steadman reached out a hand and trapped McFee's wrist in it. He tried to break free, but the older mercenary was holding him tightly. "The flame should hurt," Steadman said, conversationally. He glanced over at Cindy. "The way you hurt this young woman by slapping her face. But pain can be controlled. Would you like to try it?"

Steadman moved McFee's hand right over the candle. The thug writhed as the flame singed his hand. "It hurts!"

"Of course it does," Steadman said, reasonably. "The trick, as my friend Robert Bolt would say, is not minding! If you cannot tolerate pain, do not inflict it on others."

Steadman let McFee go. He grabbed his singed hand, staring at Steadman.

"You will pay for the champagne, won't you?" Steadman asked him, smiling now.

"For everyone?"

"Yes, I will!" McFee said, holding his wrist gingerly.

"Very good of you," Steadman murmured. "Do enjoy your evening."

Steadman smiled at Cindy, who was looking up at him with new respect. Steadman got up from the table and rejoined Caine and company at the bar. Peter handed him a beer.

"That is quite a trick," he said.

"It was not a trick," Caine said. He moved over to McFee's table. McFee and Cindy watched as Caine put his hand *right over* the candle flame. "You must embrace the pain. Make it part of yourself. Become one with it. If you can do that, the pain cannot touch your soul." Caine looked over at Steadman. "Is that not right?"

"That's right," Steadman said, and toasted Caine. Caine moved his hand away from the candle flame and moved back to the bar. Steadman took a swallow of his beer.

"Mr. McFee and I go way back." He shrugged. "He doesn't learn his lessons very well."

"I think he learned this one," Kyle remarked.

Caine turned his attention fully to Steadman. "I am told you are not a stranger to fighting?"

Steadman seemed to consider that. "Fought against Rommel in the desert, World War II. Took a hill in Korea!" He thought about that. "I can't remember *why*! Fought in Indochina in the jungle and played cold war chess with the Russians." The old spy shrugged. "Now enemies are friends, and your best friend sleeps with your wife."

"Blaisdell said you would help us," Peter said.

"Did he?" Steadman said. "How quaint. He was wrong."

Steadman finished his pint of beer and walked out of the bar. "Cheerio!"

And he was gone.

Kyle looked at Caine, Peter and the Ancient, frustrated. "This is great! We are back where we started. Any other ideas?"

Caine nodded. "Yes," he said, quietly.

Our heroes entered a gym where two boxers were fighting in a kung fu style. Other fighters were sparring, shadow boxing and hitting the heavy bags. Kyle nodded. "This is more like it! Which one is our man?"

Caine indicated a slight, bald man who was sweeping up. He did not appear to be threatening in any way, but one of the fighters from the ring approached him.

"They tell me you can throw a kick faster than a man can throw a punch," the Fighter said. "I don't believe it!"

The man was Master Khan, but he was keeping a low profile. He just shrugged. The Fighter said: "I have fifty bucks that says have been shining these boys on!"

Master Khan looked interested. "Fifty bucks?" He thought about that for a moment, then he nodded. "All right!"

He put his broom to one side. The Fighter said: "Put your hands behind your back! One punch! You won't know where it is coming from!"

The Fighter jogged in place for a second. Khan kicked out fast. The Fighter avoided his kick. He turned to his sparring partners with a smug expression on his face. "Did you see that? If I were doing it for real, he would have been on his back!"

From where Caine was standing, it did not look that way to him. He said: "He won!"

Peter agreed. "That was the way it looked from here."

Master Khan started to turn away, but the Fighter swung him back again. "Let's do it *for real*."

Khan shook his head. "Let it go. I don't want to fight you."

"Hands behind your back!" the Fighter said. He turned to one of his sparring partners. "I will give you the fifty bucks, all right?"

The other boxer nodded and took the fifty bucks. Khan had turned back to face the Fighter again. He shrugged. As if to say, if that was the way he it wanted it, that was fine with him. The Fighter jogged in place for a moment, then he lunged at Khan. Khan kicked him three times, still with his hands behind his back. That sent the Fighter back against the ropes of the ring, dazed and demoralized.

Khan turned back and saw Caine, Peter and Kyle standing in the gym. Caine bowed formally. "It has been a long time since the temple," he said, gently.

Master Khan nodded. "Yes, it has."

"The temple!" Peter said, making the connection. "That's it! Master Khan!"

Peter bowed to him. Caine glanced around the gym. "You are helping out here? And teaching?" Master Khan shrugged, not really answering. "I need you," Caine said. He gestured at Peter and Kyle. "*We* need you. There would be great danger. And the odds are very poor."

Khan looked at them, then he shrugged again. "Why not?"

Caine and Peter returned to the Dojo, which was now in shadow. Kyle was with them. A compact, ironic mercenary named James Rykker was waiting for them. This was my valentine for the *Magnificent Seven*. Robert Vaughn had played the role in the original Magnificent Seven movie as the character "Lee". His character here was more urbane, more complicated, more cerebral.

And *deadly*.

Rykker acknowledged Caine. "Kwai Chang Caine."

Caine was surprised to see him. "Rykker!"

"Except for the part where you had hair," Rykker said, "you haven't changed in fifteen years. Too bad about your temple. It was a special place."

"When we last spoke," Caine said, "you were searching for the man who had murdered your child."

"I found him," Rykker said, simply.

This was another shameful lift from the original *Magnificent Seven* movie!

Peter looked at Rykker with distrust. "If you were at the temple, how come I don't remember you?"

"I don't spend a lot with children," Rykker said with some irony. His attention was on Caine. "Paul Blaisdell tells me you are looking for some mercenaries to put out a fire. I have some equipment which would help you do that."

"So you know Blaisdell?" Peter asked him.

"You meet a great many people in my business," Rykker said.

"Mercenary," Peter said.

"Mercenaries fight for money," Rykker corrected him. "I fight for causes."

"The right ones, of course," Peter said, his tone confrontational.

"The ones that interest me," Rykker said, evenly. "I am staying at the Regency. Pick me up there tomorrow morning."

Rykker moved over to where he had laid his heavy overcoat on a chair and shrugged it on.

"Don't you want to know what is at stake here?" Peter asked him.

"I am a soldier," he said. "Soldiers need wars." He turned back. "You want to know why I am coming with you? Because I owe Paul Blaisdell a favor. And I owe your father my life."

Caine gave Rykker a small formal bow.

"Make it after breakfast," Rykker said. "The Regency does the finest Eggs Benedict in the city."

With that Rykker left. Peter turned to his father. "What did he mean when he said you had saved his life?"

"It is an interesting story," Caine said, quietly. "I will tell you another time."

Beside him, Kyle was elated. "Now we have five!"

Caine looked past them. "*Six!*" he corrected him.

Peter also turned. John Steadman was standing in the doorway. "I changed my mind," he said, simply. "I'll need time to get my little bag of goodies together. Mansfield by the lake? Charming little place."

"You talked to Blaisdell," Peter said.

"Let us just say I took the time to remind of duty," Steadman said. "Meet me at the tavern at the General Store in Mansfield after 6:00?" He smiled at them. "Game's afoot, eh? Till then!"

Steadman moved out of the Dojo. Now Caine looked at Peter and shrugged.

"*Six!*" he said.

Peter put his arm around Kyle's shoulders. "Come on, Kyle, I'll buy you a drink! We have a lot of catching up to do. Tell me about Jenny. How did you meet her?"

They exited the Dojo, leaving Caine alone.

We cut to a shot of Jenny Quinn being incarcerated somewhere in a house, alone and frightened.

Meanwhile, Caine visited the Sheriff's office in Mansfield. Sheriff Taggart looked over at him. Caine said: "I am looking for Sheriff Donovan."

"Not here," Taggart said. He took a closer look at Caine. "What monastery did you fall out of?"

"A question I am often asked," Caine said.

The Deputy Sheriff moved toward his office. Caine kept pace with him. "Your town has been assaulted not once, but four times," he said. "Are you going to organize a posse to find these marauders?"

Taggart looked amused. "A posse? Sure, I will just grease my Winchester '73 and get out my Ned Buntline colt and we will round up some Deputies. Who the hell all you?"

"I am Caine," he said.

Caine followed the Deputy Sheriff into his office. Taggart looked at him, shaking his head. "You can't be a cop. And you're not a Fed."

"I am a priest," Caine said. "Please tell me about these marauders."

Taggart back sat down at his desk. "Some towns have tried to shoot it out with them. But when the smoke clears, a lot of good cops are dead."

"So, you care nothing about a girl who has been kidnapped?" Caine asked.

"There's no report of a kidnapping that has come to this office," Taggart said. "Who are you talking about?"

"Her name is Jenny Quinn."

Deputy Sheriff Taggart reacted to that. "Jenny Quinn? The Mayor's daughter? If she were missing you could camp out in my squad right now." Taggart leaned on his desk. "I leave these survivalists alone and they leave us alone."

"Does Sheriff Donovan share this cowardice?" Caine asked him.

Taggart's eyes now were like ice. "Sheriff Donovan don't know nothing about it. He has been gone for a week and while he is away I am in charge. You give me one lick of trouble, Mister, and I will have to throw you in jail."

Caine put on his homburg hat. "A statement which I believe my grandfather heard many times."

Caine gave Taggart a small bow and walked out of the office. Taggart watched him depart with expressionless eyes.

A police car cruised down the street in Mansfield. The cop there picked up his radio.

"Taggart, he is going into the coffee shop."

In the local coffee shop, Caine was joined by the members of his *Dragon's Wing* which consisted of Peter, the Ancient and Kyle. Master Khan and James Rykker joined them. With them was Mayor Quinn, an authoritative, compassionate man who happened to be Jenny's father. Patrick Culliton, who played the Mayor in the episode, was a close friend of David Carradine's.

"So, the police have not set up a command post at your house?" Peter asked him.

"No, they haven't," the Mayor said, tersely.

Caine said: "Deputy Taggart seems to have no knowledge of your daughter's kidnapping."

"Deputy Taggart is a thug," Quinn said, "and if I am not mistaken is being paid off by these killers. When do the rest of your men arrive?"

"One more is coming later," Rykker said.

Quinn looked at him as if he had lost his mind. "*One*? *Six men*? You do not get it, do you? They have got my daughter! They will kill her, even after the ransom has been paid. Six men can't handle these animals."

"*These six can,*" Caine promised him.

"Mayor Quinn, we do not have much of a choice," Kyle said. "These men are all we have got."

One of the staff of the restaurant moved over to Mayor Quinn and handed him the phone. He took the call. "Mayor Quinn," he said.

David Macklin was in a cabin in the middle of the forest, holding a cell phone. Through the window he could see his mercenaries moving around the three black SUVs. Jenny Quinn was incarcerated in a locked room of the house. Macklin was soft-spoken and in total command of the conversation.

"Have you got the money raised, Mr. Mayor?"

Quinn gripped the receiver tighter. "I have it all."

"Noon tomorrow," Macklin said, adding with a trace of irony: "High noon. The old beer distillery. One man to carry the ransom. Not a cop."

The Mayor looked over at Caine. "How about a priest?"

"Perfect," Macklin said with a smile.

"Let me talk to my daughter," Quinn pleaded. "I must be assured that she is still alive."

"We have a code of honor, sir," Macklin said. "We don't kill hostages before the ransom is delivered."

Mayor Quinn lost it. "Honor? You're scum!"

Macklin just smiled again. "I guess that is the best you can do, Mr. Mayor. Mark Twain described Shakespearian Stratforians as Troglides, thugs, bungdaors, bandeliers and moscovites. A little salty, but rather erudite."

"Please!" Quinn pleaded.

"Soon," Macklin assured him. "She will be in your arms again soon."

Macklin disconnected the line, still smiling.

Mayor Quinn dropped the cell phone onto a table. The door opened and John Steadman entered, wearing a pea coat, carrying a slim briefcase. He was aware of the tension in the coffee shop immediately.

"Sorry I am a little late," he said. "But it took a little longer to put together my bits and pieces than I thought. It's tricky, stealing explosives." He smiled. "I wouldn't say no to a champagne cocktail." Khan brought him one. Steadman took a swallow of the martini. "If you set out a battle plan, I will work out some surprises for our guests. Cheers!"

Our heroes left the comparative safety of the coffee shop and ventured out into the maze of the streets outside the abandoned *Gooderham & Worts Distillery* where they would meet the Survivalists. There was an eerie quality to the smashed windows in the various buildings that resonated with them. A keen wind had come up that wailed through the streets. With Caine were Peter, the Ancient, Master Khan, Kyle, Steadman and Rykker. Mayor Quinn was also with them. The *"Magnificent Seven"* looked around at the streets where they would be fighting. None of them spoke. The ambiance weighed heavily on them. Peter looked up at the rooftops that surrounded the streets. Steadman and Rykker also took note of the rooftops. More of the ruined buildings crowded in around them.

It was an isolated setting that did not sit well with our heroes.

In his house sheltered in the woods, David Macklin confronted a frightened Jenny Quinn. He came from out of the shadows like a pale ghost. She reared back from him.

"Keep away from me!"

"Jenny, I am your protector," Maclin said. His voice was quiet, reassuring. "We two alone will sing like birds in a cage. When both ask, I will kneel down and ask for forgiveness. We will live and play and sing and take upon us the mystery of things. As if we were God's spies. Lear understood that the world was dying around him and that it would come to an end."

He reached out for Jenny, but she cowered away from him.

"Do not touch me!"

Macklin nodded, as if he understood. "Keeping yourself pure for---what was your man's name? Kyle? How noble." He leaned closer to her, his voice dropping to a whisper. "By the time this is over, you will beg for my touch."

Macklin got to his feet and left Jenny trembling in the shadows.

Moonlight flooded the abandoned *Gooderham and Worts* Distillery. Caine and Peter moved down one of the streets. "I've got Khan stationed in one of the streets and the Ancient at another," Peter said.

"These mercenaries will keep their word," Caine said. "You must get some rest."

"I will if *you* will. If this girl dies…"

"We will not allow that to happen," Caine assured him.

Peter nodded. "Goodnight, Pop." He corrected himself. "Dad."

Peter moved away from his father.

In the shadows of an abandoned diner, James Rykker sat at a table. He was wearing a heavy overcoat and his signature white scarf. John Steadman emerged from the darkness and sat opposite him. Their voices were hushed in the stillness.

"Everyone is asleep," Steadman said, "but not you."

"I don't sleep," Rykker said.

"Not ever?"

"Not if I can help it."

"I thought you might like some company," Steadman said.

Rykker was ironic. "Whatever made you think that?"

"I am surprised to see you on this mission," Steadman added.

"Why?"

"I know you don't do anything except for money."

Rykker's tone was still ironic, but there was an edge to it now. "Then you don't know me very well, do you?" He thought about that. "When was the last time? Kiev! A Russian scientist wanted to defect. I don't know how you got him to the checkpoint."

Steadman's tone had mellowed out a little. "I could not have done it without your help. It did occur to me that our opposition might be glad to know that this courageous band of adventurers that Kyle has hired number *only six*. I imagine that Deputy Sheriff Taggart would arrange a meeting for a price."

"Maybe I have already done that," Rykker told him. "Maybe we're all walking into a trap. You will have to wait and see, won't you?"

"I just wanted to be quite sure that you remembered why we all came here," Steadman said. "A young girl's life is at stake."

Rykker shook his head. "You've gotten cynical, Steadman. That is too bad. I no longer sell my loyalties to the highest bidder."

Steadman nodded. "My apologies. There is a human being somewhere there. I always expected it."

Now Rykker was amused. "Did you?"

He took a swallow of his ice-tea. Steadman allowed the silence between them to linger.

Later on our Dragon's Wing defenders congregated in the coffee house. Steadman was studying a diagram he had brought. "Commit it to memory," he said. "It would not do to be in the wrong place at the wrong time."

Peter turned to Rykker who sat at the bar. "You're not interested where these explosives are located, Rykker?"

Rykker looked past him at the door of the coffee house. "I am more interested in *this.*"

The others followed his gaze. Deputy Sheriff Taggart had entered the coffee shop with three of his Deputies. The Ancient offered them his sweet roll.

"Please! Join us!"

Taggart was looking at Caine. "You're under arrest, Caine."

"For what crime?" Caine asked.

"I ran your name and description through the system and came with some interesting data," the Deputy Sheriff said. "Like an arrest in Mohave Utah for attempted murder."

"Those charges were dropped," Peter said.

"All kinds of charges can be dropped," Taggart said. "I don't like killers in my town."

Mayor Quinn stepped forward. "These men are my friends. I will vouch for them."

"Stay out of this, Mr. Mayor," Taggart said. He was still looking right at Caine. "I want you and your friends to leave this town right away."

"I do not think so!" Caine said.

He tossed his felt hat in Taggart's face. Caine kicked the Deputy Sheriff to the floor of the coffee house. The three Deputies all pulled their guns. Peter drew his revolver and fired, blowing the gun from one of the Deputies' hands. Rykker drew his revolver and fired at the second Deputy, wounding him. His gun skittered to the floor. Peter moved to the Officers.

"Give me your cuffs!" Peter snapped the handcuffs on the wrists of the cops, turning to look at Rykker. "That was almost as fast as me!"

"I didn't want to spill my drink," Rykker murmured.

"As I was saying," Steadman went on, as if they had not just disarmed three Deputies and the Deputy Sheriff, "commit this to memory."

Then he set a lighter to the piece of paper he was holding and let it burn.

In the countryside of Mansfield, the three black SUVs were heading for the town.

In the coffee shop, Deputy Sheriff Taggart and his Deputies had been cleared to one side, all of them now in handcuffs. Rykker was holding an AK47 rifle and several revolvers. He looked at Caine.

"I know you can handle one of these."

Caine shook his head. "I can accept no weapon."

Peter took the AK47 rifle from Rykker's hands. "It's a Shaolin thing. Somehow he never seems to need one."

Rykker turned to Master Khan. "And you?"

Khan shook his head, not accepting a gun. "I've got myself."

"I'll take his," Peter said, taking another revolver.

Ryker offered the last revolver to the Ancient who passed on it.

"May I?" Peter said, taking the revolver that Rykker had wanted to give to the Ancient. "More for me!"

Rykker just shook his head. "You are all very strange," he commented.

"We have surprise on our side!" the Ancient declared. "They will not be expecting resistance."

Peter looked at the assembled defenders. "We've got a lot more than surprise." He glanced over at Caine. "We have a Dragon's Wing!"

Rykker looked at Peter, his expression ironic. "I didn't know that Dragons *had* wings?"

"Well, this one has!" Peter said. "And this time I want to be part of it!"

Peter gave his father's face a fond pat. Mayor Quinn moved forward, looking at Caine. He handed a briefcase to him. "Caine, there is a hundred thousand dollars in this case. Bring my daughter back alive."

Caine simply nodded.

"We're armed," Peter said. "We're dangerous! Are you ready?"

His gaze travelled to Steadman... then to the Ancient... to Master Khan... finishing on Rykker. Peter spoke for all of them.

"Let's go," he said.

The music on the soundtrack at this point was reminiscent of the "*The Good, Bad and the Ugly.*" The defenders had placed themselves around the streets at *Gooderham and Worts.* An eerie wind echoed through the silence. Like an old gunfighter, Caine stepped out alone onto the main street. He looked around him. There was a stillness to him.

Master Khan lowered himself into a sewer system in the ground, climbing down the iron rungs. Up on the roof, Peter checked his AK47 rifle. Below him, Caine acknowledged Rykker who was behind one of the doors in the complex. The Ancient lay on a bench, covered up like a homeless person. In one of the ajar windows of a room on a fourth floor, Steadman opened his briefcase. It was filled with connections wired up to explode. He proceeded to attach them.

Below in the sewer, shrouded in darkness, Khan pulled out a sleeve from his coat and opened it. Eight throwing stars were reflected briefly in the gloom.

Up on the roof, Peter checked the high powered AK47 rifle, then looked over the roof to where to Caine was standing alone. The three black SUVs turned the corner of the street and screeched to a halt. The doors opened and black-suited mercenaries jumped out, all of them carrying AK47 rifles. David Macklin emerged from the third vehicle. His mercenaries surrounded Caine, who had not moved. He watched as Macklin moved over to him.

"You're the priest? I did not see expect to see you. Give me the money."

"First let me see the girl," Caine asked.

"Guard your head, for I mean to have it err long," Macklin said.

"Henry V, Part One," Caine said.

Macklin nodded, as if he were impressed. He pulled out his radio and spoke into it. "Bring in the girl."

In one of the rooms on the fourth floor, through his open window, Steadman watched the drama unfolding below him. Three of the mercenaries dragged Jenny over to where Macklin was standing. Caine approached him. Macklin held out his hand for the briefcase of money. Caine handed it to him. Macklin opened the briefcase, noting the stacks of money inside. He closed the briefcase and looked at Caine with contempt.

"You really thought we were going to hand her over?"

"Let us talk about of graves and graves," Caine said, "Make dust our paper. Write grainy eyes write sorrow of the bosom of the earth."

"Richard II," Macklin said. "Very good." Then he looked at Caine with dead eyes. "Now watch the girl executed before your eyes."

Jenny cried out as one of the mercenaries dragged her to Macklin.

Up in his room above the streets, Steadman twisted one of the intricate connections in his briefcase. "Tally Ho!" he said, cheerfully.

An explosion rocked the street below which erupted in flame. On the roof, above the battlefield, Peter fired his AK47 rifle at the mercenaries below. The marauders fired back. Caine kicked the briefcase from Macklin's hands. Jenny tore herself free from the mercenary who had been holding her and ran into the chaos.

Peter's bullets cut down more of the terrorists. Caine kicked one of the marauders to the ground, then turned around and took out another. The Ancient came off his bench. The mercenary who had grabbed Jenny manhandled her again. The Ancient threw a rope around the ankles of the terrorist which brought him down to the ground. The Ancient took Jenny's hand.

"Come with me!"

He and Jenny ran toward the edge of one of the buildings.

On the ground, Macklin shouted: "Get the girl!"

Some of his mercenaries took after Jenny and the Ancient.

Peter continued to fire down on the marauders with his AK47 rifle.

In his window, Steadman watched the action with shining eyes. Rykker stepped out from his doorway and fired a flamethrower at three of Macklin's men. They fell back, two of them engulfed in flames. Steadman set off more explosives which took out more of the marauders. Master Khan emerged from the sewer manhole. He threw one of the throwing stars at one of the mercenaries, taking him out. He threw a second one and took out another of the terrorists.

The Ancient stumbled as a bullet grazed his head. He collapsed onto the ground. Jenny continued on through the smoke that burned the air, making it difficult to her to breathe. Caine took care of the next three mercenaries, sending them to the ground with expert kung fu kicks. Peter had leapt onto a low roof and continued to fire his AK47. More of the mercenaries fell under the deadly barrage of gunfire.

Rykker, now in the street, fired a grenade launcher at Macklin's men. They collapsed in the onslaught. Khan took a bullet from one of the marauders and fell to the ground. Peter came down a ladder from his rooftop and disappeared inside the maze of abandoned offices. Rykker had picked up his AK47 rifle and fired at more of the marauders, decimating them. One of the mercenaries tried to get a shot at Caine but Rykker cut him down.

Macklin came out of cordite-burning smoke. He lunged at Caine. Caine sidestepped the blow. Macklin whirled, staring at him.

"Who the hell are you?"

"No one," Caine said.

Macklin came back with more kung fu kicks aimed at Caine's head. He repelled them almost contemptuously. Then he dealt Macklin a blow that seemed to finish him.

Up in his open window, Steadman ignited more explosions, sending the marauders to the ground. Peter exited from the roof and found another entranceway to the rabbit warren. Rykker fired more rounds from his high-powered rifle, sending the mercenaries retreating. Peter came around the corner of the building over to where Caine had just taken care of Macklin.

"The Ancient has the key!" Caine said urgently.

Peter nodded his understanding. He needed to unlock the handcuffs from Jenny's wrists.

Mercenaries fired on Caine and Peter. Peter returned fire, shielding his father. He whirled and saw a figure on one on the low roofs firing down at the mercenaries. He was in silhouette so Peter could not see him clearly.

Then the figure was gone.

Caine and Peter ran forward. Smoke hazed through the streets. Rykker continued his assault on the mercenaries with a submachinegun. Up in his vantage point in the fourth-floor window, Steadman watched the mercenaries escaping in full retreat. Caine took out two more of them and then another two.

Peter took out the marauder who had just tried to grab Jenny. He collapsed to the ground. Caine took out last two mercenaries he faced. The Ancient was on his feet now. Jenny came around the corner and Peter grabbed her arm.

"You okay?"

She nodded, breathless. "Thank you for saving my life!"

The Ancient was a little groggy from the blow he had received. Peter took his arm, but he nodded that he was okay. "Our pleasure," he murmured to Jenny.

The remnants of the mercenaries had climbed back into their three SUVs and took off. Others were lying prone where they had fallen in the street. Caine had reached Peter, Jenny and the Ancient. Peter looked past him.

"Pop!" he warned.

Caine whirled. David Macklin was holding a submachinegun on them. Rykker came up out of nowhere with a revolver and blew the gun out of Macklin's hands. He crumpled to the ground. Rykker moved over to him and relieved him of his AR47.

"Bullets are expensive," he said. "Mind surrendering?"

Rykker straightened and looked over at Caine who was standing with Peter. "I owed you one," he said.

Caine bowed. Rykker returned the formal bow and smiled.

The marauders had all retreated.

Our heroes walked down the main Gooderham & Worts street: Caine, Peter, Rykker, Jenny and the Ancient. Peter glanced over at Rykker. "How did you get down from that tower so fast?"

"I was never *in* the tower," Rykker responded.

"Well, who was?" Peter asked him.

Paul Blaisdell, wearing black and carrying an AK47 assault rifle, walked over to them. "I thought you might need a little back-up."

Peter looked at his father and nodded. "Now we're seven."

Kyle and Mayor Quinn moved to them from the protection of one of the buildings.

"Jen!" Kyle shouted.

Jenny looked over at him. "Kyle!"

She ran to him and embraced him. When they parted, Kyle looked over at Peter and gave him a salute, kung fu style. Peter did the same.

Steadman emerged from one of the buildings. He picked up the fallen briefcase that Macklin had dropped in the street. Rykker moved over to him.

"Nice explosives!" Rykker observed.

"Nice shooting," Steadman said.

Master Khan limped up to them. Steadman turned. "Are you all right, Master Khan?"

Khan just nodded. The Ancient came over to him, breaking into a smile, giving one of his signature phrases. "Bloody marvelous!"

Caine and Peter moved past them. Caine looked at his son and the phrase was familiar. "Secure, partner?"

Peter smiled at him and nodded. "Secure!"

Peter raised his hand into a fist and Caine closed his hand over it.

Our heroes---Caine, Peter, James Rykker, John Steadman, Master Khan, Kyle Bettinger and Paul Blaisdell---walked down the street outside the Gooderham & Worts building leaving the bodies of the mercenaries behind them.

The next day, in the pub on the corner, Rykker moved over to Steadman. Both of them had martini glasses in their hands. "Just came to say goodbye," Rykker said.

"What will you do now?" Steadman asked him.

"I understand that there's some trouble getting relief supplies to Somalia," Rykker said. "Thought I might lend a hand."

"So now we know what interests you," Steadman remarked. "Saving lives." Rykker toasted him with him with his drink. "Good luck, old man. Glad I was wrong about you. Try not to get hurt."

"I have endured pain before," Rykker said.

Steadman smiled. "The trick is not minding."

Rykker nodded. "That's right." He put his glass down on the bar. "Well, we'll see other again I am sure."

Steadman lifted his glass in a toast. Rykker made a fist in the kung fu salute. Then he smiled and walked out of the bar.

In Caine's apartment, which was in shadows, Caine was playing his flute. Peter paced a little restlessly. "Five marauders killed, twenty-five wounded, fifteen escaped." He turned back to his father. "But you didn't like what happened, did you?"

Caine took the flute from his lips but did not comment. "We saved a young woman's life!" Peter said. "We broke up a gang of marauders who had been terrorizing three States. But you think that is wrong! What is wrong with that?"

"We fought violence with violence," Caine said, softly.

"Sometimes you have to."

Caine shrugged. "There is always another way," he said. Then he paused. "But... we *did* have a fine Dragon's Wing my son, did we not?"

Peter nodded and smiled. He kissed his father's forehead, then stepped aside.

"Bloody marvelous!" he said, echoing the Ancient.

Caine laughed with him.

Chapter Seven
GUNFIGHTERS

I WANTED TO WRITE AN EPISODE FOR *Kung Fu: The Legend Continues* that would be a western in every sense of the word. It would have all the elements for a regular episode, but it would be atypical in every way. It would start out as a true western and at first the audience could be forgiven if they thought they had tuned in to another show. But it was, indeed, a *Kung Fu: The Legend Continues* episode, although it would not appear that way at first. There would be a twist in the narrative which would leave the viewer no doubt that they were, in fact, watching an episode of the show. But the forward thrust would follow a western theme.

I had a number of western heroes I wanted to cast for this episode. The most iconoclastic of these potential western heroes was Clint Walker, who had played Cheyenne Bodie on television. He notched up 100 episodes of the character before he was done.

I reached out to my wonderful casting director Susan Forrest who was a joy to work with. I wanted to know how to reach Clint Walker. Susan made some phone calls and actually found a phone number for Clint Walker in Northern California. I took a deep breath, as I did not know Clint at all, and I called him. A deep, rich voice answered. I plunged into my sales pitch about *Kung Fu: The Legend Continues*, that I was the Executive Producer for the show and that we were trying to cast the leads for the next episode. I told him I had always been a fan of his, which was certainly the truth, and it would be outstanding if he would consider this episode to star in. Clint Walker was charming and soft-spoken. He confessed that he had not done a guest-role in a TV series in a long time, so he was surprised at the inquiry. I told him about David

Carradine and the fact that there would be guest stars around him in this particular episode that would be considered "western heroes". His was the first call I had made so far. I launched into my speech about how much this would mean to me personally, as Clint Walker had had always been one of my heroes. I asked him if I could send him the script. He would be playing his signature role of "Cheyenne Bodie". He laughed and said he had not expected that, but that he would look forward to reading the script of Gunfighters. I hung up and called Susan Forrest right away with my potential good news.

She said she sent the script to Clint's home in Los Angeles. I was in a state of high anxiety, but a couple of days later Clint called me back. He said he had read the script and he really liked it. He talked about how he had moved away from acting because of a contract dispute, which I gathered had yet to be settled, but he was very gracious and said he would play the role of "Cheyenne Bodie" again! I was elated. For me, this was a major coup. Clint Walker said that coming back to acting for him would be a "real pleasure". He said that if he had dealt with me before he might have considered many other roles. I took that as a real compliment. I told Clint that the episode would shoot very soon, in Toronto, where we were going to turn a Colonial location into a "western street".

So now I had my first guest star for the Gunfighters episode. The next guest star on my "westerns" list was Robert Fuller. I had met Bob Fuller two or three times over the years. Susan Forrest sent him a copy of the script, and he responded immediately. He was a lover of westerns, having starred in both "*Laramie*" and "*Wagon Train*". He loved the Kung Fu script. He was onboard.

I consulted with Susan Forrest on the viability of getting James Drury for the cast. He was a favorite of mine ever since he had starred as "*The Virginian*" on television for nine years. Susan Forrest sent him a script of the episode. He loved the script and said that he was *in*! James Drury was excited by the idea of playing a "bad guy" on the show. This was a chance for him to spread his wings a little bit. The character was a psychotic killer named "The Deacon" who hid behind the white collar of a priest.

There was a funny story about Catherine Disher who was going to play Madelaine Palmer in the episode. I had met her when she was starring in a TV series called "*Forever Knight*" which had also starred my great friend Geraint Wyn-Davies. She was a wonderful actress and a sweetheart. I remember when I was on the set of the episode, Catherine Disher took me to one side. She had met all of her co-stars for the *Kung Fu: The Legends Continues* episode, but she was not familiar with the name of *James Drury*.

I told her that he had starred in The Virginian for nine years. He was playing a very bad guy for me in our show. Catherine just shook her head and told me that James Drury scared the hell out of her! She had never heard of him before! She knew he was really a sweet, soft-spoken actor in real life, but playing "The Deacon" on the show gave her the creeps! I passed that intel over to James Drury who laughed and said that was a great compliment. He had not played many "bad guys" in his career, so this was going to be fun for him. So now James Drury was on board for our show.

The last guest star I went after for our western heroes was Clu Gulager. I had loved him as an actor when he had starred in "*The Virginian*", where he had played the role of Sheriff Rykker. It was a name I had always loved for a hero. In the Dragon's Wing episode of *Kung Fu: The Legend Continues*, Robert Vaughn had played a mercenary named "Rykker". I had high hopes for success with Clu Gulager, whom I did not know, but it was a roll of the dice and it paid off! Clu really liked the script. He was known for his "method' acting", which was fine with me. So now we had all of our old-time western heroes. Susan Forrest found the rest of the cast for me, and I was ecstatic. We had a wonderful cast, and not just our western heroes.

But we had a problem in Toronto. There was no location I could find that had a western street in it. The best option was a Colonial façade with nothing around it. There were some Colonial buildings and grass grew in abundance, but that was all. My production designer, Gavin Mitchell, came up with a way to remedy this situation. He told me to leave it with him for a couple of days. His production team set to work. A couple of days later, I took a car out to the location and saw to my amazement that it had been *completely renovated*. It was no longer just a few isolated Colonial buildings. The location had been transformed into a full western street! Dirt had been laid down in the street. The western buildings consisted of a Sheriff Office, a Bank, two Saloons, a Livery Stable, a Mercantile Store, two Hotels and a Steakhouse on either side of the street. All the locations just needed to be populated with townspeople! I was astounded! Gavin had come up with a real coup! Gavin routinely came up with great solutions for most of the troublesome problems! So now we had our great western street in the middle of nowhere! Most of action in the show would revolve around this western street.

The Director for this episode was Jon Cassar, a wonderful guy who directed twelve episodes of *Kung Fu: The Legend Continues* for me. He was a complete professional who knew the craft of filming. He was excited to be directing a "western" and entered into it with style and verve. He was my favorite director on *Kung Fu: The Legend Continues* whom I used many times. He was simply "the best"!

The episode began with Madelaine Palmer, played by Catherine Disher, careering in a buckboard through the countryside. She was being chased by two outlaws who were closing in fast on her. At the same time, Kwai Chang Caine moved through some cottonwood trees, playing his flute. He was wearing his brown shirt and a cowboy hat. Caine looked very much like he had looked in his old TV series Kung Fu. A much younger "Caine", but with all of the same mannerisms we had grown to expect from him. He put aside the flute, taking note of the drama unfolding before him.

The two outlaws caught up with the runaway buckboard, bringing it to a stop. Kyle Lefferts was a good looking, insolent outlaw in his twenties. He was played by a terrific actor named Charles Powell who tackled his role with flair and style. With him was a lean scarecrow of a man named Bone Jackson, also a terrific actor, whose real name was John Evans. They took hold of the reins and brought Maddie's buckboard to a halt. She was livid. She was an outspoken, freewheeling kind of a heroine who also happened to be the town doctor.

Kyle Lefferts took hold of Madelaine's reins as if he had just rescued her. His cohort, Bone Jackson, was more laidback and a back shooter.

"I hate to see you lose control like that, Dr. Maddie," Kyle said, grinning. "You could have taken a real mean turn. You're not going to thank us for saving your life?"

"You didn't fire those shots?" Maddie him asked, caustically.

"Hell, no!" Kyle swore.

"We'll ride with you the rest of the way into town if you'd like," Bone offered. "Just to make sure the horses don't get spooked again."

"Well, I reckon you boys have done your good deed for the day." Maddie got onto her feet in the buckboard and pointed a Winchester rifle at them. "You ride on!"

Kyle jumped off his horse onto the buckboard and disarmed her. Bone Jackson took hold of the horses.

Caine came out of nowhere, hauling Bone off his horse and sending him sprawling to the ground. Caine wielded his flute like a weapon, knocking Kyle off the buckboard. He landed heavily on the ground. Caine took the reins from Maddie and cracked the whip. The buckboard moved forward, leaving both outlaws in the dirt. They climbed to their feet. Kyle moved over to Bone.

"Let her go!" Bone said. "We have business to take care of."

Kyle just shook his head, looking after Caine. "Who the hell *was* that?"

The buckboard meandered through the countryside with Caine holding the reins. Maddie looked at him appraisingly. In answer to her unspoken question, Caine said: "I am Caine."

"Madelaine Palmer," Maddie said. "*Dr.* Madelaine Palmer. I do not know where you came from, but God love you! Are you hurt?"

Caine had a cut over his right eye. "No, it is nothing," he assured her. "You are a doctor?"

"Yeah," she said and nodded. "You got trouble with that? Like all of the other folks in this town?"

"All a physician requires is knowledge," Caine said, "and the desire to help people."

"Maybe one year in medical school is not enough," Maddie sighed. "But when my father, the old doc died, the town did not have anyone else who could stitch and sow and find a vein."

"They are very lucky to have you," Caine told her. "Why were those men bothering you?"

"The younger one, Kyle Lefferts; we have a history. Bone Jackson is a killer. You should not have rescued me. They will be coming after you."

Caine shrugged. "I will be easy to find."

Maddie pointed ahead of them. "That's Canyon Springs right up ahead."

They rode into the main street of the western town. Wide boardwalks housed two saloons, the *Silver Dollar* and the *Crystal Palace*, a Mercantile Store, a Livery Stable, a Town Hall, a Steak House, a Bank and three hotels. People were out strolling through the town. Buckboards travelled through the streets. Men on horseback were everywhere.

"I know this town," Caine suddenly said.

Maddie looked at him, surprised. "You have been to Canyon Springs before?"

"Yes."

"What brings you back?"

"Destiny," Caine said, enigmatically.

A legend appeared on the street: WYOMING TERRITORY -- AUGUST. 1905.

In the Silver Dollar saloon, the ambience was lively and boisterous. We were angled on Deputy Clay Hardin, a man in his forties, a soft-spoken, laidback Peace Officer who was drinking whiskey. It was not his first drink of the day. His hands shook from the ravages of alcohol. Kyle Lefferts entered the saloon and moved over to the bar where one of the saloon girls was just leaving with a tray of drinks. Kyle caught her arm, lowering his voice.

"Hi honey! Did you get my offer? I would sure like to see what's underneath that dress!"

The saloon girl slapped his face and moved off. Kyle grinned. We noted a lean, good-looking man dressed like a Mississippi Gambler, in a stylish waistcoat, sitting at a table shuffling a deck of cards.

His name was Daniel McBride. He dealt the cards to the other players at the table.

"The name of this game, gentlemen, is poker. Never sweat what is in your hand or in your heart. Ante up."

McBride dealt the cards. Kyle Lefferts, standing at the bar, had noted Deputy Clay Hardin nursing his drink with shaking hands. Kyle ironically toasted him. "Hey, Hardin!" he said above the noisy ambience. Deputy Hardin looked up, saw it was Kyle Lefferts at the bar and looked away again, trying to get his hands to stop shaking.

The insolent grin was still on Kyle's face.

In the Sheriff's office down the street, Sheriff Richard Blaine had just made out his Will and Testament and signed it. He sat back in his chair, a haunted look on his face. He was gathering his courage to leave Canyon Springs for good. He strapped on his holster and his .45 revolver.

Inside the saloon, Kyle approached Deputy Clay Hardin. This time Hardin did not look up, concentrating on his hands which were still shaking badly.

"There was a time when you could have taken me and the boys at the bar in one go," Kyle said, his voice mocking. "Sheriff's leaving town. Maybe you heard?"

Hardin finally looked up. "I heard," he said.

"Are you going to be filling his shoes?" Kyle asked, ingenuously. Deputy Hardin did not respond. Kyle just shook his head. "I guess not."

We were in Dr. Madelaine's house in the town. It was nicely furnished with some antiques and a good living space. Caine was standing at the window which overlooked the main street. From this vantage point we saw John Trask riding into town with two of his men. He was an older man, forceful and violent, who was used to getting his own way. Caine noted his presence. He knew a predator when he saw one. Madelaine was mixing up some medicine. Caine indicated Trask.

"Who is that?"

Maddie followed his gaze out of the window. "It has happened to every Sheriff we have had in this town in the last three years. He crosses Trask and he gets called out by Trask's cowboys. Professional gunfighters."

Caine turned back to Maddie. "Trask. I have heard that name."

"He runs stolen cattle across the county lines," Maddie said. "As long as the Sheriff turns a blind eye, he goes about his business. Sheriff Blaine is an honorable man. He led a Federal raid against one of Trask's herds."

"And no one helped the Sheriff?" Caine asked.

'Well, they helped the undertaker bury eight lawmen so far," Maddie said. "That's about as far as their honor goes." Maddie finished up with her medicine bottles. "Well, Caine, you had better get away from that window. Come over here and I will tend to that wound."

Caine did not respond. When Maddie looked back at the window Caine's figure had disappeared.

In the town main street, John Trask further rode into the town and dismounted. At the same time Kyle Lefferts exited the saloon and headed toward the Sheriff's office. In the saloon, Daniel McBride turned to Deputy Clay Hardin. The other poker players were not at the table at this time.

"You know the Sheriff is being called out?" McBride asked him.

Deputy Hardin looked up. His hands were still shaking uncontrollably. "A man gets called out," Hardin said, "he must face the odds alone."

"Not the way they've got the deck stacked," McBride muttered.

Outside on the main street, Kyle Lefferts approached Sheriff Blaine. "Well, now, Sheriff Blaine! Happy to run into you, sir! You are just the man I need to talk to!"

It was at this point that *Cheyenne Bodie* rode into Canyon Springs. There was a subtle *riff of music* to underscore the fact that Cheyenne Bodie had now arrived in our story! He wore his signature fringe jacket that he had worn during his time of becoming a western icon. He dismounted in a grove of trees. At the same time, Caine moved out into the street. John Trask approached Sheriff Blaine whose hands were coiled as if he were going to draw. Trask's manner appeared to be cordial, but there was an underlying threat to him.

"You posted my men out of town, Sheriff," Trask said, reasonably. "Now that's a ruling I just can't enforce!"

Cheyenne made his way past a barn where Bone Jackson was waiting. Two of Trask's men moved closer to the drama that was unfolding before them, guns drawn.

"Either you round them all up and put them in jail," Trask said. And his tone hardened. "Or you *leave.*"

In the Mercantile Store on the main street, one of the shopkeepers, whose name was Charlie Farrell, moved away from his window where he had been watching with his wife. He picked up a Winchester rifle.

"They're going to backshoot the Sheriff!" Charlie said. "Damn the people in this town! They're just going to let it happen!"

His wife put a restraining hand on her husband's arm, alarmed. "Charlie, what are you doing?"

Out in the street, John Trask faced down Blaine. "What is it going to be, Sheriff?"

Sheriff Blaine backed down from the confrontation. Daniel McBride exited the saloon and walked along the boardwalk, taking stock of the situation. Sheriff Blaine turned around and fled. He climbed up onto his horse. Kyle Lefferts came up to him, his mocking voice echoing.

"What's the hurry, Sheriff?"

He was laughing, having a grand time. The two of Trask's men dumped flour sacks onto the Sheriff, coating him, which made Kyle laugh ever harder. "You're looking a little pale there, Sheriff!"

From her window in the front street of the town, Maddie watched the drama unfold to her horror. Her hand came up to her mouth.

Outside, Cheyenne was also watching the events in the town. He did not like what he was seeing. Sheriff Blaine just sat on his horse, covered with flour, mortified and unable to ride away. Charlie, the shopkeeper, had ventured out of his store onto the boardwalk. He fired his Winchester rifle into the air. Kyle spun around, fast drawing his .45 revolver. Charlie held his ground.

"That's enough!" he shouted.

Kyle fanned his gun, blowing apart a rain barrel that stood beside Charlie. The shopkeeper dropped his rifle, rooted to the spot. At the horse trough, Bone Jackson drew his gun.

"Let's finish this!" he muttered.

Bone took aim on the Sheriff. Cheyenne Bodie came up beside him, disarmed him, picked him up and tossed him into a horse trough. Caine immediately attacked two of Trask's outlaws, disarming one of them and kicking the second one into the dirt. He whirled around. Charlie herded his wife out of harm's way.

Kyle aimed his .45 revolver at the shopkeeper.

Daniel McBride drew his revolver and fired, blowing the gun out of Kyle's hand. Caine leaned down, picked up the Sheriff's hat and handed it to him.

"Ride away, Sheriff!" Caine said with some urgency.

Sheriff Blaine started to do just that. In the main street, John Trask turned to McBride.

"I thought you didn't involve yourself in other people's affairs, McBride?"

"I didn't like the odds," McBride said, tersely.

The Sheriff rode away down the main street. Cheyenne manhandled Bone Jackson into the middle of the street and dumped him there, drenched from his bath in the horse trough. Cheyenne emptied Bone's gun for him. Trask turned his attention to Cheyenne.

"Who are you?"

"Name's Bodie," Cheyenne said. "*Cheyenne Bodie.*"

In a valentine to our show, Caine looked at Cheyenne with some kind of recognition in his eyes. It was subtle. Trask was still looking at Cheyenne, sizing him up.

"What's your personal stake in this?" he demanded.

Cheyenne glanced over at McBride who had holstered his .45 revolver but had it handy. "I guess I am helping him even the odds."

Trask looked over at Caine. "And you?"

Caine said: "A man, if he decides to retire from the field of battle, should be allowed to go with honor."

Trask smiled in spite of himself. "I'll remember that!"

Cheyenne and McBride entered the Silver Dollar Saloon and made their way to the bar. Deputy Hardin looked up. "The Sheriff?" he asked.

McBride could not keep the disdain out of his voice. "He rode out."

Hardin just nodded and looked back down at the whisky glass on his table. McBride turned to Cheyenne. "I'd like to buy you a drink, Mister."

"Well thanks, I don't mind if I do," Cheyenne said. "Whiskey."

"Yes sir, Mr. McBride," the bartender said.

Cheyenne turned and noted Deputy Hardin who was turned away from them, his hands still shaking as he sipped his whiskey. Then he pushed the glass away from him. The small moment was not lost on Cheyenne.

Outside in the main street, Bone Jackson, still dripping wet from his bath in the horse trough, moved over to where Trask and Kyle were standing. "You gonna just let the Sheriff ride out of here?"

"I always have a back-up," Trask said, coldly. "You know that much, Bone."

Some way out of town, The Deacon was waiting in a grove of trees for Sheriff Blaine. The Deacon was a loner, a backstabbing killer who wore a clerical collar and always dressed in black. He was a sepulchral, frightening figure who carried a Winchester '73 rifle and wore white gloves. He had a laser-sight fitted to the rifle. Through it he saw his target, Sheriff Blaine, riding through the trees. Blaine turned back, as if sensing the presence of a predator. He urged his horse on, but The Deacon had him square in his sights. He pulled the trigger. The Sheriff fell from his horse and lay still on the road.

In his Mercantile Store, Charlie Farrell emerged from out of the back of his store. "I will just close up, Mary," he said, then he stopped dead. Kyle Lefferts stood in front of him. He was chewing on a long matchstick. Charlie was immediately wary.

"Can I help you?"

"I reckon you keep that shotgun right behind the counter," Kyle said, conversationally. Charlie immediately moved over toward where his rifle was lying. Kyle turned around to confront him. "You reckon you can reach it fast enough?"

Charlie hesitated, then made a grab for the rifle. Kyle drew his gun with lightning speed and blew him away. Mary, his wife, rushed from the back of the store and fell to her knees beside her husband's body. She was distraught. "Charlie! Charlie!"

She looked up at Kyle. There was a faint smile on his lips. "Not fast enough, I guess," he murmured.

In Madeline's house, Caine had returned so that Maddie could finish treating his head wound. She sat back. "Well. You will live! Since no one in this town will thank you for what you did for the Sheriff, I will!"

Caine smiled at her. He got to his feet and returned to the window overlooking the main street of the town. Maddie looked up at him, suddenly concerned. "Caine? Are you leaving town?"

Caine turned back to her. "No. There is someone I must find."

"Maybe I can help you," Maddie suggested. "Just about everyone in Canyon Springs gets a colic sooner or later. I get to know them all."

"It is a woman," Caine said.

Maddie kept the disappointment out of her voice. "Oh!"

"Her name is Lilly?"

Maddie reacted. "Lilly Montgomery? The singer?" Caine nodded. "Well, sure, Lilly has a little farm on the edge of town." She was amazed. "You know Lilly?"

Caine put on his battered hat. "She is my *wife*."

Now Maddie looked at Caine in shock.

We went to Lilly's farm nestled in the countryside. Lilly Montgomery moved out of her modest house carrying a bucket of water. She was a beautiful woman, in her thirties, with her blonde hair piled up on her head. She had made it a few feet before the sight of Kwai Chang Caine stopped her. She gave a little cry of happiness.

"Caine!"

Caine saw her and he ran toward her, his face wreathed in smiles, as happy as we have ever seen him. He reached Lilly and embraced her. They kissed. It was a loving, passionate kiss of two people very much in love. They broke the embrace and Caine held her at arm's length. Lilly just shook her head.

"I thought you would never come back!" she said.

"The journey has ended," Caine told her. "I am peace now."

A young boy named Matthew, about six, exited the house. He was wielding a long stick like it was a hoop. He dropped it onto the ground when he saw Caine.

"Father!" the boy exclaimed.

The boy raced for Caine who held his arms for him. "Matthew!"

Caine picked the boy up into his arms and hugged him, overjoyed. This was a Caine the audience had never seen before. Caine put his arms around the boy and Lilly and held them close.

Sometime later Caine and his wife strolled through the grounds of the house.

"I need us to leave this place," Caine said.

"We've made this our home," Lilly protested. "Matthew has his school, friends, I have mine. And a contract to fulfill." Caine stopped to kiss her hands. Lilly nodded. "But you never did like the fact of my singing in saloons, did you?"

Caine said: "Ah!" and kissed her hand again. "You can bring tranquility and joy with your voice anyplace. They have beautiful theaters in St. Louis. They will welcome you."

"But I can't just abandon everything we have built here," Lilly said. "I have a life, Caine. You left for a long time."

"If I stayed in the territory," Caine told her, "I would be hunted."

Caine unfolded the old wanted poster of him and showed it to her. There was a $10,000 reward and a $5000 reward for Caine. A notice said to contact the Chinese Legation in Washington D.C. Caine refolded the wanted poster and returned it to the canvas bag he carried over his shoulder. Lilly was obviously concerned about what she had read.

"But if you can be cleared of any charge…" she began.

"I do not believe that will happen in my lifetime," Caine told her and shrugged. "Perhaps in another. The Bounty Hunters will still come. My blind Master Po would not want bloodshed on my account." He turned back into her arms. "I have squandered so much of your time… and the moments I might have spent with my son. Seek tranquility and you lose it. You can embrace it. That moment of peace we can share together."

Lilly smiled at him. "You sure talk pretty sometimes. If I don't understand it all."

"You will," Caine said, softly.

Caine and his wife kissed again, longingly.

In the town, a town hall meeting was in progress. Most of the shopkeepers were there, including Mary Farrell, whose husband Kyle Lefferts had gunned down in cold blood. The mood at the meeting was angry and confrontational. Dean Stanmore, one of the leading figures in the town, was doing most of the talking. We noted Cheyenne Bodie was leaning against one of the walls, watching the town hall meeting.

"The good people of Canyon Springs," Dean said, "this situation has gone too far!" There were murmured responses from the assembled town folks. "A man who was a friend to everyone in this town was gunned down and we do nothing about it!"

Mary, Charlie's widow, sat beside a shopkeeper named Kemp. "We don't have a Sheriff, Dean," he said. "Are you gonna walk into that saloon and arrest Kyle Lefferts?"

"We have a Deputy Sheriff!" Dean said.

Another shopkeeper named Haskell stood up. "Where was he yesterday?" All attention suddenly focused on Cheyenne. "If it wasn't for *this* fellah, the Sheriff would be dead!"

"There is no law in this town!" Dean said. "Face it! We're on our own!"

"Clay Hardin is an honest man," Cheyenne said. "As for courage, some years back I saw him walk into a saloon in Abilene that was being shot up by some drunken cowboys and Hardin disarmed three of them without firing a shot."

"Well, that must be a long time ago," Dean retorted. "Clay Hardin hasn't sobered long enough to find his boots!"

There was laughter from the townspeople. Haskell said: "His nerve broke the same time his mother's water did!" There was more nervous laughter from the assembled townspeople. "Look for him in the street with the dogs!"

Dean tried to restore some order. "All right! Settle down!"

Mary spoke up for the first time. "My husband is dead. You need to punish the man who took his life."

Cheyenne glanced away, knowing he needed to do something to defuse this situation.

"Standing up to Kyle," Haskell said, "means standing up to Trask. Standing up to Trask, means standing up to The Deacon."

The very mention of the Deacon's name brought murmurs of fear from the assembled crowd. Cheyenne said: "What is the Deacon's hand in this?"

"Know his reputation?" Kemp asked. "'Course you do! Everyone west of Wichita does! He is Kyle's Lefferts' older brother."

Cheyenne reached a decision. "I will go and talk to Clay Hardin right now."

Cheyenne found Deputy Hardin slumped at his desk in the Sheriff's office. It almost looked as if he had passed out. Cheyenne shook him.

"Hardin?"

There was no response except for an incoherent murmuring. Cheyenne shook his head. He reached into Hardin's holster and lifted his colt .45 revolver from it. He proceeded to empty the gun onto Hardin's desk.

"You can load this again when you can see the bullets," Cheyenne said. "When you're sober enough to know what you're doing."

Finally Clay Hardin looked up at Cheyenne. "Who the hell are you?"

"Name's Cheyenne Bodie," he said. He moved over to the coffee pot. "You take your coffee black? Doesn't much matter because that's way it's comin'."

Cheyenne poured Hardin a cup of coffee. The Deputy Sheriff looked as if he was in a bad way. Cheyenne filled up the coffee pot, spooned a little sugar and put the coffee mug into Hardin's shaking hands. "There you go."

Hardin took a swallow of the coffee and spit it out. "That's *salt*, not *sugar!*"

"Salt sobers a man up a mite faster," Cheyenne said. "You need to be wide awake when you walk into that saloon."

"What are you talking about?"

'Well, we have an eyewitness to the death of the shopkeeper," Cheyenne said. "His widow Mary claims that she saw Kyle Lefferts kill her husband in cold blood."

Clay Hardin pulled himself up from the desk. Cheyenne tried to help him, but he waved him away. He moved over to the jail cells and opened the cell door.

"They brought back Sheriff Blaine this morning," he said, quietly. "He was shot in the back. I have to go the undertakers. I go into that saloon there would be another wooden casket to go out right beside mine."

"I have seen you draw," Cheyenne said. "You're *fast*. You're *faster* than Kyle."

Deputy Hardin leaned against the bars of the cell. "That was a hell of a long time ago." He nodded. "I remember you now. Cheyenne! Abilene."

"Yup," Cheyenne said.

"You took out two back shooters when I drew against the Ringo Kid."

"I could stick around for a while," Cheyenne offered. "Make sure some of Trask's cowboys don't get behind you."

There was a great piece of dialogue in this scene in the Sheriff's office with Clu Gulager. The scene was a tense one. I was standing on the set. Clu took me to one side. He was a kind of method-studied actor, very self-deprecating and soft spoken. He wanted to play the scene in the Sheriff's office in a particular way. I looked at the director, Jon Cassar, and he just shrugged. He had no problem with that. I told Clu to play the scene the way it worked for him. He just nodded. I stepped away at that point. There was usually quiet on a set when we were about to roll camera, but on this particular set you could have heard a pin drop. The crew waited to see how this would play out. Jon Cassar, our wonderful director, called for "Action!"

Clu Gulager turned away from Clint Walker. He was back in character now. "You know what alcohol does to you?" Hardin asked Cheyenne. "It puts a hole, a big hole into your insides, even after you smash the bottle, it just keeps eating at you and eating at you and *eating at you*. It is like a hot, empty space that fills your soul. And then you lose your nerve."

The scene was over. For a moment no one moved on the set. Jon Cassar said very, quietly: "Cut!" The crew all exploded into spontaneous applause. Clu turned to me and murmured: "That was the way we did it in the old days!" and walked away.

It was a moment on *Kung Fu: The Legend Continues* that I will never forget.

Cheyenne continued on with the scene. "Well, you are going to have to face up to it sooner or later, Hardin," he said. "Every man does."

Hardin turned back to Cheyenne. "You didn't preach to me in Abilene. I'll wait for my sermon."

He crossed back from the jail cells and collapsed back at his desk. Cheyenne had made his decision. "Well, if you can't go into the saloon, then I'll go over there and bring Kyle back to you."

Hardin took a swig from the Jim Beam whiskey bottle. "You can't go up against him alone, my friend."

"Well, I wouldn't have to if I had a choice." Cheyenne looked at Hardin and shook his head again. "You know what, Abilene wasn't *that* long ago."

Cheyenne left Hardin alone. The Deputy Sheriff looked down at the whiskey bottle, stopped himself from taking another drink and moved the bottle away from him.

We were in a room off the Silver Dollar Saloon where Caine was packing his suitcase. He paused, seeing a poster for Lilly Montgomery, billed as the "Western Songbird". Then he moved away and entered the saloon from a back entrance. Bone Jackson was playing poker with Daniel McBride. Kyle Lefferts sat at the table with several other men. We note that they were drinking Old Raven Sour Mash Whiskey.

"I think I will raise you," Bone said.

"That suits me fine," McBride said.

Caine sat down at the table right behind the poker players. Outside the saloon, Cheyenne Bodie passed one of the saloon girls, tipping his hat to her, "Ma'am" and walked into the saloon. He went up to the bar. McBride noted his presence. At the back table, Caine was writing a letter. McBride turned his attention back to the poker game.

"Call," he said.

McBride won the hand and raked in his chips. Bone looked up at the bar. "What are you doing here, Cheyenne?" he demanded. "Some town committee deputize you?" Beside him, Kyle Lefferts grinned, enjoying this. Bone added: "I don't see no badge."

At that moment Clay Hardin entered the saloon. His hands were still shaking, but he said: "The job was already taken."

Caine looked up. McBride quickly said: "Let's take a break, gentlemen."

Bone looked over at McBride. "We don't want any back shooters."

"That's your boss's play," McBride said evenly as he got up from the table. "These odds look even to me."

McBride joined Cheyenne at the bar. Kyle's attention now was centered on Clay Hardin. His expression was not playful any longer. Kyle's eyes were like pieces of ice.

"Are you calling me out, Deputy?"

"I'm arresting you for murder," Hardin said. His hands continued to shake. "Unbuckle your gun belt and drop it on the floor."

Bone started to laugh. Kyle got to his feet, shaking his head. "Hardin, you couldn't draw that gun out of your holster without dropping it!"

Caine looked up. Bone also got to his feet. Kyle indicated Deputy Hardin's hands which still shook. "Look at your hands," Kyle suggested.

"I can't," Hardin said, evenly. "I'm looking at *yours*. You got two seconds."

Kyle drew his gun. Hardin drew his gun, a little faster, but at that moment Caine exploded into action. He kicked Kyle's gun out of his hands, throwing Bone to one side. Bone reached for his gun, but Cheyenne upended the table, sending money and poker chips flying. Bone flew back into the wall. Cheyenne drew his own gun, holding it on Kyle and Bone. Hardin grabbed Kyle.

"You're going to jail!"

Cheyenne still had the drop on Kyle and Bone. He looked over at Caine. "Much obliged, friend."

Caine nodded. Cheyenne moved away from the bar. Daniel McBride looked around, trying to diffuse the tense scene in the saloon. "If anyone is still of a mind, let's play some poker."

In the Sheriff office, Deputy Hardin threw Kyle into the jail cell. "Get in!"

Hardin locked the cell behind him. Cheyenne was beside him. Kyle gripped the bars.

"My brother is going to have me out of here before nightfall," he said.

"This jail is built solid," Hardin said with some fervor. "I have enough food for a week. I got rifles and ammo and I don't have to leave until the Federal Marshal gets here to take you to Denver to stand trial."

"What are you going to do?" Kyle asked. "Guard that jail by yourself? Against *twenty guns?*" Kyle included Cheyenne in his angry tirade. "You're both dead men!" he shouted.

Hardin crossed back to his desk in the Sheriff's office. We noted that Caine was standing beside Cheyenne. "The other man..." Caine began.

Hardin nodded. "Bone Jackson."

"Rode out," Caine said. "On his horse, very fast. I thought you should know that."

Hardin nodded. "He's got to report to Trask," he said. "And to the Deacon. Kyle might be right. His brother might be saying some pretty words at our graves." Hardin sat down back at his desk. He looked at his hands which still shook. "Maybe they'll stop."

"When the spirit is in control," Caine said quietly, "the body obeys. Look at your demons, they are formless. Listen to your fears, they are soundless. When this moment occurs, your hands will not betray you."

Caine and Cheyenne moved out of the Sheriff's office. Hardin thought about what Caine had just said. His hands closed into fists.

In the town street, Caine climbed into a buckboard where he had gathered some provisions for Lilly and himself. The Deacon watched him from an alleyway, an imposing, malignant figure. Caine spurred his horse and wagon down the street. He had not seen the Deacon yet. The Deacon mounted his white horse and rode out of town.

We were at John Trask's horse farm near the town of Canyon Springs. The Deacon was standing with Trask and Bone Jackson. Trask's wranglers were putting the horses through their paces.

"Beautiful animal," the Deacon remarked. "Such grace and majesty. But ready to be broken! To be tamed!"

"Hardin has no back-up," Trask said. "We'll storm the jail."

"The Lord abhors violence," the Deacon said. "Mind you, when Jesus threw the moneylenders out of the temple he didn't pull his punches."

Bone said: "I'll just pass the word on to the men."

The Deacon shook his head, his attention fixed on Trask. "You try to storm that jail and you'll have every Federal Marshal in the territory down on us. You have a lucrative business running here, Mr. Trask. But the Lord giveth and the Lord taketh away. We don't want to attract that kind of attention."

"Surely you do not want your brother to rot in jail," Trask asked him.

"We'll just let Deputy Hardin deliver Kyle to us," the Deacon said.

"Hardin may a coward," Trask said, "but he's sitting in that Sheriff's office and he's got no reason to go out."

"We'll offer him an exchange," the Deacon said, reasonably. "Kyle for one of our prisoners."

"What prisoners?" Bone asked.

"The ones the Lord has provided for us," the Deacon said. "He does work in mysterious ways."

He moved away from Trask.

Back in the Sheriff's office, Kyle Lefferts was lying on a cot in his jail cell. He shouted: "Hey, Hardin!" Deputy Sheriff Harden moved to the cells to see what all the shouting was about. "Hey, Hardin, what have you got guarding this jail?" Kyle was enjoying this. "You got a drunk and an old Indian fighter." He laughed. "You think that is going to stop my brother from comin' in shooting?"

"Maybe your brother won't come at all," Hardin said. "The way I heard it, you boys are like rattlers hissing at each other, is that right?"

"Oh, he'll come," Kyle said. "Then you and I can settle our differences."

Hardin had had enough taunting and moved back to his office.

Out on the street, Cheyenne moved down the boardwalk. Beside him, John Trask stepped out of the shadows.

In the small room next door to the saloon, Caine had been packing some keepsakes for Lilly. He took the poster of her as the "Western Songbird" down from the wall and carefully folded it. Lilly stood in the room with her son Matthew beside her.

"I wanted to say goodbye to this room," Lilly said, somewhat nostalgically. She smiled at Caine. "Silly isn't it?"

"Not to me," Caine responded.

Suddenly Matthew ran out of the room. Caine moved out after him, concerned. "Matthew! Matthew, come back here!"

Outside along Front Street, the Deacon rode up on his white horse, his long rifle beside him. Cheyenne stopped in the street, looking around in the shadows, sensing some kind of danger. There was no one around him. He turned back the other way and one of Trask's men jumped him. Cheyenne knocked him into the street, but three more took his place, pinning Cheyenne's arms behind him. They dragged him away.

In the small alcove room on the first floor, Lilly turned as she heard someone enter behind her. "Caine?" Then Bone Jackson grabbed her, stifling her scream. He laughed as he dragged her away. Outside in the street, Matthew was playfully trying to flee from Caine. "You can't catch me!" he called out.

Caine was right behind him. The youngster ran into the arms of one of Trask's men. In the shadows, the Deacon raised his long rifle. Matthew pulled away from Trask's thug, but there were three more men to take his place. Then Caine entered the fray. He kicked out at the attackers, hurling them onto the ground with deft kung fu kicks. He turned when he heard Lilly's screams. Bone was manhandling her down the alleyway. The Deacon took aim in the shadows and fired. The force of the bullet knocked Caine into the street. Lilly was loaded by Bone into a buckboard by three of Trask's men and the driver took off.

Deputy Hardin emerged from the Sheriff's office, summoned by the commotion. Maddie ran to Caine's side as more townspeople gathered around them.

"This man is hurt!" she cried out.

McBride moved over to Maddie's side. "I've got him, Dr, Maddie!" he said.

McBride picked Caine up from the street.

"Help me get him into the office!" Maddie said.

Maddie and McBride supported Caine down the street. Cheyenne got to his feet, clearing his head from his fight with Trask's men. He moved over to where the Deputy Sheriff had just confronted the Deacon on his white horse.

"Bring my stupid little brother to the Trask ranch," he said. "Or the woman and the boy die. Noon tomorrow. Fair exchange. No one gets hurt."

Then the Deacon rode away.

In her house, Maddie and McBride lay Caine down on a couch. He was burning up with fever. "Bullet is still in there," Maddie said. McBride straightened, moving for the door leading out into the street. "Where are you going?"

"I don't want to bust this winning streak," McBride said, but that was clearly not the reason. There was nothing more he could do. "Good luck," he said to Maddie.

McBride left the house. Caine stirred. Maddie moved over to him. He tried to stand up. "I must leave!"

"You're not going anywhere," Maddie told him, gently pushing Caine back onto the couch. "That bullet is lodged next to your heart. I do not know if I can operate. I am going to give you some morphine."

Caine slumped back down. Maddie moved over to her medicine cabinet, which was locked.

The Deacon moved into the shot *in reflection* behind her.

She whirled and gasped, completely traumatized by him.

"Ever beautiful," the Deacon murmured. "The fall of your hair, that glow of your skin. And eyes that look right through a man to his very soul."

Maddie held her ground, but it was an effort. "You don't *have* a soul," she whispered. The Deacon completely traumatized her. "When I look at you, Deacon, I see a skeleton over which the skin has been stretched too tight."

"But on our wedding night, the caress of your hands turned my skin to velvet," the Deacon reminded her.

"I must have been crazy," Maddie said, again in a whisper.

"To marry me?" the Deacon said. "Passion is the Devil's blood. It flows through the veins into the mind and fills it with dark visions." He moved over to Maddie and grabbed her hand. "Your patient must suffer his pain in His name's sake when he murdered Abel."

"You did it, didn't you?" Maddie said, accusingly. "You shot Caine!"

She turned away as Caine cried out. She struggled in the Deacon's arms, finally breaking free of him. The Deacon nodded to one of Trask's men who had entered the house with him. He took hold of Maddie and dragged her away. The Deacon moved over to where Caine lay on the couch. Caine looked up at him.

"I told Deputy Hardin that if my brother is not delivered to Trask's ranch by noon tomorrow," the Deacon said, "your family and Dr. Madelaine will die. I want you to know that they *will* die!" Caine reached up for him, but the Deacon held Caine's hand tightly. "Right after Kyle has been brought here. Think about that, as you are released from this earthly sphere."

The Deacon moved away. Caine took a deep, shuddering breath. "No!" he cried out. "Help me, Master Po! Help me!"

We are close on a pebble hitting the waters in a brook. This is a *Flashback Sequence*, but from whose perspective? The young Kwai Chang Caine sat beside the tranquil stream, listening to his Master Po's voice. Master Po said: "Does not the pebble entering the water bring fresh journey?"

Caine still lay on the couch in Madelaine's room, reliving the memories he was wrestling with. "Such is the journey to life," Master Po said to the young Kwai Chang Caine. "It begins and it ends. Yet fresh beginnings go forth. Father begets son, who then becomes son, who begets son."

"Then the roots that I have are *me*," Young Caine said, "and I am *they*."

We were back in real time with Caine. He was feverish, as if he were reaching for a dream. "My grandson…"

A moment later it appeared that Caine was suddenly in a time vortex. He spun through time, which was a really good special effect! There was a shot of the Precinct which orientated the audience to this new reality. Caine appeared behind what was basically a scrim which further enhanced the idea that Caine had made a harrowing journey through time and space.

He moved out of the scrim to enter the Precinct. Caine held his right side gingerly, obviously still in pain; otherwise he looked no different for his transformation. But he was completely disoriented. The Precinct had the usual chaos around it. Sergeant Broderick was at his counter. There were some rowdy elements in the Precinct and voices were being raised. Caine tentatively approached the Sergeant.

"Are you looking for Peter?" Broderick asked him.

Caine was a little nonplussed by the question. As if he did not know who "Peter" was. He shrugged. "*Peter?*" he asked.

"Yeah, your son, remember?" Broderick said, wryly. "He's a cop, carries a badge and a gun. Works here?" He amended that. "Sometimes!"

"*Peter Caine?*" Caine asked, again not fully understanding.

Sergeant Broderick looked up from his paperwork. Now he was concerned. "Are you all right? You don't look so good."

But Caine now understood. He nodded. "My *grandson.*"

Broderick shook his head, not tracking with Caine at all. "What?"

"He is here?" Caine asked.

"Yeah, he's back at his desk there."

Broderick had had enough of the background chatter around him. He whirled around on one of the detectives who was standing with two hookers. "Just read them their rights and gag them. That is a little gallows humor, Officer,' he added.

The Officer said: "Okay!"

"Just to keep them quiet!"

Sergeant Broderick turned back, but Caine was gone. He had moved back to Peter Caine's desk in the Precinct confusion. Peter was on the phone, nodding.

"Yeah, okay. Right."

Peter hung up and saw that Caine was standing with his back to him. "Pop? Hey!" Caine turned around. "What are you doing here?"

Still disoriented, Caine said: "Peter, I need my journal. Do you have it?"

Peter leaned back to go through some of the drawers in his desk. "Which one do you need? *Yours?* Your father's, your grandfather's, what?"

"Your great grandfather's," Caine said.

Peter collected a bunch of the diaries and handed them to Caine. Caine nodded. "Yes! Yes!"

"What is going on, Pop?" Peter got to his feet. "Sorry, don't call you 'Pop!'! I know! Are you okay? I have never seen you this pale. What's happened?"

Caine collapsed into Peter's arms. Peter held him tightly, turning back to Sergeant Broderick. "Sarge! Sarge! Give me a hand here!"

Sergeant Broderick moved to Peter's side, propping Caine up. Caine held both of their hands. He was very weak. "Take me home!"

Peter took his car to the Ancient's apartment. He lay Caine down on a table which the Ancient had turned into a makeshift apothecary. The Ancient stayed in the background. Peter examined Caine's wound.

"That's a bullet wound!" Peter realized. "This isn't going to heal with herbs that the Ancient finds in a jar! You've got to go to the hospital right now, Pop!"

Peter turned around, but Caine reached an arm up to him, turning him back. "You love your father! That would be a great comfort for me."

"What are you talking about?" Peter asked.

"You remind me of myself when I was young like you."

Peter shook his head. "You're delirious. I'll use the phone in the street." He turned to the Ancient. "Don't let him leave!"

Peter moved out of the apartment. The Ancient took his place, holding onto Caine's hands. Caine looked up at him. "You know who I am?"

The old man nodded. "Yes. I *know*! It is a shame that Peter did not. You have made an extraordinary journey!"

"I wanted to see my grandson," Caine said.

The Ancient stepped away. Caine – a *"Caine"* from the *past* – stepped through the glass doors of the apartment. This was a Caine with no bullet wound evident, a somewhat *younger version* of himself. This was accomplished by a split/screen technique of Caine and the *other Caine*.

Caine looked down at himself. "I am here," he said. "You are hurt."

"That was why I have made this journey here," the *other Caine* said. "You must take my place! Your grandfather and your father are being held hostage."

"What is the year?" the other Caine asked.

"1905."

"I have made such journeys before," the *other* Caine said, "but what you ask…" He shook his head. Caine – *our* Caine – rose up a little. "You must try! Take my journal. It will show you the time and the place."

The other Caine looked down at himself and was overcome with emotion. "It is so wonderful to speak with you!" The other Caine cradled his doppelganger's face gently. The *first* Caine nodded. "Yes! My grandson! You must succeed. Or my wife, and my son -- *your* father -- will die."

The other Caine nodded that he understood.

Sometime later, we see Caine – our Doppelganger Caine – sitting in a lotus position in his apartment. His journal was at his feet with some strange drawings and hieroglyphics on it. He was wearing his signature brown shirt and the Kung Fu symbol hanging around his neck. Caine's voice echoed in his head, remembering his grandfather's voice.

"Deputy Sheriff Hardin!" he said. "And a man named Cheyenne! Those are your allies."

The Camera *pulled back from* Caine to show him lit by myriad candles. The Ancient stood behind him in the shadows.

"You can do this, Kwai Chang Caine," he said, softly. "You can make this journey!"

Caine spiraled out of this time vortex, reversing his journey, until he was back in his room again at Madeline's place in 1905. He lay there on the couch for a moment, collecting himself for the ordeal that lay ahead of him.

In the Silver Dollar Saloon, Deputy Sheriff Hardin sat at a table with the raucous ambience around him. He fingered his badge, as if wondering if he should keep it or not. Daniel McBride was playing solitaire. Caine moved over to Hardin who glanced up.

"You're looking good for a man who got shot," he commented.

"I am healed," Caine said, gently. "Will you go with us when we bring in your prisoner?"

Caine did not get an answer from Hardin. He turned away.

"Wait!" Hardin said.

Caine turned back. Hardin stood up and put his Deputy's badge on the front of his vest. He headed for the door of the saloon. McBride abandoned his game of Solitaire and got to his feet.

"Clay!" he said. "You need another gun?"

Hardin turned around and looked at McBride. "This had nothing to do with you," he said. "Why should you risk your life?"

"Let's say I *still* don't like the odds," McBride said and picked up his coat from the back of his chair. Caine and McBride moved out of the saloon. Deputy Hardin followed them.

Outside the Sheriff's office, Hardin manhandled Kyle Lefferts into a buckboard that was waiting outside. His hands were still bound together. "All right!" Hardin said. "Up we go!"

Kyle settled into the buckboard. "No back-up, Deputy?" he asked in his insolent manner. "What happened to your friends?"

"I reckon I found out who they were," Hardin responded.

Hardin urged the horses down the main street of Canyon Springs.

Out at his ranch, Trask directed his men. "Okay, get into your positions."

His hired killers fanned out. The Deacon passed them, moving to a corral where Madelaine, Lilly and Matthew waited. The Deacon carried a gun belt over his shoulder. He leaned closer to Lilly Montgomery.

"And you will burn, Jezebel!" he said, softly. "You will *burn!*"

"Leave her alone, Deacon!" Maddie said.

The Deacon turned to Maddie. "Before this day is over, both of you will beg your Creator for forgiveness."

Out on the road, Deputy Hardin and Kyle moved to the Trask ranch. Cheyenne and McBride rode up and dismounted at a wooden fence. Cheyenne moved through the foliage around the Trask ranch, carrying his Winchester rifle. Sheriff Hardin and Kyle pulled up in the buckboard. Trask waited for them with two of his hired killers and Bone Jackson. Hardin jumped out and Kyle did the same. Hardin kept Kyle tied up beside him. Trask looked on with a smug expression on his face.

"I didn't think you would be the one to make the delivery, Deputy," he said, as if he was surprised.

Hardin did not rise to the bait. "You bring out the prisoners," he said. He took a step back from Kyle. "They start walking. Kyle starts walking."

Trask nodded. He turned to the Deacon. At the same time, Caine and McBride moved past the barn. Caine indicated for McBride to move further away from him.

McBride nodded. "Okay."

McBride found shelter in the trees. Cheyenne got closer to the exchange point. Hardin cut the bonds around Kyle's hands. Maddie and Lilly moved to where Bone Jackson was standing beside Trask. A frightened Matthew followed them.

"Start them moving this way," Bone said.

The Deacon followed the three hostages. He tossed Kyle's .45 revolver and holster to him, who strapped it on. The Deacon moved away from them. Maddie and Lilly reached Kyle, then, suddenly, he grabbed Lilly.

"No!" Hardin cried out.

Maddie and Matthew scrambled away with Matthew.

"Matthew, come away!" Maddie cried.

They knelt down beside one of the fences. Bone moved away to the barn where he had seen the Deacon. Lilly struggled in Kyle's grasp. Hardin was seemingly powerless to intervene as long as Kyle had Lilly in his arms. Kyle grinned, daring Deputy Hardin to make his move.

"You better ride out of here, Hardin!" he called to him.

Bone Jackson moved into the barn. McBride ducked down beside one of the fences, drawing his .45 revolver. A moment later Bone crashed through the window out into the dirt. Caine appeared in the smashed window behind him. Bone turned around on his back, aiming his gun at Caine. Cheyenne took aim and fired on him, blowing the gun out of his hands.

Lilly managed free herself from Kyle's grasp, ducking down at the fence. Kyle whirled to face Deputy Hardin. He grinned again.

He went for his gun.

Harden pulled his gun out of his holster with lightning speed and fired.

Kyle collapsed to the ground.

McBride came around the fences, fanning his gun, blowing Trask's gunmen away.

The Deacon retreated into one of the other barns and was swallowed up in the darkness. He emerged into the open, but Caine was waiting for him. He kicked the Deacon's gun from his hand.

"You were the man who shot my grandfather!" Caine said, angrily. "I know that!"

The Deacon pulled another gun from his pocket and pointed it at Caine. Caine passed his hand over the .45 revolver which glowed red hot in the Deacon's hands, causing him to drop it. Caine kicked out and the Deacon collapsed onto the ground.

Maddie and Lilly embraced each other while Matthew looked on. McBride moved to where Hardin was standing.

"That was nice shooting," Hardin told him.

McBride smiled. "You, too!"

Maddie knelt down and tended to Kyle's injuries. Caine moved over to where Lilly waited. She moved immediately into his arms. "Caine!"

Caine embraced her. When they broke, he looked at her. She did not know the meaning of his words, but he said: "He is a very lucky man!" He leaned down to Matthew. "Be strong for your mother."

Maddie had moved over now to Caine and examined him. "Better make sure that bullet wound didn't reopen." Then she looked back at him, astonished. *"There is no bullet wound!"*

Caine gave her one is his ionic shrugs. "I heal quickly!"

He moved past them. Maddie and Lilly exchanged bewildered looks.

Deputy Sheriff Hardin pushed Kyle ahead of him. Trask and his gunfighters had their hands in the air. "Let's go!" Hardin said. "Let's take them in."

McBride also motioned to them. "Move!"

Hardin grabbed Trask's arm. "Come on!"

Left alone, Caine made an entry in his journal. This time, we do not see Caine's journey back through the *time vortex* to his *real time*. But we are back at the ICU Ward corridor in the hospital near the Precinct. Peter was pacing restlessly. The Ancient was with him. The doors opened and a doctor in scrubs walked out. Peter moved to him.

"Mr. Caine," the doctor said. "We got the bullet out. It was touch-and-go there for a while. The bullet was pretty close to his heart, but your father is going to be all right."

At the moment Caine came through the doors of the ICU department looking fit and completely rested. "As a matter of fact," he said, "I feel *so* good, I think I will go home. Thank you, Doctor!"

Caine moved away. Peter just shook his head, just another mystery in Caine's world, and he and the Ancient followed Caine to the ICU doors out into the street.

We went to the Silver Dollar Saloon in our frontier town of Canyon Springs. Daniel McBride had just won another hand of poker. He raked the chips to him, looking at the other players at the table. "Thank you, gentlemen." He smiled at them. "What was the name of this game?" McBride started to deal the cards. "Ante-up."

Caine was in Madelaine's house. He was putting his journal into his canvas bag. Madelaine looked over at him. "All right! Somebody dug that bullet out and it was not *me*! Yesterday I could not even find the wound. Explain this to me."

Caine gave her one of his signature shrugs. "I cannot. Will you be all right when I leave?"

"All of Trask's men are being taken to the Denver Marshal," Maddie said. "Trask's ranch is up for sale and the Deacon has gone out of my life. All thanks to you." She kissed him on the cheek. "Good luck with your new life."

Caine tipped his hat to her. "Thank you."

He moved away. Madelaine looked after him a little wistfully.

Outside, in Canyon Springs, Caine climbed onto a wagon where Lilly and Matthew were waiting for him. Cheyenne Bodie rode over to them. Clay Hardin moved over to shake Caine's hand.

"I want to thank you for having faith in me," he said. "Faith I didn't have."

"It was always there," Caine said. "You only needed to recognize it."

Cheyenne said: "I reckon I'll ride with you folks for a spell."

That was fine with Caine. Lilly turned to Hardin. "Goodbye, Sheriff."

Hardin took off his hat with a disparaging gesture. "No, it's just... *just* Deputy Sheriff," he said with modesty.

"Well, the town committee just had a meeting," Cheyenne said. "Judge Worrell has already signed the papers."

Sheriff Hardin put back on his hat. Cheyenne waved him a farewell. The buckboard, with Lilly and Matthew beside Caine, pulled down the main street of Canyon Springs.

Hardin waved them away. A young woman moved past Hardin. "Morning, Sheriff."

Hardin was momentarily taken aback by the friendly greeting. Reflectively he answered: "Morning."

Another passerby greeted him. "Good morning, Sheriff."

Deputy Sheriff Hardin nodded his thanks. Then he smiled and walked away.

On the prairie Caine and Lilly rode in the buckboard. Matthew was playing with his hoop. Cheyenne rode his horse beside the buckboard. A gorgeous sunset greeted them as they traveled to a new life.

Chapter Eight
SECRET PLACE

THIS EPISODE OF *KUNG FU: THE LEGEND CONTINUES* has a special place in my heart. It was an atypical episode because of the great performances that were generated. The director of the episode was William Shatner who has been a very good friend of mine for many years. It was the only episode he directed of the series, but what an *episode* it turned out to be! He brought flair, a sense of style and chutzpah to the show. It dealt with emotional and mental health. There was a tour-de-force performance from the lead actor Craig Wasson. It appeared as if the actor was adlibbing his way through the text, but that was very deceptive. It was a very careful, thoughtful performance where Craig Wasson pulled out all the stops. His *impressions of celebrities* were rapid-fire gems, some of them exploding from his being in a staccato stream of consciousness. The actor played a manic-depressive persona that was, at times, heartbreaking.

It was a performance I would never forget.

There was also a mesmerizing performance by our lead actor, Chris Potter, who, of course, was playing Peter Caine. Chris really came into his own in this episode. Of course, David Carradine had risen to the occasion as usual, but he took a step back from the main action to lend his support to Craig Wasson and Chris Potter. David was very good about giving the other actors their day in the spotlight. My friend Richard Anderson, who had appeared in the TV Movies of The Six Million Dollar Man and The Bionic Woman for me, was also in the cast and did a fine job, as always. His role of a tough-as-nails Police Captain was right on the money. But for this particular episode, Craig Wasson was very much front-and-center.

We were in the city where a big school bus was making its way through the suburbs. It was jammed with school children, sixteen years of age, all of them in high spirits. In the first row were two best friends, Colleen and Blythe. Colleen was very pretty with a world-weary demeanor. She was a substitute teacher. Blythe was somewhat withdrawn who wore large glasses which gave her a studious look. Around them the other students made the usual snide, caustic remarks about their teachers, their other friends, all contributing to the overall ambiance.

"They're very immature!" Blythe said.

Colleen smiled. "Yeah, don't you just love them?"

"No!" Blythe said, pushing her glasses higher on her nose. "I don't!"

Colleen shook her head tolerantly. The bus driver suddenly applied the brakes. A young man was standing in the middle of the road, as if oblivious that he was about to be to run over!

"Why the hell is he standing there?" the bus driver said, annoyed.

He rolled to a stop. He had a schedule to keep. The young man's name was Max Forrester. He wore a lightweight jacket over a gray t-shirt and jeans He carried an *uzi* with a telescopic bolt design and a magazine to be housed in the pistol grip to make it a shorter weapon.

At which point Max fired the uzi into the air.

The students started screaming. Max pounded on the bus door. "Open up in there!" he shouted. "I mean it!"

The bus driver opened the bus doors. Immediately Max threw him out onto the ground. "Sorry it has to be this way!" He closed the bus doors behind him. The bus driver scrambled to his feet and took off. The students had quieted now, fearful and shell shocked. Max looked down with disdain at them, then suddenly he was *Travis Bickle* from *Taxi Driver,* raging at his passengers.

"Are you looking at me?" he demanded. "Are you looking *at me? Are you looking at me?*"

A uniformed Police Officer had pulled up in his cruiser and got out. We noted his badge said *Officer Pearson* on it. He was several yards away from the stopped bus. Warily he approached it. There is no movement inside the school bus at all.

"Everything okay in there?" the Officer shouted. When he did not get a response, he said again: "Everything okay in there?"

Max shouted from inside the school bus: "We're stranded in here, Mr. Policeman! What hell the was this driver thinking about, huh? Was he some kind of an idiot, do you suppose? I want you out of here! Do you understand me?"

The Officer did not like what he was hearing. "What is going on?"

In answer, Max strafed the window on the bus with his uzi, blowing a large hole in the glass. Officer Pearson retreated fast! He ran back to his police car and grabbed his radio. "We've got a situation here!"

At this point we were introduced to Captain Bartlett Stiles, a career Police Officer and a no-nonsense martinet. He was not one to be rifled with. He got out of his car and moved to where Officer Pearce was on the radio. Stiles took the radio away from Pearce and spoke into it. "I just got here! Fill me in! I've got a few armed police and that is it." Stiles stood listening to the Police Dispatcher's voice on his radio. "Well, he's got one uzi, enough ammunition to keep us here for a month and we've got the Swat Team on its way. What about my hostage unit, Joe? Is that on its way?" Again he listened to the voice on his radio. "I don't care what instructions I got from Chief *Strenlich*!" Stiles said. "Get it here, you got that?"

Captain Paul Blaisdell pulled up in his car. He got out and moved over to where Stiles was still listening on the radio. "Good! Block the road. I will need all the help I can get for us and I need it *now*! Thanks, Joe."

Stiles clicked off the radio.

"What have we got?" Blaisdell asked him.

"No demands yet," Captain Stiles said. "His name is Maxwell Forrester." One of the cops tried to talk to Stiles who brusquely motioned him to move on. "Over *there*!" Stiles said:" A hostage team is on its way. We're going to need a talker this time!"

"Who is he talking to right now?" Blaisdell demanded.

Stiles turned around and looked out at the school bus which stood isolated in the middle of the industrial park. We note that Max had now punched a ragged hole in the windshield.

Stiles looked as if he was going to have a fit. "What the hell! He's going to get himself killed!" The Captain motioned for his Patrolman to get out from the line of fire. "Officer Pearce!" he shouted. "Get over here!"

Office Pearce was backing away from the school bus and Max, but he would not let it go. He looked at the place he thought Max was standing in the blown-out window. "Now we are friends, right?" Pearce shouted. "Right?"

Max's answer was to fire a burst on the uzi, sending Officer Pearce running for his life to where the other Police Cars were parked around Stiles' cruiser.

"Stay down," Stiles shouted. "Block the road! Hold your fire!"

Max stopped firing. It left an eerie calm that settled on the suburban street.

At that moment Peter and Caine pulled up in Peter's sports car. They exited the vehicle and stood watching the police activity. Caine was wearing a linen shirt and carrying a canvas bag over his shoulder. Peter was casually dressed in a sport coat and jeans. He was wearing a pale, denim shirt.

At Stiles' Police Car, Stiles was shaking his head. He looked at Officer Pearce's badge number. "What the hell were you doing, Officer?"

"Trying to talk him out of it, sir!" Pearce said.

"Ten weeks of intense training with my unit and you might have a shot at it!" Stiles retorted.

"Are you hurt, son?" Blaisdell asked him.

"No, sir!" Officer Pearce said. "I thought I had him eating out of my hand! He talked about television and the need to go back to hour dramas. That was when we became friends. Not that he had anything against sitcoms, mind you. He asked me who had the better ensemble cast, *Cheers* or *Barney Miller*? I said *Cheers* and that was when he started firing at me! I guess I should have watched more *Barney Miller*!"

Paul Blaisdell and Captain Stiles just looked at one other.

One of Police Officers said: "We need more men on the other side of that bus!"

Several Police Officers scrambled to get closer to the stalled vehicle.

Stiles indicated Caine and Peter. "Who is that?"

Blaisdell followed his gaze. "Peter Caine," he said. "He was the Officer who arrested Max Forrester and put him away five years ago for armed robbery. Probably the best man for us to talk to."

Stiles turned back to Blaisdell, his manner caustic. "Oh, you did, did you?" Blasdell was not going to take the bait. He remembered the various run-ins he had had with Stiles before. "Yes, I did," he said, evenly.

"Now I've got two amateurs here!" Stiles muttered. Peter was walking toward Blaisdell. Captain Stiles indicated Caine. "Who is that with him?"

"That's his father," Blaisdell said. "They were having breakfast when I called them."

"How cozy!" Stiles muttered. "Did he bring his mother too?"

Peter had reached them. "My mother's dead," he told Stiles, shortly.

Stiles turned his attention away from Peter, virtually dismissing him and looking back at Officer Pearce. "What else was said exactly, Pearce?"

"Nothing else," Pearce said. "You could have heard the heartbeat from there," he added, dramatically.

"Well, you won't hear anything for much longer," Peter said, "unless you get somebody to talk to him. And I am that person! I know how this guy's mind works. Max has a split personality. All of them famous! He lives in the pages of TV Guide! I can deal with him."

"So you are going to talk him out of it," Stiles said, "and be the hero cop of the day, huh? Is that it?" Now he really got into Peter's face. "Let me tell you why I dislike hero cops! They get very good cops killed. You just stay out of this." Stiles moved over to Officer Pearce again, once again dismissing Peter. "I want to hear exactly what was said. Every word!"

Peter was seething. He moved forward, undaunted. "Did he carry a small bottle of colorless liquid with him?"

Officer Pearce turned back and shook his head. "That that I saw."

Captain Stiles and his Patrolman moved away. The exchange had not been lost on Paul Blaisdell. "What kind of a colorless liquid?"

"Nitro!" Peter said. "He was an explosives expert. Demolition. If I know my Maxie, he's carrying nitro."

In the stalled school bus, Max carefully took out a package from his canvas bag and unwrapped it. He held up a small vial of nitroglycerin reverently in his hands. The other students were sitting still, watching Max, as if mesmerized.

"What is that?" Colleen asked him.

"This is our salvation," Max murmured. He set the nitro bottle carefully on the rim of the windshield. "This is a just a slug on the edge of a razor blade," he said. He moved slowly down the bus, the students watching him intently, barely able to breathe. "The beauty, the incredible genius of that! To have the courage to go and blow their eyes out if necessary." Max put a set of handcuffs through the lock on the back doors of the bus. "When I compare myself to the great beauty of that I feel...*nothing!*"

"Let the children go!" Colleen urged him. "You can keep me as a hostage!" Max did not respond. "Please! You only need one!"

Max moved quickly back down the bus to where the front seats were located. He smiled at Colleen. "What a noble gesture that is... uh..."

"Colleen!" she said. "My name is Colleen."

"To be sure, darling girl that you are!" Max said, wistfully. "You can set the backpack down and go free and share the excitement with your friends." He leaned down to Colleen and his face was dangerously close to hers. "What was it like? Was it terrible? Did your eyes bug out? Oh, gross! I wish I had been there!"

"Let them go!" Colleen pleaded.

Max moved back to the front of the bus, holding onto the uzi. One of kids stood up, a good-looking dude named Jack Shepherd. Max covered him with his machinegun. Now he was Clint Eastwood. "Make my day!"

"I just had to stretch my legs!" Shepherd said.

"Yeah, stretch your legs, we can't have that!" Max was back in his stream-of-consciousness again. "Don't mind me, ma'am! He's *bad*, he's got to be able to *stretch his legs*, how long was that pass you made on Saturday, bro?"

"Four hundred yards," Shepherd said.

Max advanced on him as if he were Eddie Murphy doing a sketch on Saturday Night Live! "Yeah, yeah, yeah, give me a high five, bro! Bang, bang, you are *bad*, Jack!" Max got a high-five from Shepherd. "*Bad, bad, bad!*" Then Max's demeanor changed in the blink of an eye. Max shouted at him. "Now get into your seat!"

Shepherd sat back down in his seat. Max looked at the students. He shook his head. "Not exactly the bus from Little House on the Prairie, is it?"

We went out into the streets where Captain Stiles, Blaisdell and other Police Officers were gathered. A news van screeched to a halt. Blaisdell took one look at it and shook his head. "Oh, great! That is all we needed!"

In the school bus, eerily silent now, Max leaned down to one of the students, a sultry girl named Elizabeth who absolutely exuded sex appeal. "You like cars? Just nod, yes or no! Do you like cars?" Elizabeth looked at Max as if she were being challenged. "It is not a hard question! You know, I bet you were not even around then when they had good cars! Back in the Fifties, before they had those Japanese wind-up cars." Max retreated from Elizabeth, moving back down the aisle. "They got you high!" Then Max was revving a pretend Gran Prix racing car like he was in the Le Mans Race. "All that power between your legs! I remember…" Now he was *Marlon Brando* from "*A Streetcar Named Desire*". "I remembered when they used to ask me: 'What is it you are *rebelling against?*' And I used to say: "*What have you got!*"

In the streets, Tara Warren, an attractive no-nonsense reporter, climbed out of the news car with her cameraman filming her. "Tara Warren, filming from the streets around the hijacked school bus." She ran over to where Captain Stiles was striding past her. More Swat Officers and Police Officers were moving from their cars. Tara thrust her microphone into Stiles' face. "I understand you are in charge here. Can you tell us what negotiations have taken place?"

"I'm sorry, ma'am, there is nothing I can tell you!" Stiles raised his voice. "Listen, get that camera out of here, please!"

"The public has a right to know," Tara insisted.

"Ma'am, you have the right to stay alive!" Captain told her. "There is a man shooting at us! Now, get them behind the barricades! Behind the line of fire!"

Two of the Swat Team cops manhandled Tara and her cameraman back toward where the news team had parked. "Don't touch me! Who do you think you are?"

We went back into the school bus with Max and the students. Max gently caressed Colleen face, but there was no threat in it. Then he moved over where Blythe was sitting beside her. She immediately froze. "You are a beautiful girl too," Max said. "You know that?"

"You really think so?" she asked him, in spite of herself.

"I like you," Max said. "I really do! I think you are very pretty!" Behind him in the row, Jack Shepherd and a heavyset young man named Tim Crawford, were watching Max, looking for a way to tackle him. Now Max was *Elvis Presley*, miming a guitar. "*So lonely! So lonely!* You know what I mean?" Max paused by Elizabeth who looked at him once again with her bedroom eyes. "You are a very pretty girl too!"

"Alvin, right?" she asked him.

"How did you guess, darlin'! How did you guess?" Max was strumming his pretend guitar, but in fact he was holding the uzi in his hands. "You're a pretty gal too!" he told Elizabeth. "In fact, I wrote a song for you! There once a gal…"

"That is really good!" Tim Crawford said.

Max turned to him. "Thank you! Thank you very much. Now you watch my back, Red!"

"Who else do you do?" Crawford asked him.

Max swung back on him, like he was incensed. "*Who else do I do?* They are living inside me!"

"Can you do Johnny Carson?" Blythe asked him.

That appeared to calm Max down a little. "No, he's not on anymore!" Max moved fast down the aisle and picked up the little bottle of nitroglycerin from under the windshield. He held it up for them as if it was a trophy. Suddenly he was *Scotty* from *Star Trek*, complete with a *Scots brogue*. "I don't think I can hold her any longer, Captain!"

"I might have known he was a Trekkie!" Blythe muttered.

While Max's attention was diverted, one of the kids, a heavyset bruiser named Mickey, moved to the back row of the bus. Max did not see this as he was still being Scotty on Star Trek.

"There is too much pressure on the engines!" he said. "Can I beam up?"

Outside in the Industrial Park, a fire engine pulled up and the firefighters jumped out. Another Police Cruiser pulled up next to the bus and more cops piled out of it.

Peter and Caine waited at Peter's sports car. Peter shook his head. "This place is going to be a war zone! Everyone on that bus is going to be killed unless I can do something!"

"What can you do?" Caine asked.

Peter looked at the school bus parked at the side of the road. "Get inside!" he said, grimly.

"How?"

"He's trapped!" Peter said. "He's hurting! I've got to get his trust!" Suddenly Peter turned to his father as a memory assailed him. "You remember?"

Caine nodded. "Yes!" he said, softly.

We went to a *Flashback Sequence.* Young Peter was crouched down in some foliage in the woods beside his father. He was dressed in his grey robes, as was Caine. They were watching a wounded puma that had been trapped in a cave. Caine put a steadying hand on Young Peter's shoulder.

"I am frightened," the boy said.

"So is the animal," Caine said. "He is wounded and hurting. You must gain his trust. It will die if it stays inside!"

"You will not be far?" Young Peter asked.

"I will never be far," Caine promised his son.

Young Peter climbed into the cave where the wounded puma had been watching them.

We go out of the *Flashback Sequence* to real time again. In the school bus, while Max's attention had been diverted, Jack Shepherd leaned forward to where Elizabeth was sitting. He kept his voice low.

"Elvis could not take his eyes off you!" he said. "Give him some skin! Take him! Go!"

Elizabeth nodded and reluctantly stood up. Max had just checked his uzi. He looked up as Elizabeth made her way down the bus. She had undone two buttons on her blouse, opening it up, showing Max some cleavage. "It's getting pretty hot in here!" she said. "Can we open a window or something?"

Colleen was alarmed. "Elizabeth, sit down!" she said, but her classmate took no notice of her. Her attention was all for Max.

"He doesn't want to hurt anyone," Elizabeth said. "I know that. He just needs a little company, that's all."

Max grinned at Elizabeth's attempt to seduce him. "Oh, she wanted it, Doc! You bet she wanted it! *If you know what I mean?*"

Mickey, the heavyset kid, had been waiting for his opportunity. Now he smashed the back window of the bus and fell right down onto the ground. Max got Elizabeth into a stranglehold and marched her through the bus. "All right! All right! All right!"

Then we were back with Peter and Caine. Peter saw that one of the students had escaped from the school bus. He shed his jacket. Mickey was on his feet now, running for his life. Max reached the back window, still holding onto Elizabeth. He aimed his uzi and fired after the escaping student. Bullets kicked up the ground around his fleeing figure. Mickey fell to his knees, cringing, expecting any moment to be shot dead. Peter was coming for the kid in his sports car, at speed. Blaisdell, Stiles and two more Police Officers had hunkered down by the parked Police Cruiser.

"What the hell is he doing?" Stiles demanded. He raised his voice. "Hold your fire!"

Peter swerved to where Mickey was crouched on all fours. He turned the sports car on a dime, kicking up dirt around the kid. In the back window of the bus, Max seemed sanguine about the escape.

"That's a flag of truce, Elizabeth!" he told her and shook his head as if he had no other choice. "You can't fire on a flag of truce!"

Peter screeched to a halt in the dust. Mickey practically fell into the sports car. Peter took off again, the brakes screaming. Captain Stiles, Blaisdell and the other cops just watched the drama unfold.

At the back of the school bus, Max did a strange thing. He kissed Elizabeth's head, as if he were trying to console her. Then he ducked back into the bus and dropped Elizabeth into her seat. She did move again except to rebutton her blouse. Max still held the uzi in his hands. He moved to the front of the bus and picked up the small vial of nitroglycerin, having it catch the light.

Colleen and Blythe sat in their seats looking up at Max. "If that is what I think it is," Colleen said, "would you please put it back in the box?"

Max looked at her. He smiled and shrugged. "It's tap water!"

Colleen did not believe him. "Let the children go free!" she pleaded.

Max's mood shifted again to a more dangerous threat. "But they are not children, are they?" he said. "Never! They are old enough to steal and grab crotches and breasts and smoke pot and shoot coke!" Then he was the erudite Law Professor Charles Kingsfield from "The Paper Chase". "How should we save them? They have done nothing to warrant our trust! They have *to earn it*!"

"You should walk the streets in L.A.," Blythe started to say.

"Shut up, Blythe," Colleen said. She was looking at Max. "They are human beings. They deserve to be free!"

"Freedom!" Max said and suddenly he was quoting from the movie "The Alamo". "I like the sound of that word, Little Missy! The thing is, though, if we let them go, those Comanches are likely to storm the wagons, Pilgrim!"

"What if it was *your* child in here?" Colleen said. "How would it feel then?"

Max's mood turned in the blink of an eye. "They took her away!" he hissed at her. "And you know that, lady! They took my child away!" The other students were on their feet at this point, but Max whirled on them, raising the uzi higher. "Go ahead!" he said. "Go for it." He laughed. "You're going to be Elizabeth's hero, go ahead! I cannot get all of you. Some live, some die, that's survival! Your call!" The students sat down again. Max looked at them with disdain. "I feel sorry for you! Swear to God, I really do!"

He stalked back to the front of the bus.

"Your John Wayne was very good!" Blythe said.

Max turned back and grinned at her. "Hey, hey, oh!" he said and winked at her.

Outside where the school bus was parked, another Police Car screeched to a halt. Captain Stiles had been waiting for his "talker" to arrive. She turned out to be a round-faced, cherubic Police Officer named Molly McDowell. She was a tough negotiator, but she disguised it with an impish charm. Captain Stiles put an arm around her.

"Ready for this, Molly?" he asked her as they made their way through the parked Police Cars.

She shrugged and nodded. "Sure!"

Stiles laughed as he escorted her to where the other cops were located.

Peter pulled up in his sports car where he had left Caine and jumped out. Caine said: "I knew you would not fire on that child."

"Burt Lancaster wouldn't!" Peter told his father. "General Patton wouldn't! Those are Max's heroes! Speaking of heroes, it is time for me to be one." Peter turned and looked at the parked school bus. "What was it George said to me at the hotel? 'Heroes don't die young, they die stupid!'"

"You must approach your enemy and embrace him!" Caine argued.

"With Max," Peter said, "that might be tough! I mean, he's got so many voices in his head!"

Our "talker", Molly, approached the school bus. Max had already punched another hole in the windshield so he could look out at his accusers. Molly seemed to be sweet and unassuming, but her act was a calculated ploy to gain Max's trust. Max had a smile on his face, as if he and his "talker" had all the time in the world. He held up his uzi in one hand. The little bottle of nitroglycerin sparkled in his other hand in a sinister way. He paid little heed to it, as if he had forgotten all about it.

"Hi, Max!" Molly said, smiling.

"What was your name, Colonel?" Max asked affably.

"Molly!" she told him. "Molly McDowell."

Max nodded, as if he were sizing her up. "You don't much look like a cop! But then again, you did not look like a soldier either."

"Well, you don't look much like a kidnapper!" Molly said. "Maybe we're both new at this!" Max grinned, as if she were giving him the time of his life. "Okay if I stand here?" she asked him. "You can see me okay?"

"You bet!" Max said. "Everything's fine. Are you married, Molly? Got kids?"

"Yeah!" Molly said. "Three little girls." She measured them for Max. "Like steps!" And she laughed. "Just like their Mom! Rebecca of Sunnybrook Farm!"

"Isn't that nice?" Max said, but he was mocking her. "You are great for this, Molly! No threat! So go ahead, do your little cat-and-mouse number! Go on!"

"Well, it is really pretty simple," Molly said. "A familiar old line. You give me the kids and the teacher. And then I can come in and it's just you and me."

Max grinned. "Just you and me, huh?" Then his expression changed. He looked at Colleen who was obviously a teacher. "Well, teacher can't go, see, she has been bad! She has to stay after class!"

"How about me for the kids?" Molly asked him.

"You know, I have been here before!" Max said. "Yeah. I have! It is just like a TV scene. All the fake cuts! We watch it every night!" Suddenly Max's voice became quiet again. "All my life I wanted to do one great real thing! But this is not real! No!" Max held back up the little bottle of nitroglycerin and his voice lowered significantly. "That is real!"

Outside, in the Industrial Park, Captain Stiles and Blaisdell watched the negations between Max and Molly. Peter and Caine stood at Peter's parked sports car. Peter held up his gun, as if realizing a truth. "I don't need this, do I?"

"All you need is your own courage," Caine said, quietly.

Then we were back on the school bus. Max's attitude had undergone another significant change. He was all business now. "Just the facts, ma'am!"

"It is getting late!" Molly said, exasperated. "I can't wait here all day! Why don't you tell me want you want?"

"Gas!" Max said, immediately.

For a moment Molly was nonplussed. "*Gas?*"

"Yeah!" Max said. "Gas!" Suddenly he was Groucho, miming a cigar. "Isn't that the most ridiculous thing you've ever heard?"

"We can have a gas tanker here in fifteen minutes!" Molly said.

Suddenly Max was part of a scene from One Flew Over the Cuckoo's Nest. "Just one more thing, Nurse Smiley!" Then he was in an episode of The A-Team. "We and the boys were watching an episode of the A-Team the other morning. The boys just love it! The thing is, Hannibal and Face were commandeering a truck of liquid oxygen, but they had emptied the truck so that the Team could go inside! *If you know what I mean!*"

Molly was unnerved by Max's intensity. He gestured it was time for her to leave!

In the parking area, Captain Stiles' Swat Team had finally arrived. The Swat Officers poured out of the back of the truck. Stiles took charge, aided by Blaisdell. "Great! All right! On the roof! Take your positions over there! That's it!"

The Swat Officers started to deploy. Molly ran over to Captain Stiles. She was out of breath. "He's out of gas!"

"Out of gas!" Stiles said. "Of course!"

"We'll bring in the tanker," Blaisdell said.

"The trojan horse routine?" Molly said. "Don't bother! Lieutenant Columbo warned me about doing that!"

"Do it anyway!" Stiles said. He was getting very frustrated. "No gas. Fine! I need twenty men!" He turned to Paul Blaisdell. "Organize it!"

Then we were back on the stalled school bus. Our heroine Elizabeth, who had tried to seduce Max, had now gone over the edge into hysteria. Max was at the front of the bus with Colleen and Blythe. He was trying to keep calm. "Maybe somebody should shut her up," he said. Elizabeth was sobbing uncontrollably. "Stop that!" Max shouted. "Stop that crying!" If anything, Elizabeth became even more distraught. Max was shouting again. "Someone needs to *shut her up!*"

He moved down the aisle. Jack Shepherd stepped out into the aisle and grabbed Elizbeth's arms to stop her hysteria. He slapped her face. "Stop it! Stop it!" Elizabeth stopped crying, holding onto Shepherd's arms. Max nodded and backed way. "Well done, soldier!"

One of the other students, Tim Crawford, got to his feet. "Listen, Elvis! Or Patton, or Groucho! It is like a furnace in here! One of girls is going to faint unless we---"

Max grabbed hold of the kid and struck him, sending him into the aisle. Shepherd whirled, still holding onto Elizabeth's arms. He looked down at his friend who was out cold. Max had stepped back. He nodded, as if the situation had been temporality dealt with.

Jack Shepherd knew they were dealing with a serious psychopath.

Outside, Peter walked slowly toward the school bus. From his vantage point, Captain Stiles watched him through binoculars. He lowered them and looked up at the roof where his snipers were deployed. "One shot!" he called. "In the leg! Shoot him!"

Blaisdell defused that situation. He knew none of the snipers would shoot an unarmed man without provocation. He caught Stiles' look and the Captain backed off. He would see how this confrontation between Peter and Max played out.

Peter continued his long walk to the waiting bus. One of the marksmen on the low roof had other ideas. He raised his high-powered rifle, trying to get a shot at Max who was still inside the stalled school bus. Caine moved across the roof and kicked the rifle out the sniper's hands. The marksman fell to the ground, breaking his fall, knocking the wind out of him. Caine jumped down to the ground beside him. Three more uniformed cops tackled him. Caine took a swing with the high-powered rifle, sending the cops to the ground. Then another Police Officer got the drop on Caine.

"Hold it!" he said. "Drop it!"

Caine dropped the rifle. Two of the cops restrained him.

Then Captain Blaisdell stepped between them. "What the hell are you doing?" he demanded. "Let that man go! That is a direct order! This civilian is under my authority, now you back off!" He moved over to Caine. "This had better be good!"

"He was going to shoot my son!" Caine said, quietly.

Blaisdell looked over at where Peter had almost reached the school bus. He could not believe what he was seeing. "What the hell he is doing now?"

Caine just shrugged. "Being Peter!"

Peter reached school bus and pounded on it. "Hey, Max! Maxie! Can I come in where the action is?" He moved forward toward the front of the bus where he could see the kids through the windows. "Come on! It's lonely out here!"

Inside the school bus Max moved down the aisle with another his characterizations. "Raoul, you're a beautiful son of a gun! I read your book!" Then he was in the Twilight Zone with the Rod Serling voice. "Witness, if you will, one Peter Caine, would-be hero! What he doesn't realize is that he is about to walk into his worst nightmare right here in the Twilight Zone!"

Max opened the bus doors. His voice had gone back to normal. He just shook his head, looking at Peter. "Are you crazy?"

"Sure!" Peter said. "Aren't you?"

Max took out the small bottle of nitroglycerin from his jacket pocket and held it up, balancing the uzi with it. Now it was Peter chance to do an impression. This time it was Humphrey Bogart. "All the gin mills in the world and I have to walk into *yours!*"

Max grinned. "You have to lower the voice," he said. "Keep the upper lip moving, that is the secret, pal! You know, you are a hell of a cop! You got a lot of guts! You have a lot of style. You have to be one hell of a cop," Max said, "because you put me in prison for five years!" He nodded. "I like that! I like it that you have guts! I like that a lot! But what is keeping me from blowing you to smithereens? It has been a long day, pal! *If you know what I mean?*"

"Nothing," Peter admitted. "But I am the only person who can get out of this place alive."

He climbed up onto the bus. Immediately Max put the uzi at his throat.

"Go for it, Jack!" He looked back down at the students, shaking his head. "Kid doesn't have it, but you got to love him! Teacher?" Max asked in a sing-song voice. "You do think we should let him in with the rest of the crazies, huh?" Then he turned back to Peter, still holding the barrel of the uzi at his throat. He grinned. "You know, it has been a long time! The last time I saw you, I told myself I would kill you!"

"It is the best opportunity you are going to have!" Peter told him.

Max's mood had swung back to being The Godfather! "You know something, you're nothing but a messenger boy sent by grocery clerks to deliver a bill! Now that you are here, Mr. Hero, what did you think you are going to do? Huh?"

"Me?" Peter asked.

"Yeah!"

"Nothing," Peter said.

He pushed the uzi away from Max's hands and climbed further into the bus. "I just wanted to get on the bus! You are running the show, Max! I had a lousy seat up there."

Peter sat down at the back of the bus.

Max just shook his head. "You're as crazy as I am!"

"Well, let's not get rash!" Peter said. "I am not holding you at gunpoint. Unpredictable! Like a bottle of nitro! It will sweat. It will move. But you never know when it is going to go off."

That was when Peter realized one of the students, Tim Crawford, had been hurt. Peter got to his feet and moved over to where the teenager lay on one of the seats. He was unconscious. His breathing was labored.

"We're going to need a doctor for Sonny Jim!" Max said, unconcerned. "He had an accident."

"What was the matter?" Peter asked, caustically. "He didn't like your *Carson?*"

"No, I don't do Johnny Carson anymore," Max said. "The kid may be hurt."

"You know what, Max?" Peter said. "These kids all make me nervous. Who is going to cry? Who is going to scream? I have to go to the bathroom, that is going to start soon. Why don't you just get rid of them? Let them go! Cut yourself some slack."

"That is very good psychology, Peter!" Max said. "It will be my idea pretty soon!"

Peter laughed. "Just take me! Take me and you're going to know who you are dealing with."

Suddenly Max's mood was murderous. "Teacher stays," he said. "The teacher *has* to stay!"

Peter looked down at Colleen and Blythe. "Hi!" Then he looked back at Max as if he had reached a decision. "Okay! Teacher stays! I stay! Everyone else *goes.* What do you want, Max?"

"Gas!" Max said, immediately.

Peter laughed. "*Gas?*"

"That is what I am trying to do!" Max said, reasonably.

"Okay!" Peter said. "One gallon tank. Non-combatant to bring up it here. And I have got just the guy!"

"Who?"

"My father!" Peter said.

"Your father?" Max asked, incredulously.

"Oh, yeah," Peter said. "I bring him to all of the hostage situations."

"Are you serious?" Max said.

Outside, near the Police Cars, we move over to where Molly was standing surrounded by cops. "I was so close him!" she said. "So close!"

"I know you were, Molly," Blaisdell said. He turned away, accessing his radio. "Blaisdell!"

Peter's voice echoed over the radio. "The kids are coming out! Forget the tanker. One five gallon can of gas. And let my father bring it!"

"What about the teacher?" Blasdell asked him.

"She stays!" Peter said over the radio. "I stay! No one else moves except my father. That is the deal."

"You got it!" Blaisdell said.

Captain Stiles immediately confronted him. "The hell he does, Paul!"

"We're going to do this Peter's way!" Blaisdell said, evenly. "You got that? He is in there! Your man did not blow a hole in his leg! And there is not going to be a discussion! I am going to get him out! You understand?"

Stiles stared at Blaisdell for a long moment, then he accessed his radio. "Stand by your positions. Do not fire until I give you the signal."

Back on the school bus, Max was herding the students down the aisle. "You can stay on the bus with me, or you can face the real world!" Colleen and Blythe had not stood up yet. Suddenly Max's voice was like ice. "Not you! You two are staying!"

"Why?" Colleen asked.

"Because I like you!" Max said. "You were nice to me."

"If I kick you where it hurts," Blythe said, "can I leave?"

Max laughed. Peter crossed down from him. Max gripped his arm. He was still holding the uzi in one hand and the little nitroglycerin bottle in the other. "Hold your horses!" Max leaned down to Peter. "No tricks."

A few minutes later Caine moved toward the bus carrying a five gallon can of gas. Max opened the doors of the bus. Peter jumped down as Caine reached him. Peter twisted off the gas cap and started pumping the gas.

"Where will you go?" Caine asked him, sotto voce.

"I'll try to take him to our *secret place*," Peter said. "Do you remember?"

"A place where we have been before?" Caine said.

"Right!" Peter said. "But not for a long time."

Caine lowered his voice to a whisper. "I will find you there!"

Blaisdell and Captain Stiles were watching the drama unfolding in front of the

Police Cars. More of them were crowded into the area around them. "How long?" Blaisdell asked.

"I figure once he gets gas in that bus," Stiles said, "he is going to kill Peter, his father and all of the hostages he can lose."

Blaisdell nodded. "Yeah. Maybe. Maybe not."

Stiles said into his radio: "This is Captain Stiles. At the first shot, open fire!"

Snipers were on the various roofs, all of their weapons aimed at the school bus. One of them said: "Suspect is still on the bus."

More commands were issued over the radio from the Swat Team: "They're coming out!"

Another voice: "Okay!"

The bus doors opened and the first of the students jumped down. They were followed by other kids in a mad dash to freedom. The Swat Team and the other Police Officers were on their feet, rushing the school bus, picking the students up and supporting them. Some of the students we recognized: Elizabeth, Heather, Mickey. Max was grinning, as if he were having a grand time! Jack Shepherd was supporting Tim Crawford who was conscious now, albeit groggy. Two of the Swat Team were helping him.

Finally there was only Peter and Max on the bus along with Colleen and Blythe. Max still had the uzi in one hand and the little bottle of nitroglycerin in his other hand. The last of the Swat Team covered the school bus with their assault AK47 rifles, backing away from the vehicle. Max noted a helicopter had angled into in view. Peter slid into the driver's chair. Max turned to look at him.

"Let's get the hell out of here!" Peter said.

He closed the bus doors and a moment later he pulled away. More Swat Officers swarmed to their vehicles. Captain Stiles shook his head in disgust and hustled to his Police Cruiser to follow.

Caine and Blaisdell walked down the periphery of the hostage scene from Peter's sports car. "Every time you think you have Peter figured out," Blaisdell said, "he starts bouncing up against walls that he didn't even know existed. He has a mind like quicksilver. I can't hold of a single thought!"

Caine nodded. "It is a discovery you are both sharing," he said.

"Okay," Blaisdell said. "He is trapped on a bus with two hostages and a fruitcake. What does he do?"

"He will lead them to a *secret place*," Caine said.

That made Blaisdell pause. "What place is that?"

"A place where everyone has in his soul," Caine told him. "A locked door which no one can enter. A place of tranquility."

"Look, I am a cop," Blaisdell said. "Layman terms, okay? I get lost in your metaphysical corridors."

"When Peter was young," Caine said, "there was a *secret place* he would go to when he was confused and frightened. He will return there now."

"What do you mean?" Blasdell asked. "Back to a Shaolin temple?"

Caine shook his head. "No! But to his *secret place!*"

Now we were back on the school bus. Peter was driving through an industrial area. Colleen and Blythe were still sitting in their front seats. Max moved back down the bus. Colleen leaned forward to Peter, her voice sotto. "Can't you just flip the bus over?"

"Not with nitroglycerin on board," Peter told her, also sotto voce. Max was at the front of the bus again. Peter raised his voice. "We've got to get off these streets, Max!"

"Sure!" Max said. "I'll give you everything I got! You can trust me! Yeah, sure!"

'Either we go to ground in this bus," Peter said, reasonably "and you die and all the voices in your head die too! Not to mention your passengers and I think they would like a vote."

"Yeah, we really would!" Blythe said.

Colleen turned to her. "Shut up, Blythe!"

"Do it!" Max said. "Do what you have to do!"

"Thank you," Colleen said, softly.

Max sat down beside the two hostages. Now he was back to being the perfect host. "You're welcome, Colleen Alexanda!"

Colleen was momentarily stunned. "How did you know my middle name?"

"I know all about you, sweetheart," Max told her. "That's why I got this bus! It is *you* I had to get close to."

Colleen reacted to this revelation with a mixture of realization and fear. A helicopter angled up into the air. We saw shots of the school bus heading through a series of chain link fences. Then we were in an unmarked car speeding through the industrial area with Captain Stiles and another Detective from the Swat Team.

"He is driving into the warehouse district next to the city!" the Detective said. "A lot of cul-de-sacs there. He is going to get trapped!"

"And he is going to run out of gas pretty soon!" Captain Stiles said.

The bus reached another industrial area and crashed through the gates into one of the warehouses. The other cops were right behind it in force. Captain Stiles got out of his cruiser. Twenty more Swat Teams pulled up in front of the warehouse. Stiles had his gun out. He brought his radio to his lips. "Okay, let's get him!"

Stiles and his Swat Team ran toward the entrance of the warehouse. This became a very telling sequence. It was backlit so the figures converging on the school bus were almost *in* silhouette. William Shatner's direction for these sequences was stunning. The Swat Team stormed the bus, but Max, Peter, Colleen and Blythe had disappeared. Captain Stiles took off his reflective glasses. There was an entrance that led back into the recesses of the warehouse.

In the maze of tunnels and corridors in the subway system, Peter led the way with Colleen and Blythe. Max covered the hostages with his uzi in one hand and the little bottle of nitroglycerin in the other. He was raging at them. "Nobody sets me up. There has to be a way out of this maze!"

"There *is* a way!" Peter assured him. "We are following it!"

"What way is that?" Max demanded.

"I told you," Peter said, "it is a *secret place!*"

We went outside with Captain Blaisdell on his radio. Caine was beside him. "Okay, I got it!" He clicked off the radio. "They disappeared into that warehouse into thin air," Blaisdell said. "Stiles is having---what is the expression?"

"A *cow?*" Caine surmised.

"Yeah." Blaisdell had a sudden inspiration. "I have got an idea. Maybe you are right. Maybe there *is* a way I can get into your son's mind!"

"You can," Caine reassured him. "He is your son also."

Blaisdell ran over to his parked car and lifted the trunk. Caine moved with him. Blaisdell rummaged through some blueprints that were strewn in the back. "There is an old sewer system right under that warehouse. Miles of it! Could lead to anywhere!"

"Peter will find an artery that will take him to his secret place," Caine said.

Once again we went to a *Flashback Sequence* in the temple. Caine stood in his saffron robes with old Ping Hi.

"I cannot find Peter!" Caine said.

"Does he have a special place he goes for healing?" the old man asked him.

Caine shrugged eloquently. "That I do not know!"

"Find that place, "Ping Hi said, "and you will find your son!"

Caine moved in the shadows and knelt down. He lifted a small box and removed it. There were a number of small pebbles that he held in his hand. "Pebbles!" he murmured. "From the lake!" He stared down at a solitary pebble and caught it! The pebble disappeared. Caine nodded, as if he understood. "Yes!" he said, softly. "I see!"

We came out from the *Flashback Sequence* to where Caine and Blaisdell were looking at the map that the Captain had spread out for them on the trunk of the car. Blaisdell looked at Caine who was not looking back at him. "What do you see?"

"Come with me!" Caine said, urgently.

He moved from Blaisdell. The Captain moved off after him.

In the underground subway system beneath the streets, Colleen suddenly tripped and fell to her knees. Peter reached out for her, but Max was faster, hauling her to her feet. "Come on! Come on! Do not fall apart! You're all alike!"

Colleen pulled away from Max, trying to trip him. He fired the uzi in his hands in a staccato burst. Peter grabbed Colleen and pulled her away from him. Blythe stumbled after them. In a frenzy Max strafed the passageway, the submachine gun exploding in his hands. Then he was swallowed in the overlapping shadows.

Caine and Blasdell moved fast in a corridor in the power plant.

"We'll go to the water," Caine said. He and Blaisdell descended down some stairs that led deeper into the facility. "It is purification plant," Blaisdell said. "Too much of a leap. We're clutching at straws."

"His secret place was a lake," Caine told him.

They climbed lower into the heart of the facility.

In the subterranean tunnels, Colleen stumbled again in the semi-darkness. Blythe was beside her. Peter was not with them at this moment. There was an iron ladder that led up to the next level. Max caught up with them and shoved Colleen down into a corner of the facility. Then he grabbed Blythe and threw her up against a wall which she slid down. Max towered above Colleen, a deranged, murderous figure. Now he was Marlon Brando in "On the Waterfront".

"I coulda been a contender!" Max shouted at Colleen. "It was you, Charlie! You should have looked out for me! You should not have run away from me like that! You almost got away with it!" Now he was the comic hero from Get Smart. "Missed it by *that* much, 99!"

"What is it you want from me?" Colleen pleaded with him. "And I want *you* to tell me! I don't want to hear it from one of those characters in your mind!"

Max looked down at her, deadly serious now. He said simply: "*You!*"

"You want *me*?" Colleen said, shocked.

"Yes!" Max said.

Colleen stared up at him. Now she was putting it all together. "That is why there were no demands by the police, no helicopter, no million dollars in unmarked bills." Her voice was shaky. "You *want me?*"

"Because you took her away from me!" Max said, savagely.

"Who?" Colleen asked him, desperation in her voice. "Took who away?"

Max searched around in the pockets of his jacket, murmuring his stream of consciousness. "It was a bad thing. You almost *got* away with it!" He found a tattered picture and handed it to Colleen. Now his eyes were shining. "Jenny!" he said. "That is my Jenny!"

Colleen took the picture in her hands. Realization flooded through her. "My God," she gasped.

She recognized the photograph.

It was a photograph of *herself* as a teenager. She was standing with a young child about six years of age.

"Every day she would come home," Max said. "Mrs. Grace said this, Daddy! Mrs. Grace said that! Mrs. Grace wouldn't let you come near me, Daddy!"

Colleen looked up at Max, tearfully. "You were abusing her!"

"That's a lie!" Max shouted. "I never laid a hand on her!"

"Mentally!" Colleen said. "She was terrified of you!"

"Is that right?" Max's voice was deadly quiet now. "Her own father she was terrified of. Is that right, Mrs. Gray? You want to know what I did that was so terrible to her? What I did to her that was so terrible? Homework! For you! Homework to please you, Mrs. Gray! We watched a little television, but that was all right, but on television the good guys win. Then she would go to school the next day. Mrs. Gray, I would say to her, you know, the world is not like that," Max ranted. "In the real world, bad guys kill and maim people. Yes, as a matter of fact, that is true. But I did not need to tell her that. You know what you told my daughter, Colleen?" Max moved very close to Colleen. "That I am bad! I am a bad guy. That is part of the real world. You turned my Jenny against me."

"No!" Colleen said. "You did that by yourself!"

Max got up from her and moved into more shadows with Colleen. Peter had climbed up from the iron ladder from the floor below. Suddenly Max was behind him. He brought up the uzi into Peter's face.

"Anyone who wants to run away again and you're dead!" Peter had no doubt that the threat was real. "I will have to drop *this*!" Max said. He raised the nitroglycerin into Peter's face. Now he was suddenly President George Bush. "A whole lot of people will go up! The street above us is going to go up! A lot of good people are going to die! Wouldn't be prudent, you know!" Max pressed the uzi against Peter's throat. The soft menace in his voice was chilling. "You said you had a *secret place*! I want you to take me there! I want you to take me there right now!"

Outside, a helicopter angled over the warehouse streets. The pilot radioed to Stiles: "Alarm is sounding in the Lawrence Purification Plant!"

Stiles' voice said: "We're on our way!"

In the power plant, Blaisdell and Caine moved down more corridors. Blaisdell said: "Peter is not going to come here!"

"He will come!" Caine said.

"How can you be sure?" Blaisdell asked.

"I know our son!" Caine said.

Large hangars were opened up to the Swat Team. This was another stunning visual effect from our director, William Shatner. The Police Officers were backlit as they rushed inside the facility, led by Captain Stiles. "This way!" he instructed.

We picked up Peter and Max, Colleen and Blythe running down one of the corridors in the power plant. We noted that Peter had injured his arm fighting off Max. They were no longer in the gloom of the tunnels.

"Is this your *secret place*?" Max demanded.

"Yes!" Peter said. "You like it?"

"Oh, yeah," Max said, "I love it! Yeah, it's great!"

They came to doors that led to more corridors within the power plant. Max pushed one of them open with Colleen beside him, then he slammed it shut. The force of the doors slamming knocked Peter to the ground. Blythe ran over and knelt beside him.

"Are you okay?"

We saw Captain Stiles and more Swat Officers moving down the power plant stairs. Peter had picked himself up and had accessed the door that Max had slammed after him. Blythe was with him. More endless corridors greeted them.

Colleen ran down another artery in the power plant. Max caught up with her, swinging her around to face him. "You didn't tell him I was a bad father?" Max asked her.

"No!" Colleen said. "*Jenny* told them! She was frightened." Then Coleen's voice softened. "But she loved you! She was the sister you never had. She really does love you."

"She does?" Max said, and there were tears in his eyes. He shook his head. "Poor baby!"

Max propelled Colleen along another corridor in the cavernous facility. "I am visiting Jenny in her foster home," Colleen said, desperately. "I'll bring her to whenever you are! I promise!"

"I wouldn't let you do that!" Max said. "I'm nuts, lady, where have you been for the last five hours?" He stopped Colleen in one of the corridors of the power plant. He held her arms tightly. "You think that I want that sweet girl talking to a madman?"

Peter and Blythe ran down to a catwalk above the maze of stairs. Peter could see Max and Colleen below them in the power plant.

"Max!" Peter shouted. "Stop!"

Max and Colleen ran into another of the endless corridors. Peter had fixed Max's position. Max stopped and took hold of Colleen's shoulders again. There was no stream of consciousness from him now. It was as if the voices in his head had all vanished. He spoke quietly and rationally to Colleen.

"I want you to take care of my little girl," he said. "I know she loves you very much. Is that a deal?"

Colleen nodded, feeling suddenly great compassion for Max.

"Deal!" she said, softly.

Max gently caressed her face. "Goodbye, Colleen."

Then he placed his uzi down onto the ground. "The fault is not our stars," Max said softly, "but it is with ourselves."

Max moved over to where a hoist hung down at the floor level. He assessed it and it started to lift him up. More Swat Officers were pounding down the corridors with Captain Stiles. "This way!"

Colleen ran to the place where she could see the hoist was lifting Max high above the catwalk. This was yet another stunning visual from our director, William Shatner, where the various levels rose up to the ceiling of the facility.

Peter turned the corner of the immense facility with Blythe. She ran over to Colleen and hugged her. Peter moved over to where Max had stopped the hoist. He was fifty feet up in air. He held the little bottle of nitroglycerin tightly in front of him.

"This is *real!*" Max shouted down at Peter.

Peter pleaded with him. "Max, don't do it!"

The Swat Team had arrived and had deployed on the far catwalk. Max's attention was solely on the nitroglycerin in his hands. Peter looked up at him, precariously suspended halfway up the hoist.

Max's voice was nostalgic. "We never did find that *special place* of yours, Peter!"

More Swat Officers converged on the catwalk. Captain Stiles was with them. Caine and Blaisdell entered the facility from another entrance and moved to the catwalk railing. Blaisdell had drawn his gun.

Max shrugged, still looking down at Peter. "Well, I guess this is goodbye, Pilgrim," he said with the last of his characterizations.

Stiles took the high-powered rifle from one of the marksmen and aimed it at Max as he dangled on the hoist.

Peter ran forward. "Don't shoot!" he pleaded.

Stiles fired a single shot, hitting Max in the chest.

Max staggered and tumbled off the hoist.

The little bottle of nitroglycerin fell from Max's hand.

Immediately Peter tried to shield Colleen and Blythe from the explosion.

Stiles watched from the catwalk. Everything around him was now in slow-motion. SWAT Officers were mesmerized by the glittering bottle as it fell from Max's hand toward the ground below.

Peter had both his arms around Colleen and Blythe.

Slowly Max tumbled toward the ground, still in slow-motion.

The nitroglycerin bottle was going to crash onto the floor.

And then---

Caine reached out and caught the nitro bottle in the palm of his hand.

Captain Blaisdell took a deep breath, holding onto the guardrail of the catwalk.

Peter let go of Colleen and Blythe. Max had landed on the floor of the facility, his slight figure crumpled and lifeless. Peter looked over at his father.

"Nice catch," he murmured.

Caine gave him one of his signature shrugs.

Peter said: "I knew you would find me here!"

Caine's expression was enigmatic, but he knew that he had saved his son and all of the hostages in that moment.

Lap Dissolve to:

The scene on the riverbank, sometime in the past, was idyllic. Young Peter sat on the river's edge, throwing pebbles into the late. He was dressed in his grey robes. Caine approached him in his saffron robes and sat down beside him. Young Peter was edgy and distracted.

"You are not welcome here!" he said. "This is my *secret place*!"

"I will only come when I am invited," Caine said, quietly.

"Okay," Young Peter said, grudgingly.

Caine got to his feet and in the visual transition it was the older Peter who was sitting by the river's edge. Caine looked down and said: "Am I invited?"

Camera panned down to the older Peter who was sitting beside the riverbank. He just nodded. Caine sat down beside him. Peter was introspective and troubled. "There were so many voices in his head," he said. "They were so loud he could not hear *his own voice*. I told him I would take him to a secret place. A place where he could be safe. I just took him to the place where he would be killed."

"You did what your instincts and what your conscience dictated," Caine told him, gently. "You cannot to do more."

Peter shook his head. "It wasn't enough!" After a moment, he said: "I need to be alone right now."

Caine put his hand fondly on Peter's shoulder. Then he got up and moved away from the river's edge, leaving Peter alone with his thoughts.

Max's persona was all mixed up in his chaotic thoughts: crazy, rebellious, manic, charming, violent. All of them were mingled with his impressions of *Groucho, George Bush, Rod Serling* from the *Twilight Zone, Scotty* from *Star Trek*, the *Comancheros storming the wagons* and a generous helping of *Elvis* and the *Godfather*.

Are you talking to me?

Those images would stay in Peter's mind for a very long time.

Chapter Nine
MANHUNT

We were in a high rise building where an intruder was gathering the evidence for an elaborate frame aimed at Peter Caine. Very fast shots showed how the frame-up was accomplished. This episode had overtones of "The Fugitive" in it, which was deliberate on my part! The cast was made up of our regulars, including Kermit, with one notable exception. I wanted to cast a lead actor for the role of Marshal Jim Garrison. And that leading actor was Patrick Wayne! I had loved him in "The Alamo", one of my favorite movies. Susan Forrest, my wonderful casting director, got the script to him. The role called for charm and a larger-than-life quality. When Patrick Wayne agreed to play the leading role, I was ecstatic. He would bring a lot of charisma and style to this starring role.

This was the second episode that would feature Captain Karen Simms, played by the wonderful Kate Trotter. She played her role, as she did in the "*Quake*" episode, with a lot of charm and incredible insight. She quickly became a fan favorite with the audience. Kate was simply the best actress I had ever worked with on a continuing basis. She remains to this day one of my closest friends.

But I digress…

The episode opened with an intruder who was in Rebecca Calver's apartment, our heroine. It was deserted. She had left to go to work. The intruder had the apartment all to himself. He put latent fingerprints on a cut-glass. There was also a lipstick smudge on the glass. The intruder gathered hairs from a hairbrush he had found in Rebecca's apartment. He found some make-up in Rebecca's bathroom. He sprayed incriminating lotions on the heroine's clothing so that it would appear that someone else had been there. He worked methodically with a single purpose.

He was out to frame Peter Caine.

Peter was driving his Lexus down a deserted street. The intruder had finished in Rebecca's bedroom and was waiting in the shadows for him in the streets. Inside his car Peter reached for a DVD. "Need a little mood music!"

The intruder raised a high-powered rifle to his shoulder and fired. The impact of the bullet blew a hole in one of Peter's tires. Peter swerved and came to a halt, muttering: "Great!"

The intruder lowered the high-powered rifle and disappeared back into the shadows. Peter exited his Lexus and moved to where the tire had collapsed. "Well, this is just great!" he muttered. Peter popped the trunk to get to the spare tire, taking note of his surroundings. He was in a very rundown part of town.

Rebecca Calvert returned home and stepped into the shower. She was a vivacious, no-nonsense District Attorney, headstrong and beautiful. She wrapped a towel around herself and moved into her bedroom. We noted a photograph of her on a table with herself and Peter Caine. Both of them look relaxed and happy together. From the shadows the intruder stepped out and grabbed Rebecca. She screamed and struggled in the killer's grasp, but he was too strong for her. She slumped to the floor. We cannot see from this angle, but she was dead.

We established Chandler's Bar and Restaurant where the Precinct gang hung out. Detective Blake was sitting at the bar with Sergeant Broderick and Detective Jody Powell. Blake was advocating the necessity of wearing a bug for surveillance.

"Just wear a bug so we can monitor you, that's all I ask," he was saying. "The guy is a rapist!"

Jody was about to go undercover. She was teasing Blake, which she was very good at. Sergeant Broderick sat beside them enjoying the show. Jody gave Blake a searching look. "I will be wearing a cocktail dress the width of Kleenex, no underwear, no jewelry, high heel pumps that will clatter and an air of innocence." She smiled at him. "Where will you plant the bug?"

"I'd like the answer to that myself," Broderick chimed in.

Blake was dying at this point, stammering. "Well, we could put under your…" He did not get the words "under your dress" out, going beet red. "That is, we could put it in the curb side of your… er…"

Jody was enjoying Blake's dilemma. "Yes?"

Peter joined them at this point at the bar, looking at Blake. "Your hand would tremble! You had better let me plant the bug!"

Jody glanced at Peter ironically. "Leave it to an expert!"

"What did you do?" Sergeant Broderick asked. "Crawl in from the parking lot?"

"I changed a tire in the worse part of town," Peter said. He looked over at Terry, our friendly bartender. "Can I get a beer, please?"

"I thought you had a date with Rebecca tonight?" Jody asked him.

"Yeah, well I cancelled it," Peter said, shortly. "Went back to work."

Blake glanced at Jody. "Sounds like trouble in romance-land!"

Terry brought Peter a beer. "There you go, Pete."

Terry moved over to serve more customers. Broderick's attention had been diverted. "What's this?"

He was reacting to Chief Strenlich's entrance into the bar. He was flanked by Detective Mary Margaret Skalany and a homicide cop named Nick Drake.

"Don't run, Peter!" Strenlich warned him. "Don't make this tougher than it has to be."

Peter stood his ground, looking at the Chief candidly. "Why would I run, Frank?" he asked. "What the hell is this about?"

"Detective Peter Caine," Strenlich said, "you're under arrest."

The Precinct gang who sat at the bar were appalled by the accusation.

Peter kept his cool. "What's the charge?" he asked, evenly.

"Murder," Strenlich said.

"Who is the victim?"

"Rebecca Calvert." Detective Drake handcuffed Peter's wrists together. "You have the right to stay silent," Strenlich said, almost in a monotone. "You have the right to an attorney. If you cannot afford one, the court will provide one for you."

Strenlich allowed Officer Drake to haul Peter out of there. Detective Mary Margaret Skalany looked at the Precinct gang.

"I don't know what going on," she said, "but the Chief said that even Peter's father could not get him out of this one."

Skalany moved away, leaving Broderick and Jody totally shell-shocked.

We opened the episode on the Precinct steps. We hear Captain Simms's voice: "Nickie Elder fixed the time of death for which you have no alibi." We had moved into the interrogation room in the Precinct where Peter sat at a table. Captain Simms was on one of side him, Chief Strenlich and Detective Drake on the other. Detective Jody Powell was in the background of the shot. Captain Karen Simms was a tough, resourceful cop who had recently relocated to the 101ˢᵗ Precinct. She was questioning her top detective on the squad who happened to be Peter Caine. It was clear the Captain hated having to do this, but she had no choice. "It gets worse!" she told Peter. "Your fingerprints were found all over her apartment. You had threatened her."

"I don't care how much worse it gets!" Peter flared. "I didn't kill her. I was not even *in* her apartment! This is a set-up!"

"The evidence is all against you," Captain Simms said, "but let us say I believe you because everyone in this Precinct tells me you can't be guilty."

"Who framed you, Detective Caine?" Strenlich demanded.

"I am a hot-shot cop!" Peter retorted. "Don't you read the headlines? I got lots of enemies! Take your pick."

Captain Simms just shook her head. There was a knock on the interrogation room door which was opened by Kwai Chang Caine. Chief Strenlich said: "This is Peter's father."

"I am sorry to meet you in these circumstances," Captain Simms said.

Caine gave her a small formal bow. The Captain turned to Strenlich. "Five minutes," she said, shortly.

Strenlich, Detective Powell, Captain Simms and Detective Drake left the interrogation room, closing and locking the door behind them. Caine embraced his son. When they broke from each other, Caine asked quietly: "What has happened?"

"The woman I was involved with has been murdered," Peter told him. "I am a dangerous man. Don't you listen to Sandra Mason on the Channel Three news?"

Caine said: "No."

"Come on, Pop!" he said, "Aren't going to ask me if I did it?"

Caine shrugged. "I know you did not do it. Do you know who *did* do it?"

"Someone who hated me," Peter said. "Or hated *her*."

Caine said: "Sit down." Peter slid in behind the table and Caine sat across from him. He shrugged. "As you would say, not much to go on. What was the victim's name?"

"Rebecca Calvert. She was an Assistant District Attorney. I had been seeing her for about three months."

"Why have I not heard about her?" Caine asked.

Peter looked at him with a dismissive gesture. "I am I supposed to tell you about all of my girlfriends? I mean, there was a time when you were never there."

Caine nodded. "When motorcycles and sports cars and hockey were replaced by girls."

"When I was at the orphanage," Peter said with a catch in his voice.

"Well, I am here now," Caine said, gently.

"Rebecca was wonderful," Peter said, "but we had trouble communicating. The other night things got a little ugly."

We went to Chandler's Restaurant where Peter and Rebecca were in the middle of a heated argument. We noted Jody and Blake were up at the bar watching the drama unfolding. Peter was angry and not dealing with this situation well.

"Don't do this!" Peter told her. "Stop it!"

"Talking I enjoy!" Rebecca retorted. "Being interrogated? That grates on me! I like to be the interrogator, not the interrogee!"

Peter was trying to keep a lid on his temper. "Let's not do this for the benefit of the entire restaurant!"

"Bottom line, you want a commitment," Rebecca said. "I can't give you one."

"But that was not what you said last night!" Peter said. "So what happened? Who did you talk to today? What are you frightened of?"

"Where was I between the hours of eight and three?" Rebecca retorted. "There you go, being a cop again! Your hours are brutal, Peter! Twenty-four of them in a day. Too bad there aren't twenty-five hours for you to stop being a cop and become a human being!"

She got to her feet, but Peter caught her arm. "Please, sit down!"

"Peter, it's too late for us!" He was on his feet now, too. Rebecca struggled in his arms. "You let me go, Detective, or I'll have you on assault charges!"

"Don't threaten me!" Peter warned her. "Stop grandstanding!"

Up on the bar, Jody and Blake were watching the drama unfolding with rising concern.

"Cool it, Peter!" Jody said, softly.

Beside her, Blake said: "I'd say it's too late."

Rebecca looked at Peter. "I can't love you enough!" she said. "I can't love anyone enough!"

She moved away from him. At one of the other tables in the restaurant, Rebecca's killer, whom we have not seen clearly yet, raised his glass in an ironic toast. "Too bad, Peter."

A heavy distinctive signet ring sparkled on the killer's finger in the shape of a coiled snake. Peter did not see this in the restaurant. He sat back down at the table and took a ring box out of his pocket. He opened it. There was a diamond engagement ring in the box. He stared down at it, then closed the box up with a sense of finality.

We went back to Peter in the interrogation room reliving these memories of Rebecca. He said: "She was frightened of someone."

"The person who killed her?" Caine asked him.

Peter nodded. "Or had her killed. I would bet my badge on it. If I had one," he added. "Look, Pop, I don't know what evidence is against me, but it must be pretty damaging."

The door to the interrogation room opened and Stacy Pardcek entered. She was a compassionate defense attorney, tough and fearless. I had known Anne Lockhart for years, ever since she played a role for me on the Hardy Boys and Nancy Drew TV series. She was a sweetheart who brought flair and integrity to her role as a tough defense attorney. She looked at Peter.

"The evidence against you is very damaging, believe me," she said, quietly. Both Caine and Peter got to their feet. Stacy was looking at Peter. "I'm Stacy Pardcek, Public Defender's office. I am your attorney. You are in big trouble, Detective. You should know that Rebecca Calvert was a law student of mine and I thought she was one great lady. I'd like to think I am not defending the man who cut her heart out."

"You're not," Peter said, shortly.

She looked over at Caine. "Who's this?"

"I am Caine," he said.

"My father," Peter said.

"I need some time with your son," Stacy told Caine. "If I am going to work with him, I need to know as much about him as you do. He goes before a judge for bail in the morning."

Caine shrugged and moved toward the door of the interrogation room.

"Pop!" Peter said. "Wait a minute!"

Stacy sat down at the table. Peter's total attention was with Caine. "I can't prove my innocence in here. Maybe what I need is a *Dragon's Wing*."

Dragon's Wing was the title of one of the *Kung Fu: The Legend Continues* episodes, a pretty famous one where several of the Kung Fu guest stars came together to form what Peter referred to as a Dragon's Wing. Those guest stars including Patrick Macnee and Robert Vaughn.

But Caine shook his head. "Not this time, my son," he said. "But I will be working for you."

Caine exited from the room.

We saw the killer, shrouded by shadows somewhere in the street, dialing his cell phone. He said: "Caine's father is a priest in Chinatown. Kill him!"

We were with Caine in his apartment in Chinatown. Two thugs came to take him out. Caine nailed both of them. They retreated down the stairs. Caine did not follow them, but he was even more troubled by this new development that threatened his son.

At the Precinct Peter was still talking to Stacy Pardcek in the interrogation room. "So, when was the last time you talked to Rebecca?" he asked her.

"Let's get something straight her, Detective," Stacy said. "*I* ask the probing questions and *you* give the honest answers."

"Was she frightened of someone?" Peter pressed her.

Stacy finally nodded. "Someone in law enforcement."

"So you naturally assumed that was me!" Peter said.

"You're a cop and she was not dating anyone else."

"You're sure of that, Counsellor?" Peter asked her.

Stacy took a deep breath, then turned her attention back to Peter with a sigh. "Okay, let us start over again. I am Stacy Pardcek. You are Peter Caine. You're in a whole of trouble and I am going to do my best to get you out of it."

Stacy raised her hand and Peter took it.

We were in the Precinct sometime later with Caine and Nicki Elder. The character of Nickie Elder was a particular favorite of mine in the *Kung Fu: The Legend Continues* TV series. He was played by a very engaging and quirky actor named David Hewlett. He played the role several times during the series with an ingenious charm.

Caine was in the precinct looking at a slide through a microscope.

"You're looking at molecules that make up the skin," Nicki Elder was saying. "In this particular case, Rebecca Calvert's skin. Her skin was clinging to Peter's fingernails. Fingernails that were cut off in the bathroom."

"If the victim claws an attacker, would it not be his blood in her fingernails?" Caine asked. "Were there scratches on Rebecca's body?"

"There were small ones on the back of her neck," Nickie said, "but that might have been caused in the attack. But it looks bad, don't you see? Peter cuts his fingernails just in case her skin was underneath them."

"And then leaves them on the bathroom counter," Caine said, mildly, "and does not sweep them away?"

"I thought of that," Nickie said. "But there's a bloody fingerprint, Peter's fingerprint, in a glass in the apartment."

"But not on the doorknob," Caine objected, "and not on the door? Not anywhere else in the room?"

"Peter's hair was found clenched in the victim's hand," Nickie said, "and Peter's shirt was balled up and thrown into a corner of his closet!"

"Her blood?" Caine asked him.

"She was stabbed numerous times," Nicki said, nodding.

"An act my son would be incapable of, even in rage," Caine said.

"I know that is true," Nicki said, "and you know that, but the District Attorney of this city is one Thomas Shelton who pours ice in his veins instead of his highball glass and looks at evidence, bodies and bugs with the same analytical fascination."

"What was the type of blood found on Peter's shirt?" Caine asked.

"Same type as Rebecca's," Nickie said. "Her blood type found on Peter's shirt, not Peter's blood type, but hers!"

"It still does not prove it was Rebecca's blood," Caine insisted.

"Peter was seen entering Rebecca's apartment ten minutes before the time of the murder," Nickie said.

"Someone was seen entering, dressed as Peter, from a darkened room from across the street!" Caine objected.

Nickie Elder was ironic now. "Ever thought of becoming a defense attorney? If I am ever up for murder, I am calling you!" That did not get a rise from Caine who just looked at him. "Sure, it's fabricated evidence, but by an expert." Nickie shook his head helplessly. "It is a sweet frame."

We went back to the interrogation room where Peter was still being questioning by Stacy Pardcek. We felt that they have been at this for many hours. Stacy was pacing restlessly.

"You must have seen someone else when you were changing the tire," she said.

"There was a drive-by shooting twenty-four hours ago," Peter said, "and everyone was avoiding it like the plague and that's why they blew the tire out there."

"How did the killer know would you be driving down that particular street?" Stacy asked him.

"I got an anonymous tip," Peter admitted. "The address is around the corner from that street. I'm in a rush and that street is a shortcut."

"Who could monitor your moves that closely?" Stacy sat down again at the table. "Who could get into your apartment with no physical sign of entry? Who's got this kind of knowledge and evidence?"

"Another cop," Peter stated, quietly.

"Someone who she worked with?"

"I'm alive, she's dead, maybe it was someone *she* worked with," Peter said. "Did *she* ever talk about someone else beside me?"

Stacy got to her feet, as if the interview were over. "She never talked about you."

"Then there was someone in her life who scared her," Peter said. "You have to get me out of here Counselor so I can find him."

"Look, you've got a bail hearing at nine o'clock in the morning," Stacy said. She picked up her jacket and her briefcase. "This is murder in the first. I would not hold out much hope. Judge Sirreca wouldn't let his mother off on a parking fine." Peter put his head in his hands. Stacy knocked on the interrogation door, then she turned back to look at her client. "Peter, she did talk about you," she said. "She loved you."

The room was opened by Detective Nick Drake. Stacy moved through the ajar door and Drake closed it after her.

Lap Dissolve and we saw Peter in his jail cell with Chief Strenlich. Peter was watching Detective Drake outside the cell bars. Peter kept his voice low. "A rabbit punch should buckle him. I will try not to kill Drake when he pulls his gun. A couple of hours is all I need."

Strenlich shook his head. "I can't do it, Pete. Make a break and you will not have to worry about Drake. *I will* be the one reaching for my gun." Peter paced away from the Chief, leaning back against the far wall. Strenlich moved over to him. "Just how long do you think you'd last out there as a fugitive? You are a cop! You believe in the system. You have to. I have to! Let the wheels of justice turn, Peter." He raised his voice. "Drake!"

Detective Drake opened the cell to let Strenlich out. He did not close it immediately. Detective Jody Powell moved into the cell and Drake closed the cell door after her. Jody's mood was subdued and introspective.

"I just came by to wish you good luck, partner," she said, quietly. She gave him a chaste kiss on the cheek, at the same time palming something into Peter's right hand. "Here's your badge," she murmured.

Peter palmed it. Jody broke from him. Peter looked at her. "I could be guilty."

"I know you're not," Jody said. She raised her voice. "Drake!"

Peter looked her. "Thanks," he said, softly.

The next day, we were in the courtroom for the start of the trial. Caine entered and found a place in one of the front rows. We note Detective Mary Margaret Skalany sat beside Chief Strenlich and Captain Karen Simms. Detective Jody Powell and Detective Blake sat in the row of seats behind them. Stacy Pardcek and Peter entered the courtroom and moved to the witness table. Stacy acknowledged District Attorney Thomas Shelton, who looked away from her, busy with his court documents.

Mary Margaret Skalany sat beside Captain Simms. The Captain turned to Chief Strenlich. "You may find this surprising, but I hate to see this."

Strenlich glanced at her caustically. "Bad image for the department?"

"One of my Officers being falsely accused of anything, Chief," Captain Simms said, evenly.

"Glad to hear it, Captain," Mary Margaret said, quietly.

The court Usher stood. "Number 33258. State vs. Caine."

Judge Sirreca looked over at the defense table. "How does your defendant plead, Ms. Pardcek?"

Stacy got to her feet. "Not guilty, your honor. And we request that bail be waived so the defendant can be released in his own recognizance."

District Attorney Thomas Shelter was on his feet immediately. "Your Honor, this was a pre-mediated homicide! Prosecution demands that no bail be granted. We believe that the defendant is a high risk for flight."

"Your Honor, the defendant is a very well-known and highly respected Police Officer," Stacy argued.

Shelton moved around the defense table, playing to the jury. "Ah yes, Officer Caine's record, your honor! Investigated by Internal Affairs for the shooting of an innocent bystander during a supermarket robbery. Resigned from the force, but was reinstated by Captain Blaisdell, who happens to be the defendant's foster-father."

We went to Jody and Blake in their seats. Jody could barely contain herself. "This is outrageous!"

"Take it easy," Blake warned her.

"The defendant interfered with a hostage situation," Shelton continued, "by entering a school bus filled with children held captive by a man with a bottle of nitroglycerin, your Honor. Took his father out for the day with him, endangering the lives of civilians…"

The Judge had had enough of Shelton's rhetoric. "Thank you, Mr. Shelton, I got the picture." Judge Sirreca looked over at Stacy Pardcek. "Bail denied. Defendant is bound over for trial. Trial dates to be set for one week."

The Court Usher called for the "next case." District Attorney Shelton resumed his seat at the prosecution table. The Court Usher announced: "Case 33759 – Case vs. Kenyon."

The court doors were opened by a new defendant who entered. He was a callow youth in his twenties who looked pretty strung out. Beside Peter, Stacy Pardcek put her paperwork away. "We were expecting that," she told Peter. "Don't give up."

We were angled on the distinctive signet ring on District Attorney Shelton finger. Now we realized that he was Rebecca Calvert's killer!

Peter and Stacy both got to their feet, moving toward the door to the court. The new defendant suddenly grabbed the gun from the holster on one of the cops in the courtroom. At the same time he grabbed Stacy Pardcek and put an around her throat, holding her as a hostage. He fired the gun into the air.

"Back off!" he yelled and brandished the gun as he moved down the center aisle of the courtroom. "I mean it! I'll kill her!"

Skalany and Strenlich had drawn their guns. Captain Simms was right behind them. Then Caine got to his feet and disarmed the youth with two lightning moves that sent him sprawling to the floor. Caine steadied Stacy who was white as a sheet.

"Are you all right?" he asked her.

"Yes!" she gasped.

In the confusion, Peter suddenly disarmed one of the Police Officers in the courtroom. Caine looked up and shouted: "Peter! Peter, *no!*"

Strenlich had the punk who had attacked Stacy Pardcek in handcuffs. He saw what was happening, but it was all happening too fast. Peter ran to a second entrance to the court, smashed through the double doors there and escaped. District Attorney Shelton leapt to his feet, but there was nothing he could do in the aftermath.

That night we were in Chandler's Restaurant at the bar with Chief Strenlich, Detective Blake and Jody Powell. Carolyn Blaisdell had joined them. She was Paul Blaisdell's daughter. They were all watching a news report on the television. The newscaster was Sandra Mason who had appeared in several of *Kung Fu: The Legend Continues* episodes. I would always use her if the occasion arose. She was a terrific actress and very believable.

On the TV screen Marshal Jim Garrison was leading the investigation. He was a good-old boy, wily, astute, all of it cloaked with a charm that belied the steel beneath his words. Sandra Mason had a microphone in Sheriff Garrison's face. Two of the Federal Marshals who accompanied him, Rhimes and McKay, both in their thirties, were also good-old boys.

"What are the security precautions being taken to..." Sandra Mason said into her microphone, but Marshal Garrison cut her off.

"A rat couldn't scuttle through it, darlin'," he said, affably. "Now, before you ask me what airports I am watching and bus terminals and train terminals, so I can let the fugitive know my whole game plan, cause there's no doubt he's watching this broadcast if he's smart, which he is, let me say I'm running this here hoedown partly because the powers that be know that I can get the job done."

Detective Blake arrived beside Jody Powell at the bar with a pint in his hands.

On the TV screen, Sandra Mason said: "How long do you think Detective Caine can survive out there?"

"He can't run forever, darlin'", Marshal Garrison said. "He is scared and he's going to get caught. That's all for now."

Garrison moved out of frame. Sandra Mason moved her microphone to cover the two Federal Marshals, Rhimes and McKay, who seemed to revel in the notoriety.

"Gentlemen, do you consider Peter Caine to be a dangerous fugitive?" Sandra Mason asked them.

In Chandler's restaurant, Captain Simms moved to the bar where the television was playing, the sound low. Carolyn Blaisdell turned to her. "Why are Federal Marshals being brought in?"

"Standard procedure in a fugitive situation," Simms told her. "Also at the request of the District Attorney, Thomas Shelton."

One of the patrons turned up the sound a little. We went to the television screen again where Federal Marshals Rhimes and McKay were fielding questions from Sandra Mason. They were responding to her question about the fugitive.

"Definitely, ma'am," Rhimes said. "He's a cop, he's desperate, he's on the run."

"But he is an intelligence man," McKay said. "We hope to reason with him and bring him in peacefully."

"What other law enforcement agencies are involved in the manhunt?" Sandra pressed.

Captain Simms looked at Carolyn Blaisdell. "I thought Peter might have gone home?"

Carolyn turned to her. "Do you mean to Dad's house? I talked to Annie an hour and a half ago. She hadn't heard from him."

"Could he have gone into the house without her knowing it?" Captain Simms asked.

Carolyn smiled. "You mean because my stepmother is blind? She would hear him and would know his scent. She feels things. Peter hasn't been there."

Our erstwhile Bartender Terry brought the Captain a drink. Captain Simms looked over at Chief Strenlich and raised her glass to him. "Truce, Chief?"

Strenlich shrugged and nodded. "Why not?"

They clinked glasses. Captain Simms said: "Look, you know Peter, I don't. Where would he have gone?"

"Well, not to his apartment or to his father's place," Strenlich said. "The Marshals have them staked out."

On the television screen, Federal Marshals Rhimes and McKay were continuing their dog-and-pony act. "Yes, there are too many good men and women looking for Peter Caine for him to get far."

"Mr. Garrison hasn't lost a man yet," McKay added.

"I think that's enough questions for now," Rhimes said. "I have business to attend to."

He and McKay walked down the courthouse steps. Sandra Mason pointed her microphone at them, hoping to get one more answer. "One more thing, please!"

We went to Peter who on was on the run, finding shelter in an alleyway where boxes were stacked up. There was a homeless girl, about fifteen, amid the boxes. Peter shushed her, sending a message that he meant her no harm. A Police Car turned the corner and cruised by without seeing either Peter or the waif. The homeless girl looked frightened.

"It's okay!" Peter murmured. "It's okay."

The Police Car moved on. Peter squeezed the homeless girl's arm. "You take care!"

Then Peter bolted out of his hiding place.

The next day we established the Precinct. We hear Detective Powell's voice. "Haven't heard a word, Mary Margaret."

Jody was behind her desk. Mary Margaret Skalany moved over to her desk. Kermit Griffin entered the Precinct. He was dressed in black with a white shirt, carrying a briefcase. He was, as always, wearing his signature dark glasses. His manner was a little brusque. Jody looked up. "Hi! How has your trip?"

"Houston was hot!" Kermit said. "The computer show was hotter!"

Jody picked up a newspaper and opened it to a front-page spread. "Seen this?"

"Heard it on the radio," Kermit said, shortly. "I don't care if they found Peter standing with a bloody knife in his hands chanting Satanic verses, I don't believe it!"

When Kermit entered his office he found Caine waiting for him. Kermit sat down behind his computer and nodded to him. "Caine!"

"My son will attempt to contact you," Caine said.

"He'd go to you before anybody," Kermit said.

Caine shook his head. "He would not put me at risk."

Kermit sat back. His manner was low-key. "But I am used to taking risks?"

Caine gave Kermit one of his signature shrugs. "You were a mercenary."

"Not a widely known fact," Kermit said, glancing at the ajar door to his office. "I'd like to keep it that way. It might make the new Captain a little nervous."

"What do you think of her?" Caine asked him.

"Jury's still out," Kermit said. "What makes me special to Peter? There are a lot of cops in this Precinct."

Caine tried to find the right words. "They are all being followed. You are the only man here who could…" Caine chose his words carefully: "Shake a tail anytime you wished!" Kermit smiled at that. "Peter knows that."

In the Precinct room the Federal Marshals had arrived. Sergeant Broderick looked up from his counter. "Can I help you, gentlemen?"

"Good morning, Sergeant." Rhimes flashed his badge and ID. "We are Federal Marshals. Looking for Kwai Chang Caine."

"He's in Kermit's office at the back," Broderick said.

"Kermit?" McKay laughed. "Have you got a Missy Piggy working here too?"

The Feds moved away from Sergeant Broderick's counter. Jody moved over to him. "Wow! These guys are wasted as Marshals! Should be doing stand-up!"

In Kermit's office, Kermit still faced Caine. His manner was laconic, but Caine could see the concern in it. "So, he contacts me," Kermit said, "and I tell him what? Give himself up? You know the answer to that."

Caine took his point. "Yes! He is stubborn and headstrong. Even as a child. Particularly as a child!"

Kermit leaned forward, looking at his computer screen. "Hello! Speak of the devil! Peter!"

At that moment Federal Marshals Rhimes and McKay entered Kermit's office. Rhimes had his badge and ID in his hand. Kermit immediately turned his computer around so they could not see it from the doorway.

"Federal Marshal, sir!" Rhimes said and looked over at Caine. "You must be Caine."

"Good guess," Kermit murmured.

Rhimes turned back. "So that makes you Kermit?"

Kermit sat back. His smile was ironic. "Did my glasses give me away?"

Rhimes ignored that, turning back to Caine. "Marshal Jim Garrison would like to speak with you, sir," he said. "Would you be kind enough to come with us?"

Kermit immediately reacted to the name. "Garrison? Is he leading the special task force?" He looked over at Caine. "Worse than I thought!"

"Well, if you know Mr. Garrison," Rhimes said, "you know that he doesn't like to be kept waiting."

Caine got to his feet. "I will come." He looked at Kermit. "You will follow through with your inquiry?"

"Oh, yeah," Kermit said.

Rhimes' attention was still on Caine. "Thank you, sir," he said.

He and McKay left Kermit's office with Caine. Kermit leaned forward to his computer screen. "Talk to me, Peter!" he said.

There was indeed a deciphered message from Peter. "Meet me at our last stakeout at midnight. Come alone."

We were focused on a high rise building downtown. Peter entered from the elevator. There was a uniformed cop on duty. Peter flashed his badge and ID.

"Detective…" Peter reached out for a name from his past. "Khan! 101st Precinct. I want to take a look around."

The cop said: "I have orders that no one can go into the apartment."

"I am the detective of record now," Peter said, shortly. "You pass all of your exams, keep the graft down to a minimum, you might make 3rd grade detective before you're thirty-five. You got a problem with that call for authorization!"

Peter entered Rebecca's apartment. The uniformed cop accessed his radio. "This is Tobin. Pass me through to the 101st Precinct."

We saw Marshal Jim Garrison in his office going through some maps laid out on a table. He was talking to another Marshal in front of him. "Beef up the northwest quadrant," Garrison was saying, "and seal off the airports in the northwest and central area."

Caine entered with Marshals Rhimes and McKay. Rhimes moved over to Marshal Garrison. "Mr. Kwai Chang Caine, this is Marshal Garrison."

Garrison was still consulting the maps on the territory. We see an area marked: "*Clayfield Airport.*" "Did you check out Clayfield Airport in the Marshes?" he asked Marshal Rhimes. "Caine used to fly Cessnas out of there right after he graduated from the Police Academy."

"I will check it out," Rhimes said, "but I admit, sir, I am a little intrigued. How did you know that?"

"You stay alive two ways, son," Garrison told him, not unkindly. "You breathe and you learn." Garrison moved away from the bulletin board, motioning for Caine to come along with him. "Sit down Mr. Caine."

"I would prefer to stand," Caine said.

Marshal Garrison moved deeper into the Department. "Got any idea of where your son would be?"

"I do not," Caine said.

"You're not hiding him?"

"I am not."

"You wouldn't be lying to me, would you?" Garrison asked.

"I do not lie," Caine said, simply. "I am a Shambala priest."

Garrison turned to him. "Well, I am an old cowboy and I have been lying my whole life."

"My son is innocent," Caine said.

"Now that doesn't matter to me!" Garrison said. "I just need to bring him in. If he keeps running he is gonna die. You know where he is going, you tell me."

Marshal McKay had hung up the phone on his desk, jumping to his feet. "A Detective just showed up at Rebecca Calvert's apartment to search it again. Could be our man."

Marshal Garrison just shook his head, putting on his cowboy hat. "Return to the scene of the crime! Fugitives! I just love them!" He nodded at Caine. "You stay out of this, Mr. Caine." He raised his voice for McKay and Rhimes. "Let's go!"

We went back to Rebecca's apartment in the high-rise building. Peter was in the process of searching it. He lifted a framed picture of himself and Rebecca from the dressing table. It was the one the killer had picked up sometime earlier. Peter put it back and went through some clothes in a desk drawer and found nothing. He tried to close the desk drawer, but it was sticking. Following a hunch, he turned the drawer over and found a small notebook taped to the bottom of it. Peter pocketed it and moved over to the window. Outside he saw Sheriff Garrison, Rhimes and McKay running toward the front of the building.

Peter turned away to find the Police Officer from the hallway coming for him with his gun drawn. Peter rolled on the bed and kicked the gun of the Officer's hand. A swinging kung fu kick sent the Officer to the ground. He did not get up.

"Sorry!" Peter said. "You did a good job!"

Peter ran back to the window.

It was locked.

He leaned against the window and closed his eyes. We went to a *Flashback Sequence.* In it, Caine and Young Peter were sitting together in the temple trying to open a locked box.

"The image in your hands needs to be conducted," Caine told him. "It can break anything."

Young Peter tried again, but finally he just shook his head, admitting defeat. "I can't do it! Please help me father."

Caine took the box from him and had no trouble opening it. Inside a white dove fluttered. Immediately it flew away. Caine closed he box. Young Peter was amazed, but he knew he was going to be punished by his father.

"Who imprisoned the dove?" Caine asked his son.

"One of the other kids," Young Peter confessed. "I don't want to say who."

"Whom," Caine corrected him.

"I don't want to get him into trouble."

"Your sense of honor is laudable," Caine said.

"Will I ever able to do that?" Young Peter asked. "Open a lock? Break a seal?"

"When the situation is desperate enough," Caine told him, "you will be able to command this power, my son."

We went out of the *Flashback Sequence* where Peter was at the window. He opened his eyes and pressed against the glass, which was still locked. A beat, then the window miraculously opened. Peter climbed out onto the narrow ledge running around the outside of the building. He started to fall and clutched onto the window for support. Behind him, Marshal Garrison and the two Feds entered Rebecca Calvert's apartment. The uniformed Officer was getting to his feet.

We stayed with Peter as he held precariously to the window ledge.

"Don't look down, father!" he muttered. "Don't look down!"

In the apartment, the Feds came to a stop. "We'll have to close the window!" Rhimes said.

"No!" McKay said. "They're sealed!"

"Not this one!" Marshal Garrison said.

Outside on the ledge Peter opened his eyes, muttered: "Okay" and leapt from the ledge to the fire escape. He landed precariously on the skeletal stairs. He had only just made it! Peter climbed down and disappeared.

For a moment we do not know where we were. Tables and chairs were piled up around Peter. Obviously, it was a restaurant that was closed at this moment. Peter was reading from Rebecca's diary: "*I sound irrational, even to myself. Peter's love is so real, but my fear has been gnawing at my soul. He says he will kill Peter and then kill me. I cannot break it off with Peter! I can't confront him.*"

Peter turned another page in Rebecca's diary.

The name that jumped out at him was Thomas Shelton!

Over and over again.

Peter now realized that District Attorney Thomas Shelton was Rebecca's murderer.

We went to a rooftop where Kermit was waiting for Peter. There were more high-rise buildings around them. Kermit and Peter were right on the edge of a sheer drop. Kermit's attitude was guarded.

"Were you followed?" Peter asked him.

"For about five minutes!" Kermit said, mildly.

"Did you bring me a gun?"

Kermit's tone was ironic. "I got out of the arms business a long time ago."

Peter could not believe what he was hearing. "Dammit, Kermit, if I thought anyone would help me…"

"To save your life?" Kermit interrupted. "You bet! To help you pull a gun on a Federal Marshal, get yourself killed, you are on your own. I know the Marshal who is running this manhunt. His name is Jim Garrison. He's tough, he's relentless and he's the best."

"Yeah, cheer me up!" Peter said.

"You've got to give yourself up, Peter!" Kermit said.

"Is that what you would do, Kermit?"

Kermit smiled. "What I would do or not do in this situation doesn't count because it would be very scary. Unless you know the identity of Rebecca's murderer?"

"I know who ordered it!" Peter said. "Now I need to prove it. I need two of Blake's bugs, small, magnetic, that will affix to the inside of a jacket and one I can carry with me. I'll need a monitor."

Kermit interrupted. "Say I can get all of this stuff, then what?"

"Then I walk into the Federal building tomorrow morning," Peter said, "at 10:00 A.M."

"But not to give yourself up!" Kermit said.

It was not a question.

"To bait a killer," Peter said, tersely. "I need you to keep Marshal Garrison busy for ten minutes. I cannot afford to run into him in the hallway. Can you do it?"

"Probably for twenty minutes," Kermit said. "You want to tell me your plan?"

Peter turned away. Kermit turned him back. Peter stepped back from Kermit, saying: "Go for it, Kermit!"

There was a dangerous moment where the full weight of Kermit's anger would explode. Then he let the moment pass. "Some other time," he murmured.

"Drop those bugs and the monitor in Carolyn's mailbox," Peter said. "Do you know the address?"

"Oh, yeah," Kermit said.

Peter moved away from Kermit who watched him disappear into the shadows on the roof. There was a beat, then Caine joined Kermit. "I will accompany you to see Marshal Garrison," he said, quietly.

The next morning we were in the Federal Building downtown. Peter was wearing glasses, a jacket with a logo of a phone company on the back, and a wispy moustache. It was not much of a disguise, but Peter was improvising. The elevator doors arrived on the ground floor and some people filed out. Peter waved a greeting, even though he knew no one in the elevator.

"Hey!" Peter said. "How are you guys doin'?"

Then Federals Marshals Rhimes and McKay hustled to catch the elevator.

"Hey!" Rhimes said. "Hold them doors! Thank you!"

They got in as Peter turned away from them. Rhimes glanced at Peter, never thinking for a moment that he was face-to-face with his fugitive. McKay was mopping a handkerchief over his face. He turned to Peter. "Hot one!" he said.

"That's for sure," McKay said as he turned around in the elevator.

"I'll tell you something, Axel," Rhimes said, "this heat reminds me of Alabama. It used to bring out the critters and the villains."

We were back with Marshal Garrison in his Precinct office. He noted a pair of dark glasses beside his cowboy hat. He glanced up to see Kermit who looked at him with some disdain in his eyes.

"Kermit!" Garrison said, immediately. "Legend has it that you never let your adversaries see your eyes."

"I didn't know we were still adversaries," Kermit said, putting back on his dark sunglasses.

"Still the sun sets on one of us," Marshal Garrison said. "How's Blaisdell these days?"

"Fishing," Kermit said.

"Is that what you're doing here?" Garrison asked him. "A fishing expedition? What are you, a friend of the fugitive?"

"We work together," Kermit said.

"You're a cop?" Garrison said, amazed. "Wonders will never cease. Looking for an update on the manhunt?" Kermit just shrugged. "It's what happens when a fugitive runs for his life. Walls start closing in until the fugitive realizes he is right back where he started from."

We were now with Peter in District Attorney Shelton's office, which was deserted at the moment. He was sitting at Shelton's desk with the door open, putting the bug under the label of Shelton's suit coat. He had a 2nd bug that was designed to pick up Shelton's movements. Shelton entered his office. Peter looked up, ingenuously working on a telephone connection.

"Hey! Mr. D.A guy! How are you doin'? I have to get right on this phone here. You're not getting incoming calls."

Shelton put on his suit coat, not suspecting anything. Peter raised his voice. "I'll have to have to shut the door. Could be sparks!"

Shelton just exited the office. Peter went back to working on the two bugs that Detective Blake had left for him.

Marshal Garrison was at the 101st Precinct. Kermit was right behind him. Garrison paused when he was confronted by Caine.

"A predator stalks his prey without emotion," he said. "Survival becomes the only reality. My son is a survivor. Your compassion will betray you."

"What makes you think I have any?" Garrison said, wryly.

"Call it instinct," Caine said.

Nickie Elder barreled into the scene right up to Caine. "Caine! You were right!" He looked at Kermit who was now standing behind Garrison. "Kermit! What are you doing here?" Nickie's attention returned to Marshal Garrison. "Marshal Garrison, I took a smear from Peter's shirt and injected it with 20% hydroxychloroquine, airdried, affixed with menthol to hemorrhage the red blood cells…"

"Slow down to a gallop for me, son," Garrison asked him.

"It gives a fluorescent quality specially found in the "Y" Chromosome," Nickie said. "Male blood on Peter's shirt, not female, not Rebecca Calvert's blood."

Kermit moved closer to Garrison. "Doesn't that sound a little bit of a frame-up to you, Marshal?" he said.

We saw Peter in one of Federal Building offices with the door closed. He had found some news clippings in District Attorney Shelton's desk, all of them relating to Rebecca Calvert. He also found pieces of Rebecca's face cut-up in small pieces on the desk. That gave Peter pause, as if he were reliving moments he had spent with her. Then he stuffed the newspapers, the 2nd bug and the clippings into a briefcase and moved to Shelton's office door. He threw it open and immediately went sprawling into someone. He knocked the man down and took off down the corridor of the office suite. Federal Marshal McKay had just moved out of his office. He immediately pulled a gun on his fugitive.

"Hey! That is far enough! Turn around!"

Peter turned around and sent McKay flying with two kung fu kicks. He fell to the floor. Peter ran to one of the closed doors in the corridor.

We saw Marshal Garrison moving through some double doors putting on his cowboy hat. Caine and Kermit were behind him. "The fugitive has been spotted in the building heading for the lobby!"

Downstairs in the lobby Peter found that he was trapped with armed police at the lobby doors. There was no way out. Garrison came around the corner of the lobby with Rhimes and Kermit. Rhimes had his gun levelled at Peter.

"Don't even think about it!" Garrison told him.

At the same moment, Caine kicked the gun out of Rhimes' hands. Marshal Garrison reached for his gun. Peter smashed through a lobby window into the street outside. Garrison went after him. Peter avoided a car that had screeched to a halt and precariously hitched a ride on the back of a tow-truck.

Garrison lowered his gun. "Hell of an exit, son!" he murmured.

We were now angled on District Attorney Shelton in his office. He had discovered the papers that Peter had stolen from his desk. He was on the phone. "Yeah!" he said. "I need to see you right away! Usual place!"

We established Peter sitting in a parked car. He had the cut-up pieces of Rebecca Calvert's face on the seat beside him. Peter was tracking the District Attorney Shelton with the bug that Blake had left for him.

He shook his head. "You're a sick man, Shelton," he murmured.

Shelton emerged from a car park. Peter picked up the tracking device from the front seat and followed him.

We saw Marshal Garrison in his offices. We noted that Caine was behind him. Garrison was shouting at someone. "He's hurt and on foot! How far could he have got? Pick him up!"

Garrison slammed down the phone.

Peter continued to follow Shelton in his car through the traffic.

Caine and Kermit were in Kermit's funky green Cadillac that he called The Kermit Mobile. They pulled out into the traffic. There was a monitor on the dashboard showing the progress of the Cadillac. Caine said: "How can you be certain that this is the right man?"

"Blake gave me the coordinates," Kermit told him.

"Peter believes this person to be the killer," Caine said. "Once we reach our destination, what will happen then?"

"Mercenary rules," Kermit murmured.

"What are those?" Caine asked.

Kermit shrugged. "The man confesses to murder."

Now we were at magnificent Niagara Falls. It made a speculator backdrop to the scene. It was jammed with tourists. We spotted District Attorney Shelton waiting impatiently for someone in the crowd. Peter had to stop for some traffic lights. A Police Car pulled right beside him. Peter tried to avoid the Police Officer's gaze. The lights changed and Peter drove away. The uniformed cop also moved on, picking up his police radio.

We were back with Marshal Garrison, Rhimes and McKay in Garrison's offices. Rhimes hung up his phone. "He was just seen in Niagara Falls!"

"No way out!" McKay said.

Garrison grabbed his cowboy hat. "Fire up the chopper!"

Peter pulled his SUV into the Niagara Falls parking lot. He jumped out, still following the signal on Blake's monitor, and ran into the park.

A police helicopter headed toward Niagara Falls with Garrison, Rhimes and McKay in it.

Shelton waited for his contact to reach him in the Falls area. Peter, still following the monitor, moved further into the park. Shelton met a callow hood named Todd Ramsay who was wearing a jean jacket and cowboy boots. Shelton took his arm. "We're in trouble!" he said, tersely.

Peter spotted Shelton and Ramsey. He ditched his monitor into a trash barrel and ran into the crowd of people. Shelton and Ramsey were also on the move. "Come on!" Shelton said, urgently.

Caine and Kermit moved into the area around Niagara Falls. Caine suddenly pointed out the thug who had met up with Shelton. "That was one of the men who tried to kill me at my apartment!"

Kermit pulled out his laser gun which looked as if it would stop a rhinoceros.

Peter reached Shelton and Ramsey in the crowd. "Hold it!" he shouted.

District Attorney Shelton immediately took off. Peter took off after him, chasing him through the Niagara Falls crowd where an exit was displayed. Shelter disappeared inside. Peter was right behind him.

Caine faced Todd Ramsey, who had met with Shelton, nailing him with two fast kung fu kicks. A couple of cops ran over to them. Kermit flashed his wallet and ID. "Hey! Take it easy!"

Caine finished Ramsey off with another kung fu kick which sent him down to the ground. In the meantime, Captain Garrison, Rhimes and McKay ran into Niagara Falls Park. Inside the building, Peter descended down a huge, ornate staircase leading down to the Falls area. Shelton ran down the staircase below him.

In the park, Marshal Garrison fished the monitoring device out of the trash. He noted the scores of people who were jammed into the park. He ran past where Caine, Kermit, Rhimes and McKay were standing.

Inside the multi-story building, Shelton accessed a long tunnel that led right where Niagara Falls crashed into the canyon below. Peter came out of the entrance to the Falls and Shelton attacked him. Peter fended off the attack, getting in some speculator kung fu moves. They were fighting right on the edge of the huge falls. Then Peter slammed Shelton against the tunnel wall. He shook him like he was a rat.

"You killed her!" Peter shouted. "You killed Rebecca!"

"No!" Shelton shouted over the roar of the Falls. "I had an alibi! I wasn't there!"

Peter grabbed Shelton and moved back into the thunder of Niagara Falls. He used two kung fu kicks to send Shelton against the guard rail. He was dangling right on the edge of the precipice.

"Then you had her killed!" Peter raged at him. "Tell me! Tell me or you're a dead man!"

Peter had Shelton hanging precariously upside-down above Niagara Falls. He made it clear that he was going to drop Shelton into the raging torrent to his death. The thunder of the Falls enveloped them.

"Yes!" Shelton finally shouted. "Yes, I had her killed! She was mine! Mine!"

Marshal Garrison emerged from the end of the tunnel where it overlooked the raging torrent. He had drawn his Colt .45 revolver and reached out for Peter who was dangling Shelton as far as he could go. "You got your confession, son!" Garrison said. "Now slide him back inside. So I do not have to do something against my nature. Like shoot you!"

Peter was torn. He wanted to just drop Shelton into the raging waters. He wrestled with his decision, then reluctantly dragged Shelton back up and over the guard railing. Marshal Garrison pulled out his handcuffs.

"Appreciate that!" he said.

Peter took a very deep breath.

Outside in Niagara Falls, Marshal Garrison marched Shelton in handcuffs through some gates, followed by Peter. Caine was there with Rhimes and McKay. Garrison took one last look behind himself to see that Peter was going to be reunited with his father.

Caine put his hand on Peter's shoulder. Now that the excitement was over, Caine's attitude was lighter. He looked around them. "I have never seen Niagara Falls before! It is magnificent! Absolutely beautiful!"

Caine moved to the steps down to area below the Falls. Peter just shook his head. So much for the father-and-son heartfelt reunion! "Pop!"

He moved down the stairs. Behind him, Kermit had his dark glasses in one hand. He was smiling. "Oh, yeah!" he said and put back on his glasses.

Peter put his arm around Caine's shoulders as they climbed down to Niagara Falls. "After what I have been through, I guess it's time for us to smell the roses! Come on, let us take another look."

The next day, Caine and Marshal Garrison were standing in the lobby of the Federal Building. "I'm glad that things worked out the way they did," Garrison said.

"Truth is clarity in darkness," Caine told him. "Fear and mistrust cloud reason. Sometimes to achieve enlightenment one must embrace adversity."

Garrison nodded. "You don't get lard unless you boil the hog?"

Caine laughed. "Precisely!"

Marshal Garrison smiled and shook Caine's hand.

We were in Chandler's Bar and Restaurant that night. Peter entered to be confronted by the Precinct gang. Mary Margaret Skalany greeted him and took his arm. "Hey, partner!" Peter smiled at her, and then moved over to Detective Blake. "Did you bring the bugs and monitor back?"

"Yeah, I brought them back!" Blake assured him.

Sergeant Broderick shook Peter's hand. "Glad you made it, Peter."

"Thanks." Peter moved over to where Detective Jody Powell was standing at the bar. He gave her a chaste kiss. "Thanks."

"Anytime," Jody said. She wiped some lipstick from his lips. "Just clean it up there!"

Peter moved over to Chief Strenlich. The Chief was a little uptight. "I hope you understand where I was coming from."

Peter said: "From the heart, Chief."

Peter moved over to the bar where he found Captain Simms. "I'll be at the Precinct tomorrow for my shift, Captain."

"Make it Monday morning," Simms said.

"I don't need compassionate leave," Peter objected.

"I don't often give it," Simms said. "Make my night."

Peter moved further along the bar to where Stacy Pardcek was waiting for him. "Sorry I skipped out on you."

Stacy shrugged, but she was smiling. "You didn't trust me to acquit you."

"I didn't think I had enough time," Peter said. "But I knew you would do it. I did know that."

Stacy shook Peter's hand. "Anytime you need to be defended again, you call me."

Peter kissed Stacy's hand. "I'll remember that."

Peter moved finally over to where Caine had been sitting. He stood and Peter put his hand on his father's shoulder. He was trying to find the right words to say to him. "Thanks for not giving up on me. Not ever!"

Caine gave him one of his signature shrugs. "I love you," he said, simply.

Caine and Peter embraced each other.

Chapter Ten
BANKER'S HOURS

THIS WAS ONE OF MY FAVORITE EPISODES of the entire *Kung Fu: The Legend Continues* series. It had all of the Precinct gang in it in very good roles. Kermit had a major role in the episode. So did Mary Margaret Skalany, Chief Frank Strenlich and Captain Karen Simms. Adding to that mix were some favorite actors of mine: Nigel Bennett, whom I worked with before when he did the episode "Survival of the Fittest" with Patrick Macnee from Alfred Hitchcock Presents. Laura Press played Dr. Sabourin, a lovely actress. Catherine Blythe was playing Sandra Mason and Nathaniel Moreau was Young Peter. The leading villain in the show was Stephen Macht, a terrific actor whom I had actually met when he and I flew up to Montreal for the filming of the Kung Fu episode. The cast had responded to Stephen Macht immediately. So we had a dream cast together. I had written the episode, so I really wanted to see how it all turned out. We also had my favorite director on the show: Jon Cassar. With a director like Jon Cassar, I knew we in very good hands.

The episode started out in the city streets where Kwai Chang Caine was counseling a young, vulnerable woman named Alicia Marshall. There was a fragile quality to her that Caine was very protective of. He wore his suede coat and his wide-brimmed hat for this episode which gave him a different look. Caine and Alicia walked together on the Chinatown street.

Caine said: "It is good to see you again, Alicia."

Alicia looked around them, as if she were suddenly frightened. "Being here scares me. I am back here, living in the city in a tiny apartment, going back to school. Now all I have to do is take a deep breath and make sure I have a friend."

Caine took her hands in his. "You will always have that."

"Can I ask for your help again?" Alicia asked him. "Would you come with me to open a bank account?"

Caine took off his wide-brimmed hat. "I would be honored," he said.

We moved over to the 101st Precinct. As usual, it was the usual madhouse of people we have seen before at the Precinct. Captain Karen Simms was moving away from her office. Peter Caine caught up with her.

"Oh, Captain!"

Simms shook her head. "Not now, Detective! I am late for another meeting with the Mayor about the escalating crime rate in Chinatown and I have to go to the bank first."

Peter saw his opening. "Maple Street branch?"

"Yeah."

"That's my branch!" Peter said, ingenuously. "Could you deposit a check for me? You wouldn't mind, would you?"

Captain Simms just stopped where she stood. She could not believe her detective had just asked her to do that! Peter leaned against a desk and made out the check. Behind the Captain, Chief Frank Strenlich stared at them in disbelief. Detective Mary Margaret Skalany was behind him filing some paperwork. She was smiling to herself.

Karen Simms looked at Peter caustically. "No! Of course not! Anything else I can do for you, Detective? Pick up your laundry? Bit of cleaning?" Peter appeared oblivious to her sarcasm. "Get some milk?"

"No, that's fine!" Peter said, tearing her check out of his checkbook. He handed it to her. "Thanks!"

Peter moved back to his desk. Captain Simms just shook her head.

We went to a deserted room somewhere in an office building. A blueprint was lying on a desk. We noted a silenced gun lying beside it. Then we heard Samuel Brandt's voice. Even here, it was laced with malevolence. "Let us check out the tunnel, gang. Progress?" A man's voice replied: "One hour!" Brandt's voice said: "Keep on schedule." We noted an intense, soft-spoken killer named Kyle Hoffman sitting at the table. He talked into a two-way radio. "Nice blueprint, but computer images don't fight back. You ready for the real thing?"

Now we saw Samuel Brandt more closely. He was in his thirties, a malevolent psychopath who disguised his murderous rages with a charming façade. When Brandt spoke again into his radio there was a lilt to his voice. "Beautiful day for a robbery!"

We were angled on the entrance to a bank. It was a good size. Inside we noted the counters for the bank tellers and several desks situated around them. A bank employee named George Palmer was holding a meeting with two of his customers. Palmer had a pinched face, worry lines around his eyes and air of studied patience. Seated across from him were Tom Bellamy and his wife Krista. They were very uptight. They were desperate to secure a loan. Palmer was being tolerant, but there was no way he was going to grant these two people any slack.

"You have missed two payments, Mr. Bellamy," he said, candidly. "The bank has been very patient. I have no control on foreclosure proceedings."

"Mr. Palmer, I started a new job," Bellamy said. "Mr. Durham said I could refinance."

"What kind of collateral were you thinking of offering to secure this loan?" Palmer asked him, officiously.

Bellamy's wife Krista, who was fragile at the best of times, took hold of her husband's arm. "Tom, please!"

At the long counter one of the tellers, Jerry Maitland, was counting out some bills for a customer. He was an aggressive, uptight bank executive. Captain Simms was the next in the line. She was in a hurry because Peter Caine had made her late getting to the bank. Maitland turned to the other banker tellers and raised his voice. "Another teller up front, please!"

We noted one of the bank employees, Megan Chandler, was carrying a folder in her hands for a colleague. She was an attractive young woman in her thirties with a no-nonsense attitude, but behind the façade there was a vulnerable person who always kept herself in check. Her colleague took the file from her and nodded.

"That's fine."

Jerry Maitland looked up when his customer had departed. "Next, please!"

Megan sat down at her desk. She picked up the phone which was ringing. "Mr. Durham's office?"

A voice said: "Can I speak to him?"

"No, I'm sorry," Megan said with finality. "Mr. Durham is behind closed doors with strict instructions not to be disturbed for any reason."

We went into John Durham's office. Durham was in his fifties, a craggy face showing the strain he was under. He looked a little like the hero from that movie Blow-Up when he was younger. The actor playing the role was, in fact, David Hemmings!

John Durham had reached a decision. He opened the drawer in his desk and took out a Heckler & Koch semi-automatic pistol. He took the clip out of it to make sure it was loaded. He slammed the clip back in and turned the gun over in his hands, looking up into the shadows, wrestling with his decision in this life-or-death situation.

We went back to the Precinct. Kermit Griffin was working on his computer in his office. In this story, or in any story, Kermit did not need any explanation! Detective Blake was in the doorway of Kermit's office. "Coffee, Kermit?"

"Got to open my mail first!" Kermit said.

"What mail?" Blake asked. "I never see any mail on your desk!" Detective Mary Margaret Skalany paused in the doorway. Blake turned to her. "You know, I always wondered why no one ever wrote to him!"

"I didn't," Skalany said.

"Email, Blake," Kermit said. "People write to me from all of the world."

"What kind of people?" Blake asked.

Kermit smiled to himself. "You'd be surprised."

Skalany shook her head. "I wouldn't," she said and moved away. Blake shrugged and turned back into the Precinct. Suddenly Kermit became very still, reading a text he had just received from his old friend, John Durham who was a bank manager. Kermit read it aloud.

"The ultimate Dear John letter, Kermit. I realized when it came to say goodbye to my friends, there was only one. Now Caroline has gone, do not try to save more life one more time. Too late for heroics, but then, it always was. Your friend. John."

Kermit read the letter with a sinking heart. He picked up his phone and dialed. He checked the phone while he was listening. Then Megan connected.

"Mr. Durham's office."

"Megan, it's Kermit Griffin, let me speak to John."

"I'm sorry, Kermit..." Megan began.

A moment later Blake almost ran right into Kermit as he hustled out of his office, putting on his coat. Blake was momentary nonplussed. "Hey! Where are you going?"

"The bank," Kermit said shortly, and he was gone.

Skalany moved over to Blake who turned to her. "Is my coffee that bad?"

She considered this. "Yeah!" she said.

Out in the street, Caine and Alicia moved to the bank entrance. They almost collided with Samuel Brandt who had several of his terrorists with him. One of them was the Satanic young man we had seen earlier, Kyle Hoffman. Brandt was walking with a morose, lethal thug named Harlan Pascal. Beside him was a clean-cut young man named Barry Sutherland and another thug named Matt Benedict. Behind them was a muscle-bound woman who looked like a wrestler. Her name was Jane Kurtz. All of them looked wary except Brandt who did not look as if he had a care in the world.

Brandt was blocking Caine's way into the bank. Caine looked at him and reacted. He knew a predator when he saw one! Brandt stepped magnanimously to one side to allow Caine and Alicia to enter the bank.

Captain Simms was still waiting patiently in line for her turn with the bank teller. At one of the desks, Tom Bellamy was trying to persuade George Palmer to approve his loan. "So there is nothing you can do for us?"

"No," Palmer told him, frankly.

At the teller counter, Jerry Maitland stamped a receipt. "Okay! Next!"

Captain Simms was the next in line.

Business as usual.

Tom Bellamy was beyond frustrated as he sat with his wife Krista. He had enough of Palmer's officious attitude. "I demand to see Mr. Durham!"

Beside him, his wife Krista took his arm again. "Tom, please! Let us just…"

Bellamy cut her off. "You may have come to terms with failure, Krista, but I haven't!"

Palmer sighed patently. "Mr. Durham is behind closed doors. I am very sorry."

Caine and Alicia were waiting beside Palmer's desk. Caine reached out a hand to Alicia who was clearly nervous and on edge. She was holding a small pebble in her hands. Caine took it from her to stop them from trembling. She looked at him, a little sheepishly.

"It is a worry stone!" she confessed. "All the kung fu you have taught me, then I walk in here and I am like a pane of glass! One good door slam and I'll shatter on the floor!"

"All of us have difficulty dealing with the layers of bureaucracy," Caine told her, gently.

"Why do these situations scare me?" Alicia asked him.

"Because they are unknown," Caine said. "Once you understand the problems of others, then you can conquer your own."

John Durham sat alone in his office in the bank. He looked down at the H&K semi-automatic pistol in his hands.

He had made his decision to use it.

Before that could happen, in the main part of the bank, Samuel Brandt moved forward. He was very much the center of attention, his voice raised. "Good morning, good morning, good morning and a hot one it is! By tonight, you will be famous! I wonder who gets the best seller?"

Brandt fired his silencer gun into the air. "People, this is a robbery!"

Bellamy and Krista hunkered down in their chairs at Palmer's desk. Kyle Hoffman and Harlan Pascal pulled AK47 automatic rifles from their bags. Jane Kurtz pulled another AK47 automatic rifle from her canvas bag. Brandt continued in high spirits with his voice still raised. "We're the Brandt gang! That is spelled with a '*d*' after the '*t*'!" Then his voice took a menacing rasp. "Everyone down on the ground!"

Customers dropped down to the floor except for Captain Karen Simms who defied Brandt's order. Matt Benedict, one of the robbers, climbed on one of desks on the other side, branding his submachine gun. "Get back!"

A Security Officer came around a corner of an office and saw what was happening. He reached for his holstered gun, but Brandt shot him, sending him down to the floor.

Brandt said: "Mr. Pascal?"

Pascal fired burst from his submachine gun, decimating the counters around him. Tom Bellamy and Krista cowered down in their seats. George Palmer was down on his hands and knees in front of his desk.

"So let's all cooperate!" Brandt advised, suavely.

Caine had brought Alicia down to the floor with him. Barry Sutherland, another of the robbers, covered the bank employees and shouted: "Move it! Move it!"

Caine got to his feet and took out Matt Benedick, one of the robbers, with two vicious kung fu kicks. He disarmed Barry Sutherland and sent him down to the floor. Then Brandt fired his silencer gun into the air. On her knees, Alicia flinched. Caine swung back around. Brandt was calm and almost serene.

"Somehow I knew you would do that!" he said. "Premonition! Right in the doorway!" Brandt's moods were mercurial. Right now he pointed the silencer gun directly at Caine. "I should kill you!"

"But you will not!" Caine said.

Brandt's rage had subsided. He grinned at Caine and said: "I liked the moves! But do not try them again." He pointed the gun down at Alicia on the floor. "I'll spare you and kill your girl!" Alicia was terrified. Brandt nodded as if understood. "Not a fair trade!"

Captain Simms stood apart from Brandt. She reached for her gun that was nestled in her holster. Brandt glanced around him at his "gang". "Come on, guys, get up! This is embarrassing!"

Sutherland and Benedict got back to their feet.

Surreptitiously, Captain Simms returned the gun to her holster and buttoned her coat around it. Kurtz and Pascal covered Brandt. He moved over to Karen Simms. His manner was condescending. "Too proud to fall to your knees, ma'am?"

"Wait until I am sixty for the 'ma'am'," Simms said.

"Attractive!" Brandt said. "A woman of the 90's." Then his voice became deadly quiet. "I will shoot you as fast as I would shoot a dog!"

Captain Simms shrugged her shoulders. "I surrender!"

"On the floor!" Brandt suddenly raged.

The Captain got down onto her hands and knees.

Caine moved past the robbers. Harlan Pascal brought up his AK47 automatic weapon. "No one leaves!"

Caine pushed the gun barrel contemptuously away from him. Brandt nodded and smiled. "He won't be leaving!" he said. "He will be the last one to leave."

Caine moved to the wounded Security Officer who was lying the floor. Brandt watched him. Caine looked up. "This man is badly hurt."

"You a doctor?" Brandt asked him.

"A priest."

Brandt was contemptuous. "Going to give him his last rites?"

"Not unless your humanity had deserted you," Caine said.

Brandt thought about that. "I'll check that out. Get right back to you!"

Pascal was issuing more commands, branding his AK47. "Go! Go! Out front! Go!"

Kyle Hoffman moved with him to where Megan was standing in front of John Durham's office. His manner had a dark edge to it. "Are you going to throw yourself against the door and save a man's life?"

"If I have to!" Megan said defiantly.

Hoffman shook his head, smiling. "That must be one hell of a boss!"

John Durham moved out of his office at that moment. "Oh yes, I am," he said, quietly.

Durham's silencer gun was back in his drawer in his office. The bank executive put Megan protectively behind him. Pascal grabbed his arm. "Party time! We're rounding up the usual guests!"

Pascal motioned for Megan to come also, but an imperceptible nod from Hoffman stopped him. The terrorist moved away. Kyle Hoffman leaned close to Megan and his voice was hushed.

"I am having my own private party," he whispered. "You would be better off with me."

Hoffman propelled Megan into Durham's office. Durham watched Hoffman with growing concern. Pascal prodded him with the rifle. "Come on! Time to go!"

Captain Simms and Alicia were manhandled to the front of the crowd. Suddenly everyone turned to look at a secretary who had moved through one of the doors from another office. She was attractive, in her thirties, with a sweet face, but there was something odd about her mannerisms. Her name was Katherine Duval.

"That's far enough!" Brandt demanded, his voice coming loud again. "Get down on your knees!"

Katherine seemed to be in a world of her own, checking out some files, oblivious to the peril she was facing. Caine knew the answer immediately. He stepped forward quickly so that he was in front of Brandt. "Please! Do not fire!" Caine said. "She cannot hear you! She is deaf."

Finally Katherine looked up and froze where she stood. Caine used sign language for her. Katherine responded, using sign language of her own. Caine shrugged, following her silent commands.

"She has 100 percent hearing loss in her right ear," he said, "and can hear 10 percent in her left. She could not obey your commands."

Brandt was intrigued. He moved forward. "You can tell that by the way she walked?" Caine gave Brandt one of his signature shrugs. The terrorist grinned. "Outstanding!" He turned back to Katherine. "Can you read lips?"

Katherine responded in a halting way, using her own voice and sign language. "Yes, I can!"

"Join the party!" Brandt invited her.

Captain Simms nodded to herself. She had admired Caine even more for the way he had handled that situation. Caine moved over to Katherine protectively. Harlan Pascal propelled John Durham forward. "Move! You're wasting time!"

Durham confronted Brandt. "If your intention was to rob this bank you don't need this much firepower to open an account," he said, ironically. "You should just get on with it."

Brandt shook his head. Now he was all smiles again. "We have all the time in the world!"

Durham glanced at Caine who was standing with Katherine, his arm around her shoulders. We go to a *Flashback Sequence* in the temple.

Marauders had stolen into the temple, disturbing Young Peter who had been asleep. He got out of bed and rushed to where his father was sitting surrounded by candles.

"Bandits, father!"

Caine got to his feet immediately. "Find Master Khan! Evacuate the children!"

We came out of the *Flashback Sequence* back onto Caine's face.

In the bank, Brandt paced restlessly. Pascal was behind him. "It is a very bright year," Brandt said, enigmatically. "Not conducive for bank robberies."

"Nor for sniper fire from the rooftops across the street," John Durham suggested.

"Very good mercenary thinking," Brandt said, as if he was impressed. He moved forward to Durham. "Perhaps you haven't been a bank manager?" Brandt gave Durham an ironic salute. "Mr. Durham!" Brandt switched gears. "Are there shutters on the windows?"

"No!" Durham said.

"The face of a deaf girl," Brandt said, "is very expressive. All of the senses making up for the one." Brandt turned to her. "Do you have the key to the shutters?" Katherine just shrugged. Brandt grabbed her face with his hand, shouting at her. "You are hanging onto every syllable that falls from my lips! The key!"

"I'll get it for you!" Durham said.

Brandt squeezed Katherine's face, then, adding insult to injury, he caressed her like he was her lover, and then he let her go.

We were in the inner office with Megan Chandler and Kyle Hoffman. Hoffman sat his hostage down on a swivel chair. "I need to get into some computer files," he said. "Show me the commands."

"I don't know them," Megan told him.

"Of course you do," Hoffman said patiently, and he grabbed her.

"You're hurting me!" she said.

"Not as much as I am capable of." Hoffman gently stroked her hair. "Oh, come on! I am not asking for any secret codes! You do not know them. I will find them. Just get me into the program." His voice was suddenly raging at her. *"Now!"*

"All right!" Megan said, cowering away from him.

In the main room on the bank floor, John Durham tossed the keys to Brandt. Jerry Maitland, one of the bank executives, was behind him. "The mechanism is over there at the end of the first counter," Durham said.

Brandt turned to Maitland. He was cordial again. "Will you do the honors?"

"Do I have a choice?" Maitland asked.

Pascal grabbed Maitland and thrust him in front of him. "Not if you want to live!"

Brandt was ironic. "He knows that!"

Pascal manhandled Maitland over to the cash drawers. "Open it!"

"All right! All right!"

Maitland opened the first drawer which was stuffed with money. Pascal emptied it out. Jane Kurtz moved over to the second drawer of banknotes, stuffing them into her bag. Barry Sutherland moved to the third cash drawer, riffling through it.

Caine and Captain Simms knelt down beside the wounded Security Guard. Caine wiped the sweat from the man's face with a soft cloth. Captain Simms said: "What's that?"

"It will cool his fever," Caine said.

He got to his feet with Simms and moved over to where Alicia was waiting. He gave her a hug. She looked down at the wounded Security Officer. "Can't you do something?"

"Yes!" Caine said, quietly. "But not against so many. Innocent people will die." He looked over at Captain Simms. "Which is why you do not go for your gun."

Alicia looked at Simms, surprised. "You're a cop?"

"Yes!" Simms said, softly. "I am a cop."

We go to the Precinct where we were angled on Mary Margaret Skalany. Peter Caine was doing some filing. The television was turned up. "*This is an emergency bulletin.*" Skalany turned around and so did Peter. A Newscaster continued on the television screen. "*Word has just come into the newsroom of a robbery that is actually in progress at the Metropolitan Bank on Maple Street. A Swat Team was enroute and we'll have a report right after this.*"

Peter moved to Skalany, who looked at him. "Maple Street! Isn't that your bank?"

"Yeah," Peter said, "where I just sent the Captain with my check!"

Outside in the street, Kermit pulled up in his car and got out. Swat Officers were still deploying. A brittle, laconic Swat Officer named Jack Lasher was getting them into position. Lasher was an abrasive, edgy Police Officer, a martinet. He wore reflecting dark glasses and talked most of the time through a bullhorn.

"Go!" Lasher said. "Go! I want one team on either side of the building. Ralston, get your men onto the roof!"

Kermit's reaction was swift. "Lasher!" he said with contempt.

A reporter whom we have seen in other episodes of *Kung Fu: The Legend Continues*, Sandra Mason, moved past a uniformed Police Officer with her news team. She was stopped by the Officer. "Excuse me, Sandra Mason, I want to get a story here. What is going on?"

Lasher was still taking charge. "Get these people fifty yards back!" he shouted. "You think they got .22's in there?"

Kermit moved through the police chaos and confronted Lasher. "When does a suicide bring out a Swat Team fully mobilized?"

"I don't know what you're talking about, Kermit!" Lasher moved away from him. "I got a robbery in progress, twenty hostages, and no contact." He accessed his radio. "Harry, where is my talker?"

A voice echoed through Lasher's radio. "On his way, Captain!"

"When I say clear the area," Lasher said into his radio, "that means the Channel Three video truck and Sandra Mason and her media circus! Park them around the corner!"

Sandra Mason was still trying to get past the uniformed Police Officer who had barred her way. "What is this?" she demanded. "Let me in!"

Lasher turned his attention back to Kermit, like he was an old friend. "I wish I could stop and talk about the old days, Kermit. Maybe over a beer at Chandler's one night!"

"When I am that hard up for company I'll buy a dog," Kermit said, caustically. "A friend of mine is the bank manager of this branch. John Durham?"

"Good!" Lasher said. "Maybe there will be one cool head in there."

Chief Strenlich moved over to Kermit and Lasher. "I just got through to the bank on a cellular. A voice said: 'Brandt, I am bank robber, you're a cop' and put the phone down. Line is still open."

"I am a pretty good talker when I need to be," Kermit said, looking at Lasher. "Put me on the line."

"I have a professional team, Kermit, and you are not on it!" Lasher retorted. "Stay out of my face! Your jurisdiction around here is to direct traffic! You are making my teeth itch! I am going the old-fashioned route."

Lasher moved away from them. "Take it easy, Kermit," Strenlich advised, restraining him. "You know Lasher!"

"You don't know how well," Kermit muttered.

Back inside the bank, Brandt accessed a key to a wall panel to bring the shades at the window down. Outside, Strenlich reacted to what he was seeing. "What the hell is that?"

The shades went down to the bottom of the window. Kermit shook his head. "Don't let them seal you in there, John!"

In the bank we moved past the wounded Security Officer to where Tom Bellamy and his wife Krista sat on two chairs. Beside them, George Palmer was down on the floor with most of the other hostages. He was jumpy. When Krista moved closer to her husband, he put a restraining hand on her arm. "Don't move! They said not to move!"

Krista indicated the wounded Security Officer. "Someone has to help that poor man!"

"It doesn't have to be you!" Bellamy said.

Krista settled back into her seat. "Oh, really? I am a failure as a hostage?"

Bellamy did not respond to that. Caine stood with Alicia, who looked frightened. He took the pebble from Alicia's hands. "You will no longer need this," he told her, gently. "You are in control of your emotions. As I said you would be."

Brandt motioned to Jane Kurtz and Matt Benedict. "Come on!"

Harlan Pascal jumped the counter. Jane Kurtz and Matt Benedict moved past Brandt. Benedict helped himself to some of the cash in one of the drawers.

Durham took a step forward to Brandt. "Look, keep myself and my staff as hostages," he said. "Let the others go."

"What a grand kidder you are!" Brandt said with his infectious grin. He moved closer to Durham. "How much is in the vault? I would say at least 20 million after the delivery you received last night."

Captain Simms had been holding Katherine's hands. Now she let go of the deaf girl and stood up. Brandt ignored her, but John Durham moved forward.

"The vault is on a time-lock," he said. "It can't be opened."

Brandt was ironic. "Every secret in the world can be opened," he said. "You would save me a lot of time if you gave me the right combination."

"I don't know it!" Durham said.

"It is in your computer system," Brandt said, reasonably.

"It can't be accessed."

Brandt moved right into Durham's face. "Mr. Hoffman is a hacker. Don't you just love that word? He can access Hell!" Durham had no answer to that. "No?" Brandt shook his head. "You are not turning out to be as much help as I thought you would be. Better get down on your knees with the rest of your customers."

Brandt's gun followed Durham down to the ground. Pascal ran back over to Brandt. "Swat Team has got into position!"

"Your window of opportunity has closed, Mr. Brandt," Durham said. "You won't be going out the way you came in."

"And whoever said we were leaving to walk out the front door?" Brandt said, grinning again. He turned to Jerry Maitland, one of the bank employees. "Do you have the keys to the safety deposit boxes?"

"Find them yourself!" Maitland retorted.

Brandt struck Maitland across the face, a vicious blow that sent him down to his knees. Our deaf girl, Katherine, got to her feet, appalled by the violence. Brandt moved over to Durham, threatening him with his gun. Then Palmer, who had addressed the Bellamy's earlier, moved forward. "I have the keys" he said. "I have them! In my desk!"

Brandt motioned to Palmer to move. Tom Bellamy and his wife Krista were still waiting beside Palmer's desk. "There better not be a gun in that drawer!" Brandt warned him.

Palmer came up with a ring of keys and showed them to Brandt. The bank robber sighed as if he was genuinely grieved. "Too bad the Bellamy's couldn't get a loan this easily!"

Brandt moved past Katherine. John Durham moved over to her and signed for her. "Everything will be all right, Katherine. You understand?"

Katherine shrugged. She said haltingly: "If you say so, Mr. Durham."

Durham moved over to where Caine and Alicia were standing. "He said he was a contractor. He made some very large deposits in the last three months. Going to build a hotel complex in the city."

"Now you have seen his dark side," Caine said. "I think you have shared it with him at one time."

Durham stared at him. "How would you know that?"

"The same way I felt your pain," Caine said. "You began this day with despair. It may not end that way."

"That is not up to me now," Durham said, darkly.

"Destiny can be shaped," Caine told him. "Ours… theirs… and yours."

Captain Simms moved forward to stand with Caine and Durham. She shook her head. "I don't understand their game plan," she said. "They're surrounded now."

Durham shrugged. "Well, a helicopter to the airport, Lear jet waiting, one or two hostages along for the ride."

Captain Simms shook her head. "That scenario never works. Brandt knows that."

"It could be a suicide mission," Durham suggested. "He wants them to attack, go out in a blaze of glory."

"Suicide is the lowest form of deception," Caine said. "It does not result in death or darkness."

Durham was looking at Caine with a renewed sense of wonder. He knew Caine was talking about him. "I've never heard it put that way," Durham said, softly.

"A bottle of nitro!" Captain Simms said. "That's how Brandt strikes me. He is colorless, but you shake him up, he can explode at any point."

"It sounds as if you've examined people like Mr. Brandt before, Miss…?"

"Karen Simms," she said. She shook his hand. Then she said pointedly: "Police Captain, Karen Simms."

Durham nodded. He got it now. "Ah! John Durham."

"I have an Officer in my command," Simms said. "Kermit Griffin. Has he spoken about me to you?"

Durham laughed. Very Kermit: "Oh, yeah!"

Katherine moved forward. Her trauma level was high. She signed for Caine, who was following her words. "Will they kill us all?"

"No!" Durham said. "We're Brandt's insurance policy. He'll let us go when he gets what he came for."

Captain Simms was not convinced. "Yeah, right!"

Outside on the street, Sandra Mason was speaking into her microphone again, the video team filming her. "The situation here remains extremely tense. We have an open phone line and voices have been heard shouting. There have been no demands made yet, and we have not received official notice as to the number hostages trapped inside. Once we do…"

Peter got out of his car, flashed his police badge for the Officers there and made his way over to where Kermit was standing looking at the bank entrance.

"Captain Simms is in there," Peter said.

Kermit nodded. The situation was getting worse. "Got a friend in there myself."

Lasher was back on his radio. "Ralston, you in position yet?"

One of the Swat Team responded: "Yes, Captain!"

Another of Lasher's Police Officers moved over to him. "I've got Officers positioned where you wanted them, Captain."

Kermit indicated Lasher. "Captain Jack Lasher. Just took over the Swat gig."

"Anyone we can't see?" Peter asked.

Kermit suddenly turned back to him. "What a very good question!"

He moved quickly away.

In the bank, inside the computer room, Kyle Hoffman was working on a complicated series of algorithms and mathematical equations. Brandt stood beside him. Megan sat in her swivel chair, desperate to make some kind of a move... but to where? On the screen a list of mathematical equations came up: *Zero-Know Protocols, Strong Prime Monitor, Digital Fingerprint, Trap Door One Way Functions, Karberos Authentication, Pollard Factoring, CRL Applied, DSS Ready, MD5 Enabled, RSA Cryptos, DES Cryptosystem, Clipper Chip.* Brandt was watching the screen.

"What's that?" Brandt asked.

"Time sequence for the vault," Hoffman said. "Very complicated. Twelve floors. Not the eight that you promised. Going to take me longer."

"How much longer?" Brandt demanded.

"Well, it is not user friendly," Hoffman said, at the end of his patience with Brandt. "It won't tell me!" He looked over at Megan. "What is the next access code to the first level?" Megan did not answer. Hoffman reached out and grabbed her arm. He said in a deadpan way: "We can do this with all your clothes *on* or all of your clothes *off*! What is it going to be?"

When I was writing this episode, my story editor, Martin Borycki, came to this phrase in the script: "*We can do this with all your clothes on or all of your clothes off!*" He thought that was the best line he had ever read in a script! He even had it made up into a sweatshirt. Martin was a wonderful guy who possessed a stellar sense of humor.

In the computer room, Megan was not intimidated. She said: "We're already at level 880!"

"Keep your mind on your work, Mr. Hoffman," Brandt told him. "We don't have all day."

Caine's voice echoed from inside the bank. "Mr. Brandt?" Brandt moved over to the door of the computer room. "Mr. Brandt!" Caine called again.

The door opened and Brandt stepped out.

Inside the computer room Hoffman nodded at the information that Megan had given him. He leaned over and caressed Megan face. "Thanks, babe!"

Megan slapped his face. He took it, but he did not like it.

Outside in the bank, Brandt took another step forward. He looked around, shaking his head. "My guy just let you walk over here?" Caine shrugged. "They must be afraid of you!"

"If you allow one hostage to die," Caine said, "they will believe all will die. They will storm the building. You must get medical help for this wounded security guard and you must do it now!"

Brandt moved over to Caine. His expression was somewhat whimsical. "What did you say your name was again?"

"I am Caine."

Brandt shrugged. "Whatever you say, Caine!"

He moved away and Caine followed him.

Outside, Police Officers and sharpshooters were deployed around various police cars. A large crowd had gathered around Jack Lasher who walked forward and leaned on a cop car. Inside the bank we were close on Captain Karen Simms.

"Someone should get this show on the road," she muttered. She revealed the holstered gun in her belt. Jerry Maitland, the bank executive, took note of it. Katherine was comforting Krista in her hesitant fashion. "It is all right. People are frightened. Okay?"

Krista just nodded.

We went back outside into the street where we were angled on Lasher. He put the bullhorn to his lips. "Brandt! Need to talk!"

In the bank, Captain Simms nodded. "Thank you!" she said, softly.

Outside, Chief Strenlich was now standing beside Lasher. Peter jogged over to them. Caine emerged from the bank. There were high-powered rifles trained on him. Peter grabbed Lasher's bullhorn before the Captain could make a move.

"What the hell?" he exclaimed.

"That's his father," Strenlich told him.

Peter moved forward, bringing the bullhorn to his lips. "Mr. Caine!" he said through the bullhorn. "101st Precinct. What's going on in there?"

"There is a man badly wounded," Caine said. "We need a doctor!"

"Okay," Peter said through the bullhorn. "Will you allow a medical team to come in?"

"Yes!" Caine said.

"Okay, five minutes," Peter said. "Are you letting any hostages out?"

Caine just gave one of his expressive shrugs. Then he turned around and went back into the bank. Peter moved back to Lasher and Chief Strenlich. "Okay!" He addressed Strenlich. "Call Dr. Sabourin at Country General Hospital." Strenlich moved away from him. Peter shouted after him: "Dr. Sabourin only!"

Inside the bank, Brandt moved forward. Caine and Pascal were with him. He was playing to his audience. "Who wants to leave? Show of hands!"

Hands go up among the hostages. Captain Simms was still waiting for an opportunity to get the jump on Brandt. Krista stepped forward from the group. "Please, let us go! We're just starting our lives."

Samuel Brandt looked at Caine, then back at Krista. "I'll tell you what. I'll let your husband go!" He looked at Bellamy. "What's your name?"

"Tom," he said, hesitantly.

"Well, Tom," Brandt said, magnanimously, "walk out of the door! I am feeling in a generous mood today."

Bellamy turned to Krista. "Come on!"

"Uh-huh!" Brandt said. "You walk out of here alone. Your wife stays with us. Is that okay with you?"

"Go ahead, Tom," Krista said. "It's okay."

"He won't leave without you," Caine said.

Bellamy looked at Brandt. "You bastard!"

Brandt pointed his gun directly at him. "Go for it!" Bellamy hesitated again. "You did think about it, didn't you?" Brandt was enjoying Bellamy's crisis of conscience. "I saw it in your eyes!" Brandt looked back at Krista. "Dump him, honey! He doesn't love you." He looked at the assembled group. His eyes fell on Katherine, our deaf girl. "You can go!"

"Because I am deaf?" she demanded, using her signing skills.

John Durham moved up to her, motioning for her to leave. "Go on!"

"No!" Katherine said with some passion, still using her signing. "I work here! I know all the people here! I'm staying!"

Brandt was seriously impressed. "That's a classy lady!" He turned back to Caine. "Looks like we're all in this together."

Caine moved away from Brandt and re-emerged from the bank. The Police Officers and the Swat Team had their guns and AK47 rifles trained on him. Caine raised his voice. "He has said that no one may leave." He looked directly at Peter. "But you can come in!"

"Count on it!" Peter murmured.

Caine returned to the bank.

We went back at the Precinct where Skalany and the other members of the 101st squad were tensely watching the newscast on the television. Sandra Mason was still reporting the crisis with her news team. "*Kwai Chang Caine, a respected apothecary in Chinatown, is one of what the police are saying could be as many as twenty hostages trapped in the bank in an aborted robbery.*"

Skalany said with some despair: "Caine, what are you doing inside a bank?" Blake was watching the television screen beside her. "Don't get killed!" Shalany begged Caine on the television screen. "Just don't get killed!"

Kermit was back in his office tapping furiously on his computer. Blake moved to Kermit's open doorway. He could not believe what he was hearing. "What are you working on at a time like this?"

"Maps of the city!" Kermit told him. "Looking for Brandt's way out."

We went back to the bank. George Palmer was pouring himself a cup of coffee. His hands shook. He turned to see Caine looking at him. Apologetically he said: "He said we could have coffee!"

"It must be a great responsibility," Caine said.

"What's that?"

"The future of people's lives in your hands," he said. "When to say yes, when to say no."

"That's not up to me!" Palmer protested.

"Judgment and discretion can belong to all of us," Caine said. "Add compassion and you will always know what path to take."

Palmer paused to think about that.

In the office, with the door closed, Kyle Hoffman was working on his computer. We saw more of the algorithm that he was working on: *Digital Certificate Bypass, Private/Public KeyScan, Mass Function Digital File Stamp.* Surreptitiously, Megan eased a drawer open in the desk beside her, revealing a silenced gun. She cannot reach for it, even if she had her courage in hand, because Hoffman suddenly sat back.

"Yes!" exclaimed.

Megan withdrew her hand from the partially open drawer to look at Hoffman. "Are you into the vault?"

"One more floor to climb, angel!" Hoffman told her.

"Then what?" she said. "The bank is surrounded by armed police! How will you escape?"

Hoffman smiled. "Brandt always has an ace in his ragged sleeve!"

"And the hostages?" Megan asked him. "You'll let us all go?"

"You don't have to worry, angel," Hoffman said, leaning closer to her. "I wouldn't let anything happen to you! You just stay with me when the fireworks start."

Megan processed this. The phrase frightened her. "Fireworks?"

We are now in the main part of the bank, angled with Caine and Krista. Krista looked at Caine. "You think he would have left me? My husband?"

"I do not," Caine said. "You have shown great courage against enormous odds. It is your husband who needs faith."

"How do you know that?" Krista asked. "I guess you sense things being a priest. What about our captors? What do you think of them? Would they kill us?"

"They would not," Caine assured her.

But he saw that John Durham was watching them. His uptight manner spoke volumes. "I think that is exactly Brandt's intention," he said, softly.

On the computer in the bank offices the screen had just flashed up: *Access Permitted. Vault Open.* Hoffman was jubilant. He swung around to Megan. "We made it, babe!" He stood up and his face was inches away from hers. "We are into the vault! Come with me? Best offer you're going to get today!"

Megan was repulsed by him, but she said: "I will think it over."

"Don't take too long," Hoffman warned her.

In the main room of the bank, Jane Kurtz moved into the open vault. Barry Sutherland followed her. Brandt stepped across, talking into his radio. "ETA?"

One of the robber's voices answered: "Breakthrough in five minutes."

Brandt was ecstatic. "Nice work, gentlemen!"

In the vault room, Sutherland and Kurtz were going through drawers, taking out bundles of banknotes and jewelry. We came back into the main bank room. Katherine moved away from the gathered group, away from Caine and Alicia. She smelled something that had got her attention. She was signing in rapid signals. Harlan Pascal motioned with the submachine gun.

"Get back in there! And no signing!" Caine put a restraining hand on Katherine's arm. "You want to talk to each other," Pascal said, "do it like anyone else!"

Caine and John Durham were with Katherine. Caine nodded, speaking softly. "Your sense of smell is heightened?"

Katherine nodded. "Yes!"

"Are you certain?"

"Yes! My father was a welder!" Katherine said in her halting fashion. "I will never forget that acrid smell! What could it mean?"

"What is she saying?" Pascal demanded. He had his submachine gun aimed at her. Caine turned to him. "She is frightened!" he said. "You would be too."

Brandt was on the far side of the bank. He motioned to Pascal. "Pascal! Come here!"

The terrorist did as he was told. Caine gripped Katherine's shoulder gently. Beside them, Alicia said: "I feel like I have been listening for hours!" She looked at Caine. "Have you ever been in something like this before? A real robbery?"

"As real as this is!" Caine said.

We go to a *Flashback Sequence* to Caine and Young Peter in the temple. Caine was in his kung fu robes. Young Peter and Master Khan were walking purposefully with him.

"But I want to fight!" Young Peter was saying.

"It is not the time," Caine said.

"Do what your father says," Master Khan told him.

We went out of the *Flashback Sequence* to Caine. Katherine was listening to what Brandt and Pascal were saying some distance from them, their voices lowered. Katherine was signing. Caine knew she could hear Brandt sotto voce.

"Get the dynamite," Brant was saying softly. "When we're out of here, blow them up!"

Caine looked at Katherine's expressive face. "You can read his lips from so far away?"

"Yes!" Katherine said.

We go a close-up on Brandt's lips. "Have the explosives ready!"

Katherine turned to Caine with horror. "Explosives!" she said. "He told him to put the explosives into two places."

Katherine was shocked and deathly afraid.

Outside in the street, Peter was wearing a light jacket with a paramedic emblem on it. He opened the back of an ambulance and Dr. Sabourin jumped down. She was a compassionate doctor whom we have seen before on the show. She wore a stethoscope around her neck.

"Are you ready for this?" Peter asked her.

"I am if you are!"

"I am putting your life at risk!"

"I have been there before," Dr. Sabourin said.

Lasher grabbed Peter and whirled him around. It looked as if Lasher was going to strike him, but then he thought better of it. "Any cop goes in there it will be one of my men, Caine!" he said. "You got a hell of a nerve!"

Peter got right into Lasher's face. "You listen to me! My father is in there and my Captain! Now, this doctor is putting her life at risk! Unless you are going to give the order for one of your men to shoot us in the back, we're going in!"

In Kermit's office at the Precinct, Kermit brought up some graphics on the computer screen: "*Infrastructure – Sewers – Old Subway.*" He nodded. "The old tunnels. That is it! Brandt's escape route."

He got to his feet, pulled open a drawer and brought out his custom-made laser gun with the sight mounted on it. He checked that it was loaded.

In the Precinct room, the gang was riveted by the drama unfolding on the TV screen. Skalany and Blake were in their midst. Kermit joined them. On the TV screen we heard Sandra Mason's voice saying. "*Paramedics are getting into the bank.*" Sandra continued onscreen. "*If we could get a word with them! Excuse me?*"

On the television screen it was Peter who turned to Sandra Mason. In the Precinct, Kermit shook his head. "Don't blow his cover, babe! Brandt could have a TV hooked up in that bank hanging on every word you say!" It was obvious that Sandra recognized Peter, but she was savvy enough to know that he did not want to be on camera right now. She turned back from Peter to the camera crew. "*This seems a bad moment. We'll take you over now to the Chief of the Swat Team.*"

In the Precinct, Kermit said: "Skalany, let's go to the bank!" He moved past Blake. "Blake!"

Blake nodded. "Yeah I know. Cover for you!"

"Come with us!" Kermit said. "I need back-up. You remember how to fire a gun?"

For a moment Blake was utterly speechless. Then he reached for his coat. On the TV screen we hear Sandra Mason's voice: "*How dangerous is it for paramedics to go into the bank?*" We heard Lasher's voice: "*I would say very dangerous! But we can't let the man bleed to death in there!*"

We were back in the bank. Barry Sutherland had wired up some explosives to a timer. In another vault, Jane Kurtz had wired up another explosive charge with a timer. There was yet another explosive set in a corner of the vault. Out in the street, Lasher put the bullhorn to his lips. "Back-up unit is ready to come in!"

Peter and a Paramedic Officer moved forward carrying the gurney. Dr. Sabourin was right behind them. In the bank vault, a wall blew out, cascading debris throughout the bank. Matt Benedict said: "Brandt! Time to go!"

In the computer room, Kyle Hoffman pointed his automatic weapon at Megan. He echoed the sentiment. "Time to go!"

Outside we are at a rear entrance to the bank. Three uniformed Swat Officers have taken up their positions. Chief Strenlich was leading them with a gun in one hand and a radio in the other. One of the Officers was fitting an explosive device wired to the back of the bank.

Inside, Brandt moved forward, pulling back the mechanism on his gun. Harlan Pascal accompanied him. "Not much longer, gang!" he promised.

We saw the hostages were all lined up. Brandt nodded at the front door of the bank. "Won't you open the door, Mr. Pascal?" he said, enjoying his moment. "Invite them into our happy home!"

Pascal moved forward, past the assembled hostages. Caine came forward into the center of the group. Peter entered the bank, wheeling the gurney with the paramedic, Dr. Sabourin beside him. Peter was being closely watched by Harlan Pascal and Jane Kurtz, both holding their automatic rifles. Kurtz stopped Peter and frisked him. Then she frisked Dr. Sabourin. The assembled hostages, including Caine, watched them. Peter moved forward, memories from the temple suddenly assailing him.

We go to a *Flashback Sequence* at the temple.

Marauders were removing jewelry from the temple. Caine confronted them with Master Khan. Young Peter watched from the shadows. Caine was angry. "This cowardly act desecrates a holy place! You will leave this temple *now!*"

Caine and Master Khan fought off the attackers. Caine took one of them out on the steps to the temple. Master Khan took out another one with swift kung fu moves, then moved to aid Caine. Caine took out another of the marauders on the steps up to the altar. He threw the last of the attackers down the steps. Master Khan was there to give him back-up, but there was no need. The marauders fled with none of their spoils.

We went out of the *Flashback Sequence* and picked up Peter beside the gurney moving to where the wounded Security Officer lay on the floor. Dr. Sabourin was beside him. Peter felt Caine following his progress, although he did not say a word. Pascal and Kurtz covered Peter and Dr. Sabourin. Peter and the uniformed cop waited with the gurney while Dr. Sabourin knelt beside the wounded Security Officer. She looked up at Brandt who was also following their progress.

"This man will die unless we get him to the ICU Ward in minutes!" she said, urgently.

"Then get moving!" Brandt said, reasonably.

Jerry Maitland suddenly wanted to be a hero. He moved forward and grabbed the gun from Captain Simms that had been nestled in her holster. He shoved her away into a filing cabinet. Caine turned and kicked the gun out of Maitland's hands. He fell heavily to the floor. One of the thieves fired into the air which sent Alicia and Katherine to the floor.

In the computer room, Hoffman reacted to the gunfire. He grabbed Megan.

In the main bank, Matt Benedict let loose with his AK47, strafing the glass cabinets. Caine ducked away from the carnage. Captain Simms cowered down while the bullets decimated the furniture and glass cases around her. Bellamy and Krista covered their heads while the hail of bullets rained around them. Peter threw himself over the body of the guard who was lying on the gurney now.

Outside, Lasher picked up his bullhorn. "Go in!"

Strenlich was wearing a gas mask and so were the Swat Team. They blew the lock on the rear door of the bank. The Swat Team stormed inside. Inside the bank, Matt Benedict's AK47 gun had jammed. Peter climbed the counter and leapt at him, kicking the terrorist to the floor. George Palmer, seeing his opportunity to be a quasi-hero, jumped down on Matt Benedict.

"I got him!"

The Security Officer was lying on the gurney. Dr. Sabourin shouted: "Go! Go! Go!"

Palmer wrestled with Benedict, but Jerry Maitland and another hostage pounced on him, pinning his arms down at his sides. It took four of them to do it. "All right!" Maitland said. "I've got a gun!"

"Where did you get a gun?" Palmer asked, bewildered.

Maitland had no answer for that.

Peter ducked down under the counter in the bank and turned the key there. The blinds there slowly ascended, clearing the window. Outside Lasher motioned to his men. "Fire! Now!"

Three of the Swat Team fired, blasting the windows, sending tear gas cascading into the bank. Three of the tear gas canisters exploded.

"Go!" Lasher shouted. "Go!"

The Swat Team ran forward.

Strenlich and the Swat Team entered by the back door into the bank itself.

Inside, Captain Simms kicked the AK47 from Jane Kurtz' hands and knocked her out. The three hostages were still grappling with Sutherland, holding him down. One of the Swat cops motioned to the hostages to get out. "Okay, everybody out! Move out!"

John Durham manhandled one of the hostages to his feet. "Get back out!"

He helped two more of the hostages get to safety.

"Go!" The Swat Officer ordered. "Move out!"

Caine moved around the corner to face Barry Sutherland. Caine took him out with two kung fu kicks that sent him over a desk onto the floor. John Durham, coughing in the tear gas, looked to where Megan had been held prisoner and moved toward her.

Sutherland, recovered from his fall fighting with Caine, came through the smoke to where two more of the robbers were waiting for him at the blown-out wall. "Where's Brandt?" he demanded.

"Don't know," one of the terrorists said. "Let's get out of here!"

We were in the subway tunnels with Kermit, Skalany and Blake. Kermit had the blueprints of the bank in his hands. "This tunnel leads right now to Maple Street," Skalany said.

"It is part of the old subway system that was abandoned," Kermit said.

Blake was shaking his head. "Pretty long shot!"

"It's the only one I got!" Kermit told him.

In another part of the subway system, Barry Sutherland and the other robbers were running flat out. Brandt paused in the huge hole that has been blown in the wall of the bank, his gun held high. He was holding a canvas bag in his other hand. "Hold on, gang!"

Brandt ducked down into the gaping hole blown in the wall and moved to where there was another hole leading down into the subway system.

We were angled on John Durham, coughing in the tear gas, moving forward. Katherine Duval was kneeling beside one of the file cabinets. Suddenly Harlan Pascal reached down and pulled her up beside him. She was terrified.

"You're coming with me!"

Peter came for him. He raised his AK47 at Katherine. Peter took him out with two swift kung fu kicks.

"That felt good!" he murmured.

He grabbed Katherine and hauled her out of there.

John Durham threw open the door to his office. Megan was there, but Hoffman grabbed Durham. He threw him on top of the desk.

"Leave him alone!" Megan cried.

Hoffman laughed. He looked at Durham scornfully. "She must love you, Durham! I guess you did not notice, did you, old man? You probably don't love girls the way I do!"

Durham was hanging at the top of the desk. He looked down and realized that the desk drawer was open. Durham noted the automatic revolver resting there. Hoffman shoved Megan away. Durham steadied her on the desktop, putting Megan behind him. Hoffman pointed his gun at both of them.

"She goes first!" Hoffman said.

Durham pulled the revolver he had taken from the drawer and shot Hoffman, hitting him in the shoulder. He collapsed onto a couch. Megan hugged Durham to her.

In the subway tunnels, Barry Sutherland and the two other robbers reached a crossroad of pipes. "This way!" Sutherland said. They ran down the echoing pipes. Kermit, Skalany and Blake reached a skeletal staircase in the subway system, clinging to two ladders there.

"Police!" Kermit shouted.

The thieves turned and starting firing. Kermit and Skalany fired back. From his position on the second skeletal staircase, Blake fired his gun. All three of the robbers collapsed under the barrage of fire. Skalany climbed to the underground passageway. Blake climbed from his vantage position further along. Kermit reached the top of the iron staircase. He was smiling. Skalany had the drop on the thieves. Her voice echoed in the tunnels.

"Did I forget to say please?"

Kermit followed her and Blake down the echoing tunnel. "Nice shooting, Blake!" Kermit dragged one of the robbers off the railing where he was suspended. "You have the right to hang there!" Kermit hauled him right over the railing. "You have the right to hang here!"

Then we were back in the bank. Peter was trying to disarm one of the explosive devices. Strenlich moved to him, removing his gas mask. More Swat Officers were behind them.

"Everybody out?" Strenlich asked.

One of the Swat Team said: "Everyone is outside, Chief!"

Peter, with some difficulty, managed to disarm the explosive device. He leaned against it, taking a deep breath.

"How did you know which wires to pull?" Strenlich asked him.

"I didn't!" Peter confessed.

Brandt ran down one of the subway tunnels carrying a large canvas bag filled with jewels and cash. He turned to make sure no one was behind him. When he turned back around he found Caine waiting for him. Brandt leveled his gun at him. Caine kicked it out of hands.

"Would you have denoted the explosives," Caine asked him, "before or after?"

"Guess you are never going to know!" Brandt said, smiling. He reached into his pocket and came out with a small electric device that fit in the palm of his hand. "Since that was the very thing I am going to do right now!"

Caine grabbed the small device out of Brandt's hand like lightning. In the same instant, Brandt opened his hand to show the small device had gone! It had been replaced with a smooth pebble! Brandt was stunned. He lunged at Caine. Caine disarmed him with two vicious kung fu kicks. He collapsed onto the ground. Peter reached the underground subway through some double doors and pulled up beside Caine. He looked down.

"Brandt?"

"Yes!" Caine said.

"The last time we faced odds like these you wouldn't let me help you!" Peter reminded him. "At the temple."

Caine turned to Peter. "This time I could not be happier to see anyone!"

Caine and Peter embraced.

Outside in the street in front of the bank, one of the hostages ran to his wife shouting: "Karen! Honey!"

Strenlich and Captain Lasher were moving past one of the parked ambulances. "Nice work, Frank!" Lasher said. Strenlich said: "I had help, Lash!"

The camera settled on Caine, who was again wearing his fedora hat. He moved from where Dr. Sabourin was treating one of the hostages. He passed Sandra Mason and her camera team. She was interviewing Jerry Maitland.

"Is there a way you can tell me how all this happened?"

Maitland was having his moment in the sun and loving every minute of it! "I grabbed the gun from the robber," he said. "I actually I took two of them out! They did not like that! I don't want to be called a hero, but, you know, if the situation calls for it..."

Caine was past him at this point. Captain Simms stood a little apart with Krista and Tom Bellamy. Krista touched Caine's arm. "Thank you!"

"I'll add to that!" Captain Simms said.

"Both of you showed great courage," Caine said.

"I would have stood by my wife through anything!" Bellamy said.

Krista put her head on Bellamy's shoulder. Caine nodded. George Palmer moved over to them. The bank executive's mood was introspective. Caine knew what was coming next. "Mr. and Mrs. Bellamy, I am approving your loan! We can work out the details later. Let us say the points will be low." Palmer glanced over at Caine. "Some points take time to learn," he added.

Caine gave Palmer a small kung fu bow. He passed Captain Simms who shook her head. She had liked that! Caine moved over to where Alicia and Katherine our deaf girl were standing. Katherine was signing furiously. Alicia looked at Caine for a translation. "What is she saying?"

"She said perhaps you should find yourself another bank?" Caine said.

"Why?" Alicia said and laughed. "I love this bank!"

Katherine laughed. Her laugh was infectious. She gave Alicia a hug. Caine moved on through the aftermath of the robbery. Kermit and Blake stood in front of one of the police cars. Skalany was with them. Kermit was shaking his head. "It's boring!"

"Really?" Blake asked.

"You have to work at it."

Kermit may have been giving Blake a speech about risking their lives. John Durham and Megan moved over to them. Kermit turned to look at Durham.

"Ah!" Durham said. "I take it you received my letter?"

"What letter?" Kermit asked, innocently. "I was just in the neighborhood so thought I would drop in." Kermit's voice was quiet now. "I know the death of your wife has been on your mind."

Durham looked at him and nodded. "A stranger helped me through it."

Skalany smiled, looking at Caine. "I wonder who that could have been."

"Good to see you alive and kicking, John," Kermit said.

"It's good to be that way!" Durham responded.

Megan took Durham's arm. "He was incredible! He saved my life with one gunshot without having to kill that creep who was molesting me!"

"Well, you know old spooks never die," Kermit remarked. "They just get spookier!" Kermit noted Megan's startled reaction. "Oh, you didn't know. John was a member of the Circus in London."

Blake was having trouble following this. "You mean like in Barnum and Baileys?"

Kermit sighed. "No, I mean like Mi6!"

Megan looked at Durham in astonishment. "You were a spy?"

Durham was looking at Kermit with irony. "I'll get you for this!"

Kermit laughed. Skalany moved away to where Caine, Alicia and Katherine were standing together. She hugged Caine. "Don't you ever scare me like that again!" she said. "Now, this doesn't mean you're going to cancel our date for tonight?"

Caine put an arm around her shoulders. "Of course not!"

"Good!"

Peter walked over to them. Caine gave Peter a shrug and walked off with Skalany. Katherine moved forward and gave Peter a kiss. "What's that for?" he asked her.

"Saving my life!" she said. She looked over at Caine. "He is your father?"

"Yes," Peter said. "He is."

"You're very lucky," Katherine said.

"We all are," Alicia said, looking at the place where Caine and Skalany had disappeared.

The camera pulled away from the scene where Jerry Maitland was still telling his tall stories for the benefit of Sandra Mason and her news team.

Chapter Eleven
STORM WARNING

A STORM WAS RAGING IN THE CITY outside the 101st Precinct. Inside in the squad room the Precinct gang was watching a breaking bulletin on the storm. Detective Blake was riveted as was Detective Mary Skalany who was sitting facing the television screen. Peter had sat down at his desk. He was more concerned about the violent argument that was taking place in the Precinct room between Kermit Griffin and his sister Marilyn. Peter did not like the sound of it, but it was none of his business. The newscaster's voice echoed.

"*The resort hotel, the Meriden in Paradise City Beach, has been abandoned. Hurricane Amy is sweeping through the panhandle.*"

Kermit's voice came through from the ajar Precinct room. He was shouting. "It is not open for discussion!"

Kermit slammed the office door. The violent argument had brought Captain Karen Simms out of her office. Detective Blake got to his feet to get a cup of coffee. Mary Margaret Skalany was philosophical about the argument that was taking place in the Precinct.

"I argued with my brother all the same," she recalled. "Usually it was about who got to use my Dad's ancient De Soto on Saturday."

Peter was interested. "What year?"

Blake indicated the closed door of the Precinct where he could see Kermit and his sister still in a heated discussion. "What is going on in there?"

Peter shook head, picking up some files from his desk. "Brothers and sisters fighting. I did not have brothers and sisters, but if I did, I'm sure I would be fighting with them."

"Well, maybe not," Skalany said. "Especially if one of them was an ex-mercenary who killed people."

Captain Simms waded into the argument. "Kermit has his own sense of justice. When he kills people…" Then she faltered. "You know…" She kept the sentence hanging there.

Peter looked up at her. "Bad guys?" he said, ironically.

Simms just handed him a stack of files. "I wouldn't worry about Kermit, Captain," Peter said. "He's mellowed!"

In the Precinct office, Kermit took his state-of-the-art modified gun which he carried at all times. It had a laser sight attached to it which turned it into a very lethal weapon. He was seething. "The subject is closed!"

Marilyn Griffin, Kermit's sister, knew this was a battle she was going to lose, but she had to make the effort. She was feisty and beautiful, but when it came to dealing with her brother she was at a loss. She was also very pregnant at this point. As Captain Simms had just stated, once upon a time her brother had killed people. Bad guys, as Peter said, which Marilyn knew was the truth.

Kermit moved to door of the office and slid his gun into a leather bag. His anger was a palpable force threatening to consume him. Finally he turned back to his sister.

"It's fine for you lecture me, Marilyn!" he said, tersely. "We exorcised the demons from your house, you got a new husband, you got a baby on the way, your life is hunky-dory now. But I got memories that eat at me, they gnaw at me like a cancer and I'm going to kill them before they kill me!"

"So you are going to going kill him!" Marilyn said, horrified.

"I'll do what is right." Kermit said.

"What's right for you!" she exclaimed. "Kermit justice! Can you guarantee me that you will come back, Kermit?"

Kermit zipped up the bag and heaved it upon his shoulder. His rage had somewhat subsided. He looked at his sister with compassion. "If I've learned anything in this life," he said, "it is that there are no guarantees." He pushed some of Marilyn's hair out of her eyes. "Kiss Mitch for me."

Kermit opened the office door leaving Marilyn in tears. He knew the Precinct gang had been listening to every word they could hear through the closed door. "No questions from the floor, please!" Kermit said. He looked over at Captain Simms who had been waiting for him to exit his office. "Captain, I'm going to take that vacation that I've got coming." He looked over at Peter. "Peter, do me a favor, make sure that Marilyn gets back to the Gables safely?"

Kermit was referring to the time when he had visited a house in the country where Marilyn had been living with her daughter Mitch. He had been accompanied by Kwai Chang Caine and Peter to the house where Marilyn had been dealing with some terrifying demons. But that was for another chapter in the book!

Captain Simms fell into step with Kermit as he walked toward the door to the squad room. "I thought we were friends?" she said, quietly.

"We're more than friends!" Kermit acknowledged.

"Then tell me where you are going?"

"I'm just a snowbird flying south to Florida!" Kermit said, wryly.

"I'm not sure that is where I would go for my vacation!" Blake muttered.

On the television screen, the newscaster said: "*Hurricane Amy continues to cut a swathe in the Mid-Atlantic. The storm is expected to make landfall in force in 24 hours.*"

Captain Simms said: "I could stop you from going!"

"No, you couldn't!" Kermit said, darkly.

It was an empty threat. Kermit knew that his Captain only had his best interests at heart. He looked over at Peter. "Don't even ask Marilyn what is going on. She lies outrageously!" He turned back to his Captain. "Goodbye, Karen!"

And then Kermit was gone. Captain Simms was nonplused by Kermit's behavior, but there was nothing she could do about it. On the television screen, the commentary continued: "*And Amy was returning for more punishment!*"

We had a terrific cast for this episode of *Kung Fu: The Legend Continues*. The lead was played by a wonderful actor named Kent Staines. Predictably, the actor himself was a sweet guy who relished playing "bad guys" with psychotic tendencies. I got to know Kent quite well during the filming of the episode. I remember I went to the theater with him where he was playing a major role in a new play called "Poor Superman". It was a great night at the theater. The other members of our *Kung Fu: The Legend Continues* cast were all solid performers. I had a lot of time for one of them, Krista Bridges, who was playing Lorraine Larson. She brought an emotional tour-de-force to her role. Another outstanding performer was Bridget Hanley who played a novelist named Jennifer Campbell. She brought a lot of chutzpah to her role. The other leading heroine in the episode was an edgy, charming actress named Claire Ranken who played the role of Susan Benedict. She was the owner and receptionist for the Coral Reef Hotel on Adderbury Island.

But, as usual, I digress...

We were outside another bar which was a frequent hangout for the Precinct gang called Delaney's Bar and Restaurant. Inside, Terry, our friendly bartender, brought over a cocktail for Peter. "There you go, Pete!"

Peter was sitting at the bar with Marilyn Griffin. On the television screen over the bar they were listening to the news about the hurricane. "*Again, here are the pictures of the devastation brought on by the storm!*" Peter shook his head somewhat ruefully. "If your brother knew I was sitting here in a smoky quiet bar with his sister he'd kill me! What brought you into town and sent him away?"

"It's nothing!" Marilyn said. "Family stuff."

"Family stuff?" Peter said, skeptically. "I know about family stuff! My father would say you are 'extinguishing the light of truth from your chi'!"

Marilyn looked back at him wryly. "Is that the Shaolin way of calling me a liar?"

Peter shook his head. "No, it's my way of telling you that I care about your brother and what happens to him. Help me out here, please. Why did Kermit go to Florida?"

Marilyn took a deep breath. She had reached her decision. "To kill a man named Douglas Larson," she said. "The man who had my younger brother murdered four years ago."

Peter was shocked by the revelation, but he just nodded. "Where is Kermit going to be?"

"At a resort hotel on the gulf coast," she said. "Adderbury Island?"

Peter looked back at the television above the bar. "It looks like he is not going to have trouble finding a room," he remarked with irony. Then he looked back at Marilyn. "And neither will I!"

Caine moved right up to the bar. His manner was ingenuous. "Hi!"

Peter was startled to see him. "Pop! How did you...?" Then he just shook his head. "I don't know why I ask anymore!"

"As a mole senses the rain," Caine said, "I have sensed this storm coming." He looked at Marilyn Griffin. "This storm that will consume and destroy your brother unless we can stop it."

"I can't ask you to risk your lives for him!" Marilyn objected.

"We won't have to," Peter assured her.

"What are you going to do?"

"Help Kermit find the calm within the storm that consumes him," Caine said with finality.

Terry continued to watch the news coverage of the storm on the television screen. "*This is the scene at the beach coast. The National Weather Service has upgraded Hurricane Amy to a four-force hurricane and the full impact of it is expected it in the next few hours.*"

The Florida coast was still reeling from the elements that were pummeling it. Palm trees swayed in the 100-mile-winds that were assailing the hotels on the island. The boulevards were awash with rain that pounded the coast. Tourists were escaping from outside the Coral Reef Hotel where the full brunt of the storm had not yet been felt. Some workers were bringing shutters to nail down the windows. Lou Sheridan, the hotel owner, carried suitcases to a car where a husband and his wife were fleeing the high winds that whipped through the façade of the hotel. The actor playing Lou Sheridan was a larger-than-life character named Peter Jason. He happened to be a close friend of David Carradine and he did a terrific job with his role. Occasionally David Carradine would seek me out about a piece of casting on the show. This was an occasion where his "old friend" Peter Jason came through for us with flying colors.

Lou Sheridan was an affable, gregarious hotelier with a ready smile. One of his guests had just thrown open his car door so his wife could climb inside. Lou had to shout to be heard above the wind that was lashing the front of the hotel.

"Sure I can't talk you into riding it out, Mr. Kendrick?" he asked him. "For no extra charge?"

"I know you've got more sense!" Kendrick said. "This is the worst storm I've seen in a long time!"

Lou dismissed his protests good naturedly. But Kenrick just shook his head. "You would be crazy to stay!"

Lou shrugged. "Where else would I go?"

We go into the Coral Reef Hotel where we establish Bridget Hanley who was playing the role of Jennifer Campbell. She was an eccentric, larger-than-life personality who had been staying at the Coral Reef Hotel for eight months writing a mystery novel and enjoying herself immensely. More guests were leaving the hotel. A man came to the desk where Susan Benedict, the co-owner and receptionist, was checking guests out. He said over his shoulder: "Janet, wait here!" He was carrying a poodle in his arms.

"Checking out, Mr. Morgan?" Susan asked him.

The man nodded and moved briskly away. Jennifer Campbell approached the front desk. "Does this mean I won't have to wait for a table for dinner?" she asked, wryly. "Maybe room service will show up before noon?"

Susan had been dealing with Ms. Campbell for months, but she actually liked the eccentric mystery writer. "Ms. Campbell, will you be needing help with your bags?"

"You mean the ones beneath my eyes?" she asked. Susan suppressed a smile. "Listen, a little Max Factor works wonders. The bags in my room are staying there!"

Susan was amazed. "You're not leaving?"

"Not a chance!" Jennifer said. "A writer needs a little rough sailing to get the juices flowing!"

Carlos, the lone bellhop left at the hotel, waved at some guests as he moved past the reception desk. "Be right with your folks!"

"Listen, I have been here eight months," Jennifer said, "writing a mystery novel in the same room! I don't walk beneath ladders and I just know if I don't finish this book in room 205 I will never know who committed the crime in the last chapter!"

Susan gave her a chit for her room, amazed. "You mean you still don't know?"

"So many suspects," Jennifer sighed, "so few chapters! I just keep changing my mind!"

Susan smiled at the iconoclastic writer as she moved away from the reception desk. Then she went back to work at some cards that were on her desk.

We were at a rental place on Adderbury Island where Peter was pacing restlessly. Rain lashed the opaque doors. The manager, Frank Morgan, who had a major attitude problem, was shaking his head.

"Rent a car to the Coral Reef Hotel on Adderbury Island? In a couple of hours there won't *be* a Coral Reef Hotel there!"

Peter showed the man his wallet and ID. "Police emergency!"

"That isn't valid here!" Morgan said.

Caine entered the rental place completely drenched in the deluge. He shook the excess rain from his fedora. Peter looked at him.

"Pop!"

Caine was looking at the manager. He was all business. "We will take the blue sedan!"

"I can't send you out in this." the manager said. "Company policy."

"Does your company policy cover the renting of unsafe cars?" Caine asked him.

"Three of the seven cars parked outside have bare tire treads. Two others have faulty brakes and three have expired reservations."

Frank Morgan caved in. "I'll get you the keys to the blue sedan!"

"Thank you," Caine said.

The manager proceeded to go outside into the elements. Peter was ironic. "Have you ever thought about being a cop?"

Caine gave him a scathing look.

Rain continued to violently lash the Coral Reef Hotel. Inside the hotel, Lou Sheridan was sitting up at the bar nursing a cocktail. His daughter Susan sat with him. The hotelier had a drinking problem which had worsened since the advent of the storm. Susan did not relish having to deal with her father when he was brusque like this.

"What are you doing, Dad?"

"First break I've had since Art and Jennie left in '94," Lou said.

"Dad, you know what alcohol does to you!" Susan leaned forward to take the highball glass away from her father. "Please don't do this!"

Lou shied away from her. "Beside you, the Coral Reef is all I got! She has survived hurricanes before, but…" He shook his head. "But this one is a doozy!"

He knocked back his cocktail. Someone called from the lobby. "Hey! Anybody home?"

"Do your best, Dad!" Susan implored him.

She moved from the bar through the lobby. Lou finished his glass and got to his feet to follow his daughter. In the lobby area, a man pushed a trolley loaded up with bags. His name was Carl Drake. He had the languid demeanor of a killer. Behind him was another hoodlum, Darin Coltrane, who sported a buzz cut and had an edge of violence. Both of them worked for Eric Larson, the man who had murdered Kermit's brother David some years before. Larson was edgy and given to temper tantrums. Beside him was his wife Loraine, a gorgeous brunette with many anger issues, most of them relating to her husband. She had a petulant quick temper and she made it clear that she was suffering the company of these killers at the Coral Reef Hotel with disdain. Standing beside Larson was a psychotic killer named Mallory who had a veneer of urbane sophistication.

Eric Larson moved over to the desk where Susan was waiting. She was immediately backed up by her father. Larson had a way of unnerving people with his attitude, but right now he was keeping his cool.

"We have reservations," he said.

Beside him, Mallory jabbed at the open register on the desk. "Right there!"

"Perhaps you are not aware that there is a voluntary evacuation order being issued at this hotel?" Susan Benedict said.

Larson's voice was icy. "We're volunteering to stay. And obviously you weren't scared away." He turned to his gorgeous wife whose attitude was even more standoffish. "I told you the reputation of the Coral Reef would not allow a little rough weather to shut it down!"

Behind the reception counter, Lou Sheridan shook his head, smiling. He was proud of the fact that the Coral Reef Hotel was still standing! "No, sir!"

"So they're as crazy as you are?" Lorraine said with an edge to her voice.

Larson kept a rein on his temper, turning to Mallory. "Pay the hotel in advance, would you, Mr. Mallory? Just so they don't think we'll skip out in the middle of a stormy night!" He turned to Lou. "Cash be all right, sir?"

"Fine!"

Mallory took a fat envelope from his coat and deposited it on the reception counter.

"Carlos!" Lou called. He smiled at his new guests. "Carlos will help you up with your luggage!"

Lou moved away and Carlos took his place. He greeted the new guests with a smile. "Yes! Great! Makes me feel it was worth it setting up those tables!"

Carlos left, leaving Larson and Lorraine to see about their luggage. Mallory was watching Susan behind the desk with a predator's air of malevolence. If Susan noticed it she kept it to herself. Drake and Coltrane followed Larson and Lorraine from the lobby area.

Outside the ravages of the storm were massive. Palm trees bent under the weight of the elements. Rain sheeted through the shrubbery on the coast road. Through the deluge Peter's rental car was buffeted by the storm. The windshield appeared to be completely opaque. Inside the car, Peter drove with Caine beside him. The noise of the storm was overpowering. Visibility was down to a few feet.

"Pop, I don't want to alarm you," Peter said, "but I can't see a thing."

"Simply stay on your path." Caine told him.

Peter looked at him. "Is that metaphorical or literal?"

"Both!" Caine said. "We must get to the hotel to keep Kermit on his." He indicated the road ahead which at first glance seemed to be underwater. "Fast!"

Peter turned on the road ahead. Caine knew that something was really bothering him. Finally Peter said: "You know that Kermit's younger brother died of a heroin overdose provided by a man named Eric Larson."

"A scenario suffered by many people in this country," Caine countered.

"Marilyn told me the kid was an undercover cop," Peter said. "They turned him back into a junkie before they killed him. I think you more than anyone would understand Kermit's rage. Now Kermit has somehow found the guy who was responsible for that rage. He is going to kill Larson and I think you would do the same thing."

Caine looked at him. "Blindly seek revenge?"

"I prefer to think of it as getting even," Peter countered.

"You sought out revenge once before," Caine reminded him. "Do you remember, my son? The scroll of Dulay?"

We go a *Flashback Scene* in the temple. A much younger actor, Robert Bednarski, had replaced Young Peter for this one episode only. He did a fine job. Young Peter was dressed in gray robes. Caine wore his saffron robes. Young Peter was cleaning the tiles on the temple floor. Obviously, this was a punishment that Caine had given him. He was not happy about it, but he was resigned to his task. Caine approached Young Peter.

"You have almost completed your penance," he said. "But you harbor vengeance in your heart against your friends."

"They are not my friends anymore," Young Peter said. Then he looked up at his father. "Besides, I said nothing!"

"To suffer in silence will only make the pain greater," Caine said. "I know you did not take the sacred scrolls from the room of antiquity."

"If that is true," Young Peter said, reasonably, "then why am I scrubbing the floor!"

Young Peter went back to his scrubbing with a vengeance.

"You chose to pay penance rather than betray your friends," Caine said. "You feel that once that debt has been paid you can seek vengeance. But vengeance only returns when one is not consumed by it."

Young Peter looked back up at his father. "But I have done nothing!"

Caine knelt down to Young Peter. "That my son is my question! What will you do?"

"Walk away!" he said.

"All right!" Caine said and nodded. "Your penance is completed!"

Young Peter grinned with relief. Caine looked at the tiles with a wry expression. "And I have never seen the stones so clean! You may walk away!"

Young Peter grinned again. "Thank you, father!"

He got back up to his feet, carrying his scrubbing brush with him. "Take your bucket with you!" Caine directed.

"Oh, yeah! Later, father!"

We come out of the *Flashback Sequence* to Peter and Caine driving through the torrential downpour.

"Yeah! I remember!" Peter said. "Do think that general philosophizing is going to work on Kermit?"

"Kermit must carry the burden of his past in his heart," Caine told him. "But perhaps you are underestimating him. He does see his past clearly." Suddenly Caine said: "Turn here!"

Peter turned onto another road which was absolutely deserted. "Please don't tell me that through the eyes of Kwai Chang Caine this is going to be a clear, dry road filled with sunshine."

"Left!" Caine directed him. "Now!"

Peter turned onto another stormy road in the deluge.

We were in the lobby of the Coral Reef Hotel. There were small sounds of activity, but they were muted. Susan Benedict was at her cash register counting money. Above her the lights in the lobby flickered and then went out. Susan looked up. "Oh, great!" she muttered. "Oh, that's great!" She picked up the phone on the desk and sighed. "Dead phone!"

Susan suddenly jumped at the sound of Kermit's voice from out of the darkness. "I didn't mean to startle you!" he said. Susan looked up at him. He did make a striking figure, all in black wearing his trademark dark glasses. "I need a room and refuge from the storm," he said.

"Well, you're in luck!" Susan said, wryly. "I just had a deluxe cancellation!" She indicated the register. "Here!" Kermit signed the hotel register. Susan looked at him as if intrigued. "Do you always wear dark glasses in sunshine or storm?"

"My life gets filtered that way," Kermit said, with no sense of irony. "Do you always ask personal questions of your guests?"

"Sorry!" Susan said. "I am little edgy today!" She reached into a drawer and brought out a key for him. "Here! Room 332. We have one member of staff left, Carlos, who was seeing some diehards up to their rooms. He'll be down to help you with your luggage."

"I travel light," Kermit told her.

The lights came back on in the lobby. Susan nodded, as if to herself. "Back-up generator."

"Good to know," Kermit said.

He moved away. Susan looked after him, still intrigued by his mysterious persona.

The storm continued to pound the Florida coast, bringing with it sweeping rain and more palm trees swaying in the onslaught of the hurricane winds. The front of the Coral Reef Hotel was flooding. In the lobby, Jennifer Campbell came around the corner. "Hi honey," she called out. "I'm home!"

There was no response. Jennifer moved past the reception desk and noted Kermit sitting on his own at one of the tables in the lobby. He was immediately pounced on by the loquacious Jennifer. "Would you like some company?" He was the absolutely the wrong person for Jennifer to accost, but she did not know that. "You look a little lonely." Kermit just looked at her. She turned away quickly. "Perhaps not!" she murmured.

Carlos, the bellhop, moved to the bar where Kermit was sitting. He was carrying three plates of food in his arms. "You ready to order, sir?"

"Coffee is fine," Kermit said.

Carlos moved over to where Jennifer Campbell was sitting at one of the tables. "Carlos, I'll take the usual!" our mystery writer said. "Cripple the steer, leave it at the table and burn those fries!"

Carlos laughed, turning his back to her as he made his way to the other occupied tables. "Yes, Ms. Campbell."

Kermit was watching the three people at one of the tables in the dining room, his expression unreadable. They were drinking coffee. Eric Larson was talking on the phone. Lorraine sat beside him with Mallory on the other side.

"Just after dawn?" Larson was saying. "We'll be waiting." Carlos set the food down at their table. Larson was oblivious to the intrusion. "There is a small airstrip eight miles from here."

Mallory said: "What good does that do for us?"

At this point Larson's attention had been fixated on Kermit. Something about him had unnerved the mobster. He could not take his eyes from the mercenary. Carlos set up the last plate of food for his diners and left. Larson hung up the phone. "Patience was never a virtue of yours, was it, Mr. Mallory? We're going to wait out the storm, then take off at first light."

Carlos came by with hot coffee for Kermit. He reached into his pocket for the check. At his table, Larson was looking at Lorraine who also had also noticed Kermit. "What are you looking at him for?"

"I wasn't!" Lorraine said, defensively.

"Would you like the gentleman to join us?" Larson asked, sarcastically.

"Of course not!" she said.

Mallory smiled, but there was not a shred of humor in it. On the television the commentor's voice continued with the newscast: "*The eviction order to evacuate Adderbury Island has been changed to mandatory. All residents and tourists on Adderbury Island will be evacuated.*"

Carlos dropped the check off for Kermit. "Thank you, sir." He moved away. Kermit got to his feet, putting his wallet away. Across from him, Jennifer Campbell looked up from her dinner as the lights suddenly came back on. She applauded enthusiastically. Having checked out the guests and their threat potential, Kermit moved away from his table. At Larson's table, Lorraine tried to leave but Larsen dragged her back.

"No one is leaving this hotel!" he hissed at her.

Mallory opened his jacket, revealing the gun he carried there. He waggled his hand at Lorraine as if to say: "Naughty, naughty!" Lorraine pulled from Larson's grasp.

Outside in the violent rainstorm a cop car pulled up in the monsoon. A cop climbed out of the vehicle. He wore a Sheriff's uniform and hat and donned a rain slicker. His name was Jack Thorpe. He ran for the shelter of the hotel.

Inside, Lou Sheridan was talking to Susan and Jennifer Campbell. "Well, we have some bad news," he said. "The chef up and quit and he took Carlos with him!"

The Sheriff approached. "Mr. Sheridan?"

Lou turned around. "Yeah?"

The Sheriff took off his hat, facing the guests. "I'm sorry, folks, but you're going to have to leave the hotel right now. I've got a van waiting outside."

Larson got to his feet. "Out in the cold cruel elements? I don't think so, Officer."

"I'm sorry, sir, but I have my orders. It's for your own protection, so if you like to move quickly and quietly."

Larson turned to Mallory. "Mr. Mallory, please do what you do best."

Mallory nonchalantly got up. Loraine jumped up, crying out a warning. The Sheriff pulled out his firearm, but Mallory aimed and fired his weapon in one smooth motion. The Sheriff collapsed to the floor.

"My God!" Susan called out.

Jennifer was rooted to the spot in horror. With the same indifference, Mallory put his gun away again. Susan rushed to the Police Officer while her father knelt beside her.

"Jack!"

"How bad is it?" Lou asked.

Susan had no immediate answer to his question, but it looked very bad to her.

Peter and Caine got out of their car. They walked along the façade of the Coral Reef Hotel in the driving rainstorm.

"Was that thunder or a gunshot?" Peter asked.

"A gunshot," Caine responded. "Someone is injured."

"This way!" Peter said.

Caine restrained him. "There are three men with guns! We must find another way into the hotel."

Caine moved back across the façade, Peter keeping up with him.

More lightning and thunder exploded over the hotel. Rain was sweeping through the foliage. Inside the hotel, Susan brought out a first-aid kit while Larson, Lorraine and Mallory watched. Jennifer Campbell and Lou Sheridan were setting Sheriff Thorpe down on a couch. "That's it, put him down!" Lou said.

The lights flickered, and then came back on again. Susan looked down at the fallen Officer.

"He's in shock!"

In complete control, Larson stepped forward, his voice a husky rasp. "Let us lay down some rules. I am expecting some people to meet us here as soon as the storm breaks in the morning. Everyone stays put and gets along and everyone stays alive!"

Jennifer looked up at Larson, her manner subdued. "I had a villain in the Red Corpse Murders who made a similar speech, a little less stilted, to my heroine and assorted suspects in a hotel very much like this one." The lights flickered once again, more violently this time while Larson watched her. "Then he proceeded to kill them off one by one!"

"I can always revise the chapters with your help!" Larson said, dryly. He turned to Mallory. "Make sure no one goes for a walk in the rain!"

"Oh, I'll keep a close watch of them." Mallory promised. "Fun way to pass the time."

Susan looked back up at him, unnerved and frightened.

We realize that we were now inside the hotel with Caine and Peter, hidden away behind some screens. Chairs were stacked and part of the lobby could be seen. Larson grabbed Lorraine's arm and propelled her forward. Coltrane followed them.

Peter shook his head. "Pop! We've got get to a doctor," he said, urgently.

"No one could reach the hotel until dawn," Caine said. "The bullet did not exit the man's body. I will administer to him when I can reach him without casualties."

"There are only two of them," Peter argued. "We can take them out."

Caine said: "And risk stray bullets?"

Peter sighed and nodded. "You're always right."

"This is not what we came for," Caine added, quietly.

Up in his suite in the hotel, Kermit checked his monster gun to make sure the sliding mechanism was working. A floor beneath him, Larson moved through the lobby. Lorraine was trying to keep with him. She was caustic. "Is the best place you could find on the Florida coast?"

"It suited my purposes," Larson said.

"Why did you want me to come here in the middle of a hurricane with you?"

"You always were begging me to come along on my trips," Larson said. "But not this one?"

"I'm just asking why?" Lorraine said. "You're the one who likes the sound of a human voice."

Larson swung back so Lorraine could face him. "Why are you frightened, Lorraine? Not of me, surely?"

Larson held her in a vice-like grip. She struggled to break free. "You're hurting me!" Then she said in a whisper: "Don't kill me!"

Larson still held her tightly. He appeared to be genuinely appalled at her words. "Kill you? I love you, Lorraine! I do not kill the things I love! We are inseparable, you and I. Get used to that idea. You're never leaving me!"

Larson let her go and started climbing the staircase that led up to the first floor. Lorraine trailed behind him. "Eric, tell me why you wanted me to come with you this time?"

"Because we are not going back," Larson told her. "Not to what we have known. I'm here to collect 20 million dollars in chemicals from our Mr. Dassas." They reached the top of the staircase and Larson strode along the passage. "But the strangest thing is going to happen! The plane goes down in the storm with the goods and the two of us simply disappear!"

Lorraine grabbed Larson's arm. "You're insane! Dassas will find us and kill us!"

"He will not know where to look," Larson said, reasonably.

We noted Kermit moving down the corridor of the hotel carrying his gun pointed down at the ground. He could hear the voices raised in the other corridor that dissected this one. "Trust me, baby!" Larson continued with the same low-key intensity. "I am your meal ticket! I am your life! I've got to be able to trust you!"

Larson suddenly kissed Lorraine. When they broke her voice was somewhat breathless. "You can trust me!" she said. "You know that! Let us go to the suite."

In the far corridor Kermit had Larson and Lorraine in his telescopic sights. As soon as they cleared the passage it was obvious he was going to kill Larson. Then strong arms wrapped around him. They forced Kermit to hang on to his weapon. Larson and Lorraine were now moving down another corridor in the hotel. Momentarily they would be within a few feet from Kermit.

"Kermit, no!" Peter said, urgently.

Kermit allowed himself to be propelled back into another suite. The glass door distorted the images of Larson and Lorraine as they made their way further down the corridor. Kermit turned and slammed Peter against the wall of the suite. His hand was at Peter's throat. Caine was right there with them.

"What the hell are you doing?" Kermit raged at him.

"Saving a life!" Caine said, quietly.

"Saving the life of Doug Larson!" Kermit said, still keeping his choking hold on Peter.

"No!" Caine said, evenly. "Yours!"

Finally Kermit released the pressure on Peter's throat. He moved further into the hotel suite. Caine closed the door behind them. Kermit turned back to face them.

"You just can't help it, can you?" he said, savagely. "You have to play the white knight riding to the rescue!"

"Larson is a killer in his heart," Caine said, his voice still quiet. "You are not!"

Kermit moved away from them. He leaned against the wall of the room as if he had suddenly been depleted of energy. Peter took a tentative step forward.

"Look, Marilyn told us the basics," Peter said. "What don't you tell me the truth about your brother?"

"David," Kermit said, as if he were talking to another person who was not there. He did not continue for a moment. Peter wanted to give him his space. Caine watched the struggle that Kermit was having with his soul.

This sequence had a stellar performance from Scott Wentworth, one of the great actors I have had the pleasure to work with on *Kung Fu: The Legend Continues*. Scott was simply at his best in this heart-wrenching scene. Personally, I thought he should have been nominated for an Emmy for his fine performance.

Kermit took a breath. Slowly he let it out and took off his dark glasses. Memories assailed him about his brother. "It was 15 years ago when he got hooked on heroin." Lights were flickering on and off in the hotel at this point. Kermit barely noticed them, lost in his remembrances. "I was off fighting in some dirty war in a third-rate country that nobody had ever heard of. I was not there for him. Marilyn, she could not handle it. She was just starting out. So finally I got home. I helped David to kick the habit. I got him into the Police Academy with Blaisdell's help. He got stationed in the Panhandle. I went back overseas with Blaisdell to put out another fire in another hellhole. And David, he…" Kermit shook his head. For a moment he could not go on. Then he nodded to himself and turned back to Peter and Caine. His expression had softened. "He was a really good cop! And they assigned him to narcotics to go after Eric Larson. Larson found out about it. And he…" This was very hard for Kermit to put into words. Finally he said: "They shot him full of heroin."

The revelation of that stunned Peter. Caine, however, had been expecting it. Kermit nodded. "So it would appear he had gone back to his old ways." Thunder echoed through the hotel in a loud crescendo. "He died in his own vomit."

For my money this was hands-down the best scene ever filmed for a *Kung Fu: The Legend Continues* episode featuring Scott Wentworth as Kermit.

Caine and Peter reacted to this harrowing story, not really knowing what so say. Kermit put back on his dark glasses. We heard a woman's voice shouting: "No!"

Peter and Caine left the suite with Kermit right behind them.

In the lobby, Susan Benedict was being manhandled by Mallory. His voice was ironic. "Did you think that someone was going to rescue you from the storm?"

"Keep away from me!" Susan warned him.

"Don't worry," Mallory said, taking off his coat. "I'll be gentle!"

Lou attacked Coltrane, one of Larson's hoods, who threw him onto the lobby floor. But then Peter, Caine and Kermit had arrived. Peter faced off with Coltrane. Kermit brought out his gun. "Room Service is really terrible in this hotel. Who do I have to kill to get a sandwich?"

Drake disarmed Kermit with a lighting move. Peter took care of Coltrane with two swift kung fu kicks. Caine fought against Mallory, taking him out. Drake came back, but Kermit knocked him out with a vicious right hook. Peter took care of Coltrane, sending him to the ground. Larson entered from another room with a gun in his hand. Caine turned around and so did Kermit. Larson looked as if he were intrigued.

"Mystery guests in the middle of the night!" he murmured. "You just never know who will come in from the storm!"

Kermit muttered: "Oh, yeah" as he realized the odds were stacked against them.

We do a *Time Cut here*. The Coral Reef Hotel was awash with the rain sweeping across the grounds. Back in the bar, Eric Larson still had the drop on his guests. He did not realize, of course, that the man he really needed to deal with was Kermit, who was there to kill him.

"Who are you people?" Larson asked, as if it was a perfectly logical question.

Lou Sheridan was standing at the back of the room with Jennifer Campbell. Caine and Peter were facing the mobster. Caine gave one of his iconic shrugs. "Travelers. Searching for shelter from the storm."

"Do you usually fight your way into places?" Mallory asked.

"You threatened a woman," Peter said.

"How noble," Larson said. He turned to Mallory. "Search them!"

Larson moved to the desk in the corner of the lounge and picked up Kermit's gun, turning it around in his hands. "Impressive piece of artillery. Going to hunt crocs after the storm?"

"I can't seem to leave home without it!" Kermit murmured.

Malloy had finished frisking Peter. "No ID!" Kermit opened his coat to show them he had no other concealed weapons. "They're clean!" Mallory said.

"Real mystery guests!" Larson observed. "You travel without identification?"

"No, we've got our identification," Peter said. "It's in our rental car which is sitting in a ditch about half a mile down the road."

Mallory turned to Kermit. "And you?"

"I don't carry ID," Kermit said.

"No identity?" Larson asked. "What a wonderful way to go through life! Anonymous! Mr. Invisible! What do you think, Ms. Campbell? You're an expert at reading strangers."

"It's right out of my fourth Jackie Trent novel," Jennifer said. "Death Begins at Forty."

Caine took a step forward toward Sheriff Thorpe who was lying on the couch. Suddenly Larson was screaming at him: "I didn't tell you to move!"

Caine turned back to him. "I am a Shaolin priest," he said. "This man is seriously injured. I can help him."

We saw Susan sitting on the couch with the Sheriff. His eyes were closed, his breathing shallow. Mallory muttered: "He's going to need a priest!"

Larson grabbed Mallory and slammed him against the reception desk. "Touch the girl again," Larson said, tersely, "and you'll find my blood pressure is very high! And you will be wandering in the storm!" Larson turned back to Susan. "My apologies."

"She doesn't need them!" Lou said, vehemently.

"Perhaps you should have your daughter speak for herself," Larson said. "Or don't you communicate? I am a firm believer in paying back for one's actions! 'For there are slaves who fear to speak…'"

Kermit finished the quote for him: "For the fallen," he said.

Larson looked at Kermit, as if gauging his threat potential. "Maybe I should see the eyes behind these glasses!" Larson moved over to Kermit and removed his dark glasses. Kermit's expression was unreadable. Larson was contemptuous. "Not very scary!"

Larson put Kermit's dark glasses back on again. Peter moved up to Larson. "Look, I don't know who you people are, or what you are doing in this fleabag mausoleum, but I need a shower and to get some sleep and I assume you have some rooms?"

"Take your pick!" Lou said, magnanimously.

"All right!" Peter moved Larson's hand away. "Why don't you stop waving the gun around because we are no threat to you."

"I am gratified to hear that!" Larson said. He moved away from Peter. "Enjoy the rest of your night! Help yourself to food and wine. Put it on the tab!"

"I'll do that!" Lou said, truculently.

Larson moved away from Mallory. "Come with me."

Larson was striding down the lobby. Mallory's attention was fixed on Susan. "When I'm done with Larson," he said, his voice like silk, "I'll be back for you."

Susan was unnerved by his intensity. Then Mallory followed Larson out of the lobby. Peter watched his departure and nodded. He felt he had defused the situation for now.

But for how long?

More thunder exploded outside the Coral Reef Hotel. Lightning seared through the clouds, seeming to set them on fire. There was no respite in the elements as they continued to lash the hotel façade.

Caine sat on the couch in the hotel with Sheriff Thorpe. Susan leaned on the couch looking down at the Peace Officer. Lou Sheridan had stepped back. Peter knelt beside the couch. Caine had some herbs in his hand.

"Put this under your tongue," Caine said softly to the fallen Officer. "It will help the pain."

Sheriff Thorpe was delirious. "Trying to think… guests… no strength."

Peter squeezed his arm. "Hang in there! You are doing great."

Lou was restless. Finally he turned to Jennifer Campbell. "Would you care to join me at the bar?"

"It will take the chill out of the night," she admitted, "and my nerves needed coating!"

"Go on!" Lou said and shepherded her toward the bar.

Susan looked up at Peter. "Is he going to die?"

"No!" Caine said, gently but firmly.

Peter got to his feet. Susan looked from him to Caine. "You weren't just travelers caught in the storm."

Peter shook his head. "No! We were not." He indicated Caine. "My father." To Caine he said: "You took my ID and my badge when we came out."

Caine shrugged. "A precaution."

Peter nodded and moved away. Susan looked at the fallen Sheriff as if her heart were breaking. "It was always my fear! That he would get shot in the line of duty. But to think it was here at our hotel!"

"You are very much in love," Caine said.

"We're engaged," Susan said. "My father doesn't know. He wouldn't approve."

"Perhaps he will after tonight," Caine said.

"Dad needs me to help him run the hotel," Susan said. "It's his life! And I need to keep him sober. I can't leave him!"

"Perhaps you must leave him," Caine said.

Susan shook her head. "He's suffered too much."

"Suffering can only be cured by experiencing it," Caine countered. "He needs to face his demons and conquer them."

Susan thought about that. Caine turned to look at the bar area where Peter and Kermit were standing. Peter was trying to get through to Kermit.

"You're a cop!" Peter said. The lights flickered on and off again in the hotel lobby. "You have an obligation to protect innocent civilians."

"I have an obligation to my dead brother!" Kermit said tersely. Peter tried to restrain him, but Kermit pulled out of his grasp. "You stopped me once! You won't do that again."

Kermit moved away from Peter.

Outside the Coral Reef Hotel the storm still raged against the elements. If anything, it was even more violent and terrifying. We found Jennifer Campbell in her room in the hotel sitting at her computer. She was proof-reading a passage from her mystery novel.

"*Jackie Trask was once again caught up in other people's lives and deaths...*"

Around her the lights in her room once again flickered on and off.

We picked up Kermit moving through the bar area. Jennifer's voice continued as she read aloud from her book. "*Who was the stranger with the green glasses?*"

Drake, one of Larson's hoodlums, stopped Kermit. "Where do you think you're going?"

We noted that Larson and Mallory were sitting on a couch in earnest conversation.

"Upstairs!" Kermit said. "It's drier than outside," he added, wryly. He was playing to the others in the lobby. "I'll have room service at 9:00. The usual. Caviar and Dom Perignon."

We hear Jennifer's voice reading from her mystery novel. "*What were these Key Largo gangsters waiting for? What was the mesmerizing power of the Shaolin priest over everyone in the hotel?*"

We went down to the bar where Lou Sheridan was drinking a cocktail. Caine joined him. He stirred his straw vigorously. "This will improve the favor," he said. "Drink! If you believe that is where your courage comes from."

We went back to Jennifer's hotel room where she was reading more from her thriller novel. "*Jackie needed answers! What could she do?*" Jennifer took off her glasses and came to a decision. "She could investigate."

Jennifer moved out into the hotel corridor. She knelt down and proceeded to pick the lock of one of the hotel rooms. She was having trouble with it. "It worked on Murder Train," she murmured.

Finally Jennifer got the hotel door open. For a moment she hesitated, then let herself into room 205. Down in the lobby, Peter moved past Coltrane and Drake. Larson and Malloy were going through a blueprint laid out on a table. Peter moved past the two hoodlums. "Insomnia. I wanted to see if there was anything to eat."

The two hoods looked at Larson and Mallory for guidance. Larson said: "Get him!"

Drake followed Peter as he went into the kitchen, but he was just helping himself to a ham sandwich with mustard.

Up in suite 210, Jennifer Campbell moved to a computer up on a table. Quickly she assessed it, bringing up a screen. A graphic was prominently displayed: *Michaelanglo Dassas Corporation*. Beside it were the letters: *MDC*. Then she brought out another graphic: *ABT-DZP-LSP*. Jennifer wrote the letters down as quickly as she could. Behind her, Lorraine moved into the suite. She had on a full-length sheer nightdress and a flowered-patterned robe. Oblivious to this, Jennifer lifted a suitcase that she had found beside the computer. She looked inside it and gasped.

The suitcase was filled with banknotes!

"Jennifer Campbell," she said with wonder in her voice, "you're playing in the big leagues, babe!"

"Find what you were looking for, Jackie Trent?" Lorraine asked, wryly.

Jennifer whirled around to find Lorraine pointing a gun at her. She tried to regain her composure. "Oh, great! Curiosity of the cat! I am a writer!"

"That's debatable," Lorraine murmured. "I read your last book."

"Murder in the Ruins didn't work for you?" Jennifer asked, horrified.

"It did until the hero got in and out of the lion's den unscathed with the one piece of evidence to convict the villain." The lights in the suite went on and off again. Lorraine looked at Jennifer. "You enjoy living dangerously?"

"It gives me my edge," Jennifer said, as if that was all that mattered.

Lorraine motioned with the gun. "Get out of here!" Jennifer hesitated. "Look, I'm not going to kill you. If my husband finds you in here he will!"

"Thank you!" Jennifer said. She moved past Loraine, then turned back. She could not help herself. "I'll send you an autographed copy of the book I started tonight!"

Lorraine put the gun down onto a table. "Don't bother!"

"Hardcover!" Jennifer said, as if that were an incentive that she knew Lorraine could not resist. Then our erstwhile mystery writer realized it was time for her to leave. She exited the suite through another door. Lorraine moved to some shelves in a closet and picked up a highball glass. She did not hear Kermit entering the suite behind her. We knew she was referring to Larson.

"Dammit, Kermit, why don't you just kill him!"

Kermit moved behind her. "I will!" he promised. Lorraine turned around, startled. "It's what you want. That was why you emailed me!"

"Yes!"

Lorraine moved into Kermit's arms and hugged him fiercely. Then she let him go, pacing restlessly. Kermit waited for the revelation that he knew was coming. "I knew my husband had murdered your brother," Lorraine said. "Doug bragged about what he had done. How David's brother was a mercenary named Kermit Griffin who was searching for him to kill him. I'm sorry about had happened to your brother."

Kermit was unmoved by her words. "No, you're not. You are sorry for what happened to yourself. I have been looking for Larson for a long time. You contacted me yesterday. So why did you need a hitman, Lorraine?"

"He's going to kill me!" she said. "I know too much about him! The odds are about a hundred to one." She swung back to him. "But you can save me! Set me free!" She moved back into his arms again. "Kermit!" She kissed him passionately. Kermit broke her embrace immediately.

"You're grateful to me because I contacted you?" Loraine asked him.

"Just for being a part of it!" Kermit said, dispassionately.

"I am not a part of Larson!" Lorraine said, desperately. She wrapped her arms around him. "I'll give that up."

This time she really kissed Kermit. A noise broke them apart. Loraine was panic-stricken. It sounded as if Larson was coming back into the suite. Lorraine moved to where she had left her gun and pressed the weapon into Kermit's hands. "Here's my gun!"

Kermit glanced at it as he moved away. "Not even loaded."

He moved to the sliding door out to the balcony.

"You will kill Mallory too?" she pleaded.

"He is not part of the equation!" he said.

He climbed out onto the balcony and edged along it, rain sheeting against him, drenching him. Inside the hotel suite, Larson and Mallory entered. Larson stopped in the overlapping shadows, noting that Lorraine was at the balcony window.

"What is the window open for?" he demanded.

Lorraine shrugged. "I needed some air."

Larson grabbed her. "And the rain on your face?"

Behind him, Mallory closed the sliding window.

Kermit climbed up onto the next balcony window and opened the sliding door. In her room, Jennifer Campbell whirled, startled to see Kermit come through the window. He closed it behind him. He looked like a drowned rat.

"Oh, my!" Jennifer exclaimed. "Are you all right?"

"Yeah!" Kermit said. "I like to make a splashy entrance!"

"You're a cop, aren't you?" Jennifer said, sounding excited. "Working undercover?"

"I guess you could say that much," Kermit agreed.

"And that young man, too?" she asked. "Not the priest, his son?" Kermit just nodded. Jennifer was elated. "I knew Jackie – I mean, that my instincts were right!"

"I think you need to stay in your room!" Kermit said. "You'll be safer that way!"

Jennifer had a note for her to give him, but he had already felt the room.

Downstairs in the bar, Caine stirred up another cocktail for Lou Sheridan. He looked as if the flavor and the alcohol were not agreeing with him at all. He indicated the glass. "More?"

Caine just stirred the cocktail and shrugged. Lou drank it all down.

We picked up Jennifer Campbell moving down the corridor in the hotel until she found Peter. He moved her quickly into a billiard room off the lobby. Jennifer was undaunted. "I know that you're a cop!"

Peter shushed her. "Keep it down, please!"

"I've got some info for you!" Jennifer said. "One investigator to another! Read this! I got it from Larson's computer in his suite!"

Peter took a look at the message. "These are all prototypes for designer drugs."

"And Larson's briefcase is filled with money for the purchase!" Jennifer added, dramatically. She lowered her voice to a whisper. "What do we do now, partner?"

"You go back to your room!" Peter told her. "Where it is…"

Jennifer's face fell. "Safe!" She finished the sentence for him. She shook her head. "This never happens to Jackie Trent!"

Peter looked after her as she departed. "Thank you!"

In the lobby, Susan Benedict was giving Sheriff Thorpe a glass of water. At the bar, Lou Sheridan shook his head. Caine was watching him carefully. "I can't see very well!" the hotel manager said. "I feel sick! It doesn't taste good to me anymore!"

"I doubt if it will ever again," Caine said.

Suddenly Lou jumped off his stool and went charging to the restrooms. A moment later Peter found Caine at the bar. "I know why our happy band of gangsters are here. To pick up a ransom. There are exits all over the hotel, so what do we do, Pop?"

Caine was no longer paying attention. He looked up and Peter followed his gaze. "What is it?"

"The storm!" Caine said. "It has broken!"

Peter nodded. "So whoever is waiting for us will be here in a couple of hours."

Caine shrugged. "So, we wait."

We went outside for the first time to see the devastation outside the hotel; fallen tree limbs, palm fords strewn around the grounds. Then we went back into the hotel where Eric Larson was sitting in his hotel suite checking his gun. A restless Lorraine paced in front of him.

"It looks as if we survived another storm, babe," Larson commented.

She swung back to him. "Did we? I don't think so!"

Mallory entered the suite. Larson got to his feet.

"Mr. Dassas landed safely," Mallory said. "He'll be here in an hour."

"Have Drake and Coltrane round up the usual guests," Larson said, "and put them in the bar and keep them there. You and I will await our visitors in the lobby."

Downstairs in the lobby, Lou Sheridan and Jennifer Campbell were manhandled by Coltrane into the bar. Susan Benedict sat on a couch with Sheriff Thorpe who was conscious now.

"All right!" Lou said. "Just take it easy!"

"Sit down!" Coltrane said brusquely and pushed them onto another couch. Then the hoodlum sat down, covering them.

Up in the hotel suite Caine and Peter had found Kermit. "We must make certain that these drugs do not reach the street!" Caine insisted.

"That's all right," Kermit said. "I am a cop! I will do everything I can to help these people! After that, all bets are off! I hope you two do not try to stop me again!"

Caine did not respond, just looked behind him. "Someone is about to enter!" he said, softly.

He stepped to one side. The door opened and Drake entered, pointing his gun right at Kermit. "Hey!" he said, affably. "I wondered where I had left that!"

Hidden behind the door, Peter slammed the door into Drake, knocking him out. Kermit reached down and picked up his huge gun and moved away from Caine and Peter.

Outside in the ravaged grounds of the Coral Reef Hotel, Mark Dassas, the gangster who Larson had been waiting for, stepped out of his rental car. He was a dapper, violent man, well-dressed with no soul. With him were two more hoodlums. Dassas carried a heavy briefcase.

"What is that smell, gentlemen?" he asked. "That sweet smell in the air? Is it the aftermath of the rain? Or the scent of betrayal? Go in first."

"Yes sir, Mr. Dassas," one of the hoodlums said.

In the Coral Reef Hotel, Mark Dassas and his two men were confronted by an angry Eric Larson who was also carrying a briefcase. "What the hell is going on? What are you doing in here?"

Dassas was cool and unperturbed. "A successful businessman always anticipates the competition. Did you really think I would leave this hotel with 20 million in drugs? And the 20 million I already gave you to pay for them?"

Larson pulled out his gun, but Mallory disarmed him and pointed the gun right at him. Larson was livid and seething. "You bastard!"

Mallory's tone was mocking. "You just figure that out?"

Dassas's voice had an edge to it. "Thank you, Mr. Mallory. You just got Larson's job."

Then Drake moved Dassas out of harm's way as Peter and Caine entered the fray in the lobby. Caine disarmed Mallory and knocked him to the floor. Peter took care of Drake. Mallory was back up on his feet at this point, but Peter sent him back to the floor with two vicious kung fu strikes. Lou Sheridan moved forward to where Coltrane was covering him. Sheriff Thorpe managed to get to his feet and rush the hoodlum, knocking the gun out of his hands. Susan and Jennifer Campbell were also on their feet. Lorraine ran into the action. She was casually dressed now but kept in the background.

Lou knocked Coltrane out cold. Then the Sheriff collapsed back onto the couch. Lou tossed Sheriff Thorpe his gun. Mark Dassas just walked away from the mayhem. Peter whirled. He executed two more kung fu kicks that sent Dassas to the ground. Larson had recovered his briefcase and was headed for the door.

Outside, the mobster was confronted on the grounds by Kermit Griffin. He had his gun trained directly at Larson's chest. Kermit's voice had no emotion in it at all.

"You know who I am, Larson?" That brought Larson up short. He had no idea who Kermit was. "The name's Griffin. You remember my younger brother? Detective David Griffin? The cop you turned back into a junkie."

Now Larson had put it all together. He was suddenly terrified. He fell to his knees, still clutching his briefcase. "Please, don't!" he pleaded and set the briefcase down. He knew he was staring death in the face. "Don't!"

Behind Larson, Peter emerged out of the hotel with Lorraine and Jennifer Campbell.

Kermit was in total control. "You are a firm believer in being paid back for one's actions. 'For there are slaves to fear to speak for the fallen.' I am speaking now for my brother!"

Lou Sheridan joined the others standing in front of the hotel. Kermit aimed his monster gun right in Larson's face. Larson cringed where he was kneeling. Peter took a step forward.

"Kermit!" he shouted.

Caine stood beside Kermit now. He motioned for his son to back off. "Peter! Do not interfere!"

"Don't get cute, Caine," Kermit said. "No melting the gun and burning my hand!"

"I will not," Caine promised him, quietly.

"Pop!" Peter said, taking another step forward.

Caine's tone was resolute. "I will not!"

Larson was pleading for his life. "Don't let him do this to me! You can't stand there and watch him execute me!"

In front of the hotel, Lorraine and Lou continued to watch with a morbid fascination. Peter stood his ground. Kermit had his gun aimed down at Larson who was groveling now, gasping for air. Caine just watched. Kermit wrestled with his life-and-death decision. Then he brought his gun away from Larson's face and took a deep breath. "I guess my brother speaks to me louder than anyone," he said, softly.

Kermit lowered his gun.

On his hands and knees, Larson glanced up. Kermit turned away from him. Larson took out a small gun from his pocket that he had been concealing and aimed it. Kermit turned back and fired, blowing the gun out of Larson's hand. Then Kermit walked away.

Peter hauled Larson onto his feet. "Get up! Time to go!" He picked up the fallen briefcase and manhandled Larson back to the front of the hotel, his hands behind him.

Kermit leaned against some ornate scrollwork. His fury had been spent. Caine moved over to him.

"Did you know the path I would take?" Kermit asked him, softly.

Caine nodded. "I did," he said.

"Well, I didn't," Kermit confessed.

He watched Peter, Lou Sheridan and Lorraine move into the hotel with Larson with them. Jenner Campbell hustled to join them.

"Not until the last moment," Kermit said." He looked back at Caine. "Thanks, Caine." Caine gave him one of his elaborate shrugs. "Listen, would you do me a favor?

I would like to keep my reputation intact. So if anyone asks how you stopped me, could you just tell them that you wrestled me to the ground?"

Caine smiled, very much a la Kermit. "Oh, yeah!"

The two of them shook hands.

A clean-up crew had moved to the front of the Coral Reef Hotel. A taxi pulled up at the hotel façade. Things were getting back to normal. The guests and residents were all gathered in the lobby area. Susan Benedict held Sheriff Thorpe's hand. He was wearing a sling and looked as if he had recovered somewhat from his injuries. Peter sank down onto one of the easy chairs.

"I just got off the phone with the Chief of Police," he said. "I guess these other mobsters were surprised to find a hotel of cops waiting for them!" Peter turned to the Sheriff. "How is your shoulder?"

"It is good enough to keep me out of ICU," he said.

"Well, thanks again for your help," Peter said. "We would never have made it without you!"

"I hate to say this to a fellow cop," Sheriff Thorpe said, "but I've decided to quit the force."

"Jack is going into the hotel business," Susan said. "Maybe the three of us can make this hotel into a profitable business."

Lou was in deep discussion at the bar with one of the guests. "Should have the place up and running by tonight!"

Jennifer Campbell jumped to her feet. "Before the two of you return to wherever you are from," she said, "I just need a few hours of your time!" Caine glanced over at Peter. This did not sound too promising. "I am making you guys the heroes in my new novel: 'Coral Reef Murders!'"

"Who is the hero?" Caine asked, mildly.

"Why Kermit, of course!" she said.

Caine shrugged. "Of course!"

Carlos, reinstated, came around the corner carrying some suitcases, followed by Kermit and Lorraine. "Your taxi is waiting, Mrs. Larson."

"Call me Lorraine," she said. "Thanks, Carlos." He moved away. Lorraine turned to Kermit. "I'm sorry I made you clean up the mess I have made of my life! At the same time, I couldn't trust a stranger."

"My life got destroyed a long time ago," Kermit told her, gently.

"I don't believe that!"

"So are you going to testify?"

"I am going to sing my head off!" Lorraine promised him.

"The authorities will protect you," Kermit said.

Lorraine moved closer to him. "Can I talk to you sometime?"

"You know where to email me," Kermit murmured.

Lorraine gave him a chaste kiss on the lips. Then reluctantly she moved away from him.

"Goodbye, Kermit."

Before Kermit could even acknowledge the tender moment, Jennifer Campbell had pounced on him. "I am just going upstairs to get my cassette recorder. Do not go away." she threatened him. "I shall return!"

Further down in the lobby, Caine and Peter walked away from Susan Benedict and Sheriff Thorpe. Something was on Peter's mind.

"When it looked as if Kermit was going to blow Larson away," he said, "why didn't you do something Shambala-like?"

"If you understand this, you must understand the nature of the hurricane," Caine said. Kermit pushed his dark glasses higher on his face and just smiled.

"Explain," Peter said.

"The raging storm gathered its power over the water and released its fury on the land," Caine said. "Once it had run its course, it became a nourishing rain again."

Peter smiled. "I like that."

Caine nodded. "I knew you would."

"So Kermit is safe?" Peter asked him.

"For the time being," he said, quietly.

Peter nodded and put his arm around his father's shoulders. "It felt good being able to rescue Kermit from himself."

"That was the general idea," Caine said. "I am glad it worked out so well."

Peter nodded. "Like you knew it would," he said.

Caine just shrugged and smiled.

Chapter Twelve
DRAGON'S LAIR

THIS EPISODE OF *KUNG FU: THE LEGEND CONTINUES* contained classic elements of mystery and suspense. It featured the Precinct gang in a way that uniquely showcased their talents: Captain Karen Simms, Detective Jody Powell, Detective Mary Margaret Skalany, Chief of Detectives Frank Strenlich and Detective Blake. It was a lot of fun for me to write. The episode also introduced a great of friend of mine, Patrick Monckton, who was a quirky and a one-of-a-kind performer. He had been one of my best friends since we were thirteen years old. A very funny guy who brought some chutzpah to his role. My friend Simon Williams had described Patrick Monckton in a great quote: "*Monckton Come, Buffalo die!*" That always made me laugh!

Another member of the cast of *Kung Fu: The Legend Continues* was a young Ryan Gosling. He went on to perform as an actor in *The Notebook, First Man, Blade Runner 2041, Half Nelson* and *La La Land*. He played one of the teenagers caught up in this dark tale of a demonic game that was being played in an abandoned mansion surrounded by overgrown grounds. Kermit was the only member of the Precinct gang who was relatively unscathed, but I do not want to give too much of the plot away!

We started on the abandoned old mansion where the grounds were unkempt and overgrown. The windows of the house looked foreboding. We saw a *For Sale* sign among the tangled weeds. The whole place had an air of decay and desolation. We went inside the house where the shadows were myriad and eerie. A group of teenagers had entered the house. They were led by a brash, cocky young man named Rick, although at this point he was wearing a frightening demonic mask. With him was Cindy, an attractive teenager who was more than a little skittish. Wally was their leader, a studious young man who should have known better than to enter a haunted house. The last of our stalwart band was Kevin, a shy, unassuming young man who had already decided that this haunted house gig was a very bad idea. But their sense of adventure was not going to be deterred. Our band of intrepid adventurers moved further into the mansion. They were carrying four powerful flashlights.

"I don't believe we're doing this," Cindy said in hushed voice.

"I don't think this a very good idea," Kevin added, the most intimated of them. "I heard this place was haunted!"

"It's just abandoned!" Wally, who was their leader, said. "It's been this way since the Chung family moved out years ago."

"Yeah, Wally's right, it just old," Cindy said.

A voice echoed in the creepy stillness. "And *Damned*! Damned!" That was followed with a burst of maniacal laughter. The kids trained their flashlights on a hideous face leering out at them from the darkness. It had glowing red eyes with massive teeth and the snout of some Devil Monster. The rasping voice echoed in a sing-song cadence: "I have come for your souls!"

Then the "monster" removed the frightening mask which had hid his face and dropped it onto the floor. This was Rick, the last of our fearless band of entrepreneurs. He was a snide, nasty piece of work who reveled in being an outcast.

"Very funny!" Cindy said, but the incident had, in truth, scared her. "You can take off the other death mask now!" she added.

"Nice one, babe!" Rick said, knowing he had just scared the hell out of her.

"Midnight at the old Chung House!" Wally said, moving to the front of the group. "Okay, we're here! Love the ambiance. Chills down the spine. So what?"

Rick shone his flashlight ahead of them. "See that door? I was in here last night! That room wasn't there!" Cindy tried the door. "It's locked!"

"I know!" Wally said. "That was the reason I told Rick to bring his tools. Because there isn't a room he cannot get into!"

And just like that the room opened up, although none of them had entered it as yet. For the first time, Rick looked a little intimidated. "Nice one, Wally!" he murmured.

The inherent evil had not registered with any of them as yet.

The four teenagers ventured into the room. Myriad candles were burning everywhere. Their flashlights probed the darkness, revealing tapestries on the walls, old rusting trunks and grotesque masks.

"I recognize this stuff!" Cindy said. "It's like we're in a museum! How did it get here?"

"Who has the keys?" Kevin asked, his voice betraying his emotions.

"Very good question!" Rick said.

The foursome moved forward through the overlapping shadows, and then Cindy's flashlight landed its glow upon an old trunk in the center of the room.

"Check this out!" she exclaimed. "This trunk must be a million years old! There is writing and some kind of strange hieroglyphs written all over it."

"Actually," Wally said, "this is written in an ancient dialect that I can actually understand! I took some courses while I was researching Egyptian hieroglyphs." He read the Change Cards as if this was a game of monopoly. "*Roll the dice if you dare and face the Dragon in its lair!* This is kind of a game."

"Let's play it!" Rick urged.

"Look guys, let's just go!" Kevin said.

"Are you as chicken as your brother?" Rick asked him.

"Open it up!" Cindy urged.

The four adventurers opened up the Game Box. Immediately a choking mist arose from it. The game was laid out in various compartments with the demonic game pieces separated and Dragon's Lair Cards were neatly stacked. "Like no one has opened this box for centuries!" Cindy exclaimed.

"Look at these playing pieces!" Wally said. "Lawyers, knights, demons! All of them life size!" Rick turned the playing piece around in his hands. "I wonder who he is?"

From there we went to Kwai Chang Caine's apartment in Chinatown. Caine was playing his flute, as he does from time to time. He stopped playing as a sense of foreboding came over him. He looked around the apartment. He could not see anyone threatening, but he felt the demonic power of the game pieces weighing heavily on him. He suddenly staggered as if he had been struck in the face. In a few moments he had recovered. The Ancient stood in front of him with a grin on his face. He was holding a Japanese Bonsai Tree in his hands.

"Happy Birthday!" the old man said.

Caine accepted the Bonsai tree. "I am honored!"

The Ancient bowed.

"If there are other gifts here I will strangle you!" Caine warned him.

The Ancient laughed. "I have followed your wishes! No one knows of this momentous occasion!" He lowered his voice conspiratorially. "Not even Peter!"

"It has always been our secret!" Caine said.

Cheryl Hines, who was being played by Calista Carradine, David Carradine's real life daughter, stepped out of the bushes. She was also grinning. "Until now!"

We went back to the haunted room where the Game Players were gathered. Wally was the leader. "The rules for the Dragon's Lair!" he read. "A game of peril!" Beside him, Rick was getting impatient. "Come on! Come on! What else does it say?"

"These are not exactly the rules for Monopoly, you know," Wally said, irritated with Rick. "Which would be in English! Okay, I got it! The object of the game is to destroy the Dragon Lord and his allies by casting spells of ever-increasing power." Our Game Players set out the life-size figures. Wally said: "The Dragon Lord was found in his temple. He must identify his troops: *The* Virmin, the Princess Morgana and the White Prince. Then he may enter the temple and fight the Dragon Lord to the death. Roll, Cindy!"

Cindy rolled four of the many-sized dice.

Back at Caine's apartment, Caine had suddenly become faint and disoriented. Cheryl and the Ancient helped him sit down in a couch in his apartment. He was feverish and it did not seem as if he knew where he was.

"Caine!" Cheryl said. "What's happened to you? What is it?"

"I don't know!" Caine said. "A great force blinded my senses, obliterating them with a light so bright it overwhelmed my eyes."

"What is it you can feel?" the Ancient asked him.

"I can feel... *nothing!*" Caine said.

Then we were back around the Game Table in the haunted house with our four heroes. Wally was reading the hieroglyphs and arcane symbols that covered whole pages. "We travel through the realms on the way to the Dragon's temple."

"Something about this game sends chills down my spine!" Cindy said. "I mean, who did light those candles? And what was that light coming out of the game? It is like someone was waiting for us. Like he's watching us right now!"

"Come on, guys," Rick said, "we're playing this game! Look at all this cool stuff! Warriors battling it out with evil wizards. This is a blast! Read on, Wally!"

"Everyone has to become a character in the game," Wally said. "One person acts as the Game Master and runs the game and reads the rules."

"That would be you, Wally," Cindy said.

"Well, I don't speak Chinese!" Wally said. "But okay! Everyone has to pick a character."

Rick picked up his character, a black-suited warrior who is at least seven feet tall. "That's cool!"

Cindy chose another of the life-sized figurines. "Sorcerer!" she said. "Pretty neat!"

Kevin picked up a monk! "No way!" he said. "Does this mean I am going to die?"

Which brought peals of laughter from the others. At this point we traveled past the Game Board where the shadows had taken over the room. A strange figure had materialized out of the gloom, a demonic, frightening monk in black robes with a mask that covered half of his face.

"Play the game, children!" the monk said in a harsh voice. "Destroy the Dragon Lord! Begin with his friends! With Caine's friends!"

We tracked back through the shadows. Kevin rolled the dice. "Think of a deadly spell!" he said.

He picked one of the Game Cards which was sitting in a pack and turned it over for the others to see. "Confusion!" Wally said. "You begin in the realm of the Dragon Warriors. The one who protects the Dragon Lord."

"You make them sound like cops!" Cindy said and laughed.

We went to Delancey's Restaurant and Bar near the Precinct. The Precinct gang was moving to a table, led by Chef of Detectives Strenlich, Detective Jody Powell and Detective Blake. With them with was the museum curator, a larger-than-life, droll figure named Martin Blythe who wore a bowtie at all times. He was full of good humor, which sometimes abandoned him in moments of stress.

"What a splendid place!" Blythe enthused. "It reminds me of my little pub in Popplewich. That is the English village I am from in England. Yes, it is quite…" Blythe shook his head and removed his glasses, which was a habit he had picked up over the years. "Actually, it is not like that at all! I'm sorry; I tend to ramble like this when I am nervous."

Terry, our friendly bartender, came over to the table. "Usual, kids?"

"Yes!" Blythe said immediately. "A whiskey, some Benedictine and a large ginger ale."

"That's what we call a Bobby Burns," Terry said.

"That's splendid!" Blythe said. Terry made his way back to the bar. We had the feeling that the museum director was searching for the right words. "It's like a Rusty Nail or a Harvey Wallbanger!" Blythe elaborated.

Jody and Strenlich exchanged glances.

"What are you so nervous about, Mr. Blythe?" Strenlich asked him. "We didn't invite you here to give you the third degree."

"Just to ask you some questions," Jody said, reasonably.

"Like how a large valuable Chinese exhibit can disappear from a museum overnight!" Chief Strenlich said.

"Cameras picked up zilch!" Blake added.

"I'm leaning to the idea of an inside job," Jody said.

Blythe was affronted. "That is preposterous! My employees' credentials are impeccable!"

"But are yours?" Strenlich asked him.

Blythe looked at the Precinct gang. "Am I under arrest?" he demanded.

"If you were under arrest, Mr. Blythe," Chief Strenlich said, "we would be having this conversation at the Precinct and not in a bar that reminds you of your little pub!"

We were back in the Game Room with our four Game Players. "We introduce the Dragon's Lord son, the White Prince!" Wally said.

Around the Game Table, one of the huge figures was set down by Cindy.

In Delancey's, Peter joined the Precinct gang, giving Terry a wave. "Terry!"

"Hey, Peter!"

Peter sat down at the table. "Hey! I just spent ten fun minutes under a bridge with Donny D where the graffiti had graffiti. Word on the street that no one has any knowledge of the artifacts in the hothouse."

"Hothouse?" Blythe asked, confused.

"Street slang for black market operations," Jody said.

Blythe nodded. "Ah!" he said.

For the first time we noted that Captain Karen Simms was standing near their table.

Peter said: "What we were looking for is a collector, someone who knows the value of the shipment."

"Kermit says it is priceless," Strenlich added.

Captain Simms moved over to their table. But this was a Karen Simms we have never seen before. Her expression was distracted. "The only collection of Chinese artifacts that I know of belongs to the Ancient," she said.

"That's right!" Blythe said. "He was at the museum yesterday! He spends all day in the Chung Room!"

"Captain, are you saying that you suspect *the Ancient*?" Peter asked her.

"Well, I don't know," Captain Simms said. "But it fits the profile you have described." Peter glanced away. He was not buying it. "He is obsessive about Chinese history," the Captain added. "Magical, in fact."

Jody echoed her word. "Magical?"

"Well, yes, he is just like…Caine," Captain Simms said. "Isn't he? I mean, he gets in and out of places and no one knows how he does it." She thought about that. "Doesn't he?"

Blake reacted with skepticism. Captain Simms seemed to be very distracted now. "I'm sorry," she said. "I am a little confused. I think I have to leave now."

She turned away from the table, then she started to inexplicably rearrange the settings at another table.

"I'll go and check on the museum stuff," Peter said. He got to his feet and followed Captain Simms. "Captain?" He reached the other table and stopped the Captain from leaving. "Captain, is there something wrong?"

"No, I am fine, Detective," she said. "I just needed to get out of a smoke-filled room and get some air!"

We went back to the mansion and the Games Room. Wally had picked up one of the massive figurines to place on the game board. "Morgana, the Witch, not remembering any of her spells! 15-point advantage to the Dragon Warrior! Nice one, Kevin! You move forward!"

We went back to Captain Simms and Peter. She had moved away from him and collided with a guy who was very drunk. She was not looking where she was going. The drunk was very apologetic.

"Sorry! Look, leave me your jacket and I'll get it cleaned!"

Simms reared back from him. Then she slapped his face. "Stay out my way!" She turned back into the room. "I am a Police Captain!" she shouted. Strenlich and Jody were staring at her. "Don't you forget that!"

Then we were back in the Games Room. Kevin was elated as he got into Rick's face. "I told you Morgana can kick butt!"

"Oh yeah?" Rick retorted. "Well, wait until you see what my assassin does! My roll!"

Cindy suddenly looked at her watch. "Oh, my God! Is that the time? Mom is going to kill us! Come on, Kev!"

"Okay, everyone must leave everything the way it is! We will pick it up in the morning!"

"Okay, ten o'clock," Wally said. "And don't tell anyone. We might have to move our stuff."

The Game Players got to their feet. We went through the overlapping shadows in the room until we were close to the Demon who was controlling the game. His eerie mask still covered half his face. "No, we mustn't break the spell, children!" he said in his sing-song voice. "I feel the presence of Kwai Chang Caine. You seek me, but you will never find me!"

We went to Caine's quarters where he sat in meditation. The Ancient and Cheryl sat in front of him at a series of screens. "I can see my enemy location!" Caine said. "But is it enough?"

"Where is it?" the Ancient asked him.

"I don't know," Caine said. "A corridor that leads to a room." He shook his head, as if in despair. "You must leave me now!"

"Very well," the Ancient said.

He and Cheryl got to their feet and left Caine isolated and alone.

We went to Cindy Foster's house, a modest, two-story townhouse in the suburbs. Cindy was engrossed in some drawings of demonic symbols at her desk. Her mother Rachel entered her room. She was a loving, carefree spirit, in her thirties, with a sense of adventure and humor.

"How is it going?" she asked her daughter.

Immediately Cindy gathered her drawings and stuffed them in the top drawer of her desk. Her mother approached her. "The Sandman has been trying to get back to you!" she said.

"And little girls should be on the boat to Sleep Byes Island before it sails without them!" Cindy sighed. "How many years have you been saying that to me now?"

Rachel flopped down on Cindy's bed. "Since you were born! Where did you go out? I thought you were going to the mall?"

"You're checking up on me now?" There was an edge to Cindy's attitude, but Rachel chose to ignore it. "I was out walking the dog," her mother said. "Can I see your drawings?"

"No!" Cindy said, quickly. "I'm just fooling around with these images. We were at Rick's place, shooting basketball hoops."

"I thought you didn't like the quarterback with an attitude very much?" Rachel said.

"What is it with the 3rd degree?" Cindy asked.

"I am just doing Mom in the bed stuff," Rachel responded. Her daughter's attitude was starting to worry her. "What's wrong? You seem edgy."

"Nothing!" Cindy said, as if it was no big deal. Rachel got up from her bed. Cindy gave her Mom a kiss. "I'm going to brush my teeth before Sleep Byes Island!"

Cindy moved away. Rachel looked after her, concerned.

We hear the Game Master's Voice. "We'll play the game tomorrow, children!" he said, hoarsely. "So that Kwai Chang Caine may die!"

The next day we returned to the Game Players in the Chung House. Our four Games Players were gathered around the game board. "Now we send the Dragon's troops into full disarray," Wally said. Rick picked up the dice. "Playing out their fantasies!"

We moved over to the Precinct building where we can see that the usual chaos reigned.

"Where's Broderick?" Peter asked, heading to his desk.

"Gone fishing," Strenlich answered, shortly.

"I didn't think he had any days off?" Peter said.

"He doesn't!" Strenlich said. "That's my concern as Chief of Detectives, not yours, Peter!"

Peter was surprised by the tart response, but he decided that was Strenlich just having a bad day. He paused beside Detective Blake. We note that he was impeccably dressed today. "Something wrong?" Blake asked.

"That suit!" Peter said. "Did you take out a second mortgage for that, Blake?"

"You know I like to look good, Pete. You might think about starting a new wardrobe for yourself!" Blake took out a card from his pocket and handed it to Peter. "See my tailor! A well-dressed cop is an efficient cop."

We returned to the Games Room with our teenage players. Cindy rolled the dice. "Nice roll, Cindy," Wally said. "With seduction you weaken the Dragon Lord's son and the Dragon Master himself!"

"Sixteen points!" Cindy exclaimed.

Back at the Precinct, Jody moved up to Peter who was sitting at his desk. She was dressed in a jean jacket with a disturbingly low cleavage. It was all Peter could do to keep his eyes on her obvious attributes. "Here are you!" Jody handed him some files and leaned over him so that her breasts were literally in his face. "I was hoping that you and I could work these files together! Very closely together." Peter was having trouble keeping his eyes focused where they should be. "I thought that you and I might look at the Tao-Chung exhibit. There might be a secret room." She leaned down. "Of course, I wouldn't want to get trapped with you! But, then again, that might not be so bad!"

"What the hell is going on around here?" Peter demanded. "Broderick takes a trip on his vacation days! Strenlich just took my head off! Which he usually does but he did not have a good reason. Blake looks as if he was out of GQ and you're…" Peter faltered. Jody leaned down again. "Very close!" Peter murmured. "Aren't you and Skalany supposed to be working on a jewelry robbery?"

"Who?" Jody asked.

Peter looked at her as if she had lost it. "Skalany?"

Mary Margaret Skalany entered Caine's quarters. This was a Skalany we had never seen before. She was wearing a short-flowered dress and carrying a picnic basket and there was a kind of whimsical expression on her face. Caine was going through his kung fu exercises, wearing his silk Kung Fu shirt. At first he did not see her, or rather, if he did he ignored her.

"Hi there!" Skalany said, all smiles.

Caine still ignored her. Skalany would not take no for an answer. "You look as if you need to take a break!" She opened the picnic basket. "Champagne? Truffles? Tofu?" Finally Caine looked at Skalany, somewhat nonplussed. Skalany tried again. "Picnic at the park! You and me!"

"But don't you have to work?" Caine asked her.

"I took the day off!" Skalany said.

Caine warily approached her. "It is very sweet of you to ask, but I cannot." He gave Skalany a kiss. "It is time well spent," he said.

Skalany gave him a wistful smile. "Story of my life."

Then she moved away from Caine's quarters.

Back in the Games Room in the abandoned mansion, Cindy said: "The Dragon's Mistress beguiles and smothers him!" But it was Rick who was livid at one of Wally's moves. "This is a joke! Assassins use emotions to their advantage!"

"Well, pick a card," Kevin urged.

Rick turned his next card over and showed it to the table. Wally was following the game in his large book of spells. "The spell of treachery!"

"Merlin, the Dragon's magician, is about to be betrayed," Rick said.

We went to a Tarot Room where the Ancient and Cheryl were facing a young Oriental woman. Her name was Yo-Nee. Cheryl leaned over to the Ancient. "I feel stupid doing this!"

"Do not mock the power of the cards!" the Ancient said. "They can tell us what is afflicting our dear friend Kwai Chang Caine."

Yo-Nee turned around more of the Tarot cards she had dealt. "The cards talk about great danger," she said. "And a magician! A Games Master! Playing with people's emotions and their vulnerabilities. Their very lives!"

"Does this Games Master have a name?" the Ancient asked.

"The cards will not tell me this!" Yo-Nee said.

"Turn the next card, Yo-Nee!" the Ancient urged her.

Yo-Nee turned over the Tarot card. "You!" she said. "The old one! You know of this evil Games Master. He will strike at you next!"

The door opened and Chief Strenlich moved into the room with Jody, who was still wearing her low-cut outfit. The Ancient stood. Strenlich was all business. "Chief of Detectives Strenlich, 101st Precinct. You are the one they call the Ancient?"

"You know that as well as your name, my friends!" the Ancient said.

"We're not your friends today!" Jody told him.

"You're under arrest on suspicion of robbery!" Strenlich said.

Cheryl jumped to her feet. "What are you talking about?"

"Stay out of this!" Jody advised her.

"The Tao-Chung exhibition at the Museum of Life had been robbed," Strenlich said.

He shook out his handcuffs to take the Ancient away.

"There's no need for that!" Cheryl exclaimed.

Strenlich ignored her and moved away with the Ancient. Jody got into Cheryl's face. "Don't make me pull my gun!" she warned her. Cheryl backed off. Jody turned to Yo-Nee. "Sorry to break up your little card game."

Left alone, Yo-Nee turned over the next card in the Tarot pack. She reacted to it. A foreboding, malevolent card. "Wei-Chi!" she said, softly.

The Games Master's room was still wreathed with shadows. Our Game Players were playing the Dragon's Game with a frightening intensity. "Old Merlin is spinning in his square!" Rick chortled.

"Yeah, that's a good square, but wait until I roll," Cindy said. She checked her watch. "After lunch!"

"Do we have to go now?" Kevin demanded. "Let the Dragon Lord get into the realm of anarchy in the next roll!"

"This from the kid who didn't even want to play!" Wally murmured.

"Meet back here in two hours?" Rick said.

Camera tracked back in the shadows to where the Demon Lord was waiting. "They're closing on the temple," he said in his hoarse voice.

In the Precinct, Kermit Griffin was at his computer. His door was open. He was dressed in his usual black suit with a slim tie, his hair long, wearing his trademark dark glasses. Martin Blythe entered his office carrying four large books.

"Ah! There you are!" he said. "Great to see you again!"

Blythe dumped the heavy volumes on Kermit's desk. Kermit reacted. "I asked for the history of Tao-Chung, not the entire 16th Dynasty that preceded it."

"Very droll!" Blythe said. "Actually, I rather wanted to be interviewed by you at Delancey's last night. Chief Strenlich can be somewhat intimating. Ex-marine, I understand."

"I am an ex-mercenary," Kermit said. "I don't intimidate anyone." Kermit paused. "I kill them!"

"You must be a joy at parties!" Blythe murmured.

"I don't get asked to many of those," Kermit said. "I just finished War and Peace last night. What's in here?"

"Oh yes, now then, everything about Tao-Chung," Blythe said, tapping the books on Kermit's desk. "He was a strange young man. Died mysteriously at the age of seventeen. Playing a game of all things."

"What kind of game?" Kermit asked.

"Well, you know, just folklore, sort of a Dungeons and Dragons I suppose you would call it today," Blythe said. "Yes, very odd. Emperor Tao-Chung was obsessed with this game. Played it day and night. And when he finally came into the inner sanctum, the temple, and found himself face to face with the Lord Dragon…"

"He died?" Kermit said.

Blythe nodded. "He could not take the excitement, do you suppose? Of winning?"

"What's the name of this game?" Kermit asked.

"It will be in here," Blythe said and assessed the large volumes he had brought. "Let me see."

"I need a word code," Kermit said, "something to access the Timeline database."

Blythe glanced up. "What?"

"Chinese secret service."

"Oh!" Blythe murmured.

"It could be in cyberspace if it's not in their program." Kermit smiled. "If not, I'll spend the rest of my natural life in a Mongolian Goulag." Blythe chuckled. "Along with you!"

Blythe looked back at him. "Good Lord!"

Blythe found the book he was looking for on Kermit's desk.

Captain Simms was in Caine's quarters. She was extremely distraught. Caine watched her carefully. "I can't reach my decision!" the Captain said. "I can't let them see me like this!"

Caine moved over to her. "Please! Sit down!"

Captain Simms moved to a chair. She was wearing a gray shirt and a pair of slacks. Her hair was disheveled. She had been crying. "Caine, I think I am having a crisis of confidence. I am not sure I am able to command any longer."

"These cannot be your words!" Caine objected.

"Last night I slapped a man in Delancey's because he tipped a drink on my shoulder," Captain Simms said. "He was a little bit drunk. It was an accident, but I was out of control."

"At times we are all like that," Caine said.

"Not you!"

Captain Simms got to her feet. She was very teary now. "All of the crime and violence and hatred. I am being overwhelmed by it! Because I have no one in my life! A broken marriage. A military man I never ever see. I have no personal life. I have no feelings."

"You have feeling for Kermit," Caine said.

She turned back to Caine. "You know about that?"

He gave her one of his iconic shrugs. Captain Simms sat back down again. "Does everyone know about that?" She reached into her purse for a tissue. "My feelings can be so intense! I cannot go on like this! I am going to offer my resignation to Commissioner Kincaid this afternoon!"

Caine knelt down beside Captain Simms, taking her hands in his. "You are in control of your emotions and fears. I can feel your tension being affected by someone else."

"But why would some dark force be controlling my emotions?" she asked, holding back her tears.

"To get to me," Caine said. "Others may be afflicted as well."

"What can I do?" Simms asked him.

"Understand these conflicts will pass," Caine told her. "Be calm in yourself. Know that your chi is protected in the inherent goodness that is within you."

Captain Simms took hold of Caine's hands. "Thank you, Caine." She kissed his hands. "You might forget to mention to your son that his Captain broke down and wept."

Caine nodded and smiled at her.

We were at the Museum of Life with Blythe and Peter. They moved toward the Tao-Chung exhibit in one part of the room. "Going through the Tao-Chung texts I came up with a name," Blythe said. "Wai-Chi. Rather inspired, I thought. Anyway, Wai-Chi was the inventor of a board game called Dragon's Lair."

"Board games!" Peter said. "I didn't think they had board games back then."

Peter and Blythe moved further into the museum where a death mask was prominently displayed. There were similar exhibits in glass cases around them. Blythe nodded. "Oh yes, board games were invented with the Pharaohs."

"I guess people had to amuse themselves before the days of ER and Melrose Place," Peter commented.

"Here we are!" Blythe said. "Now then, take a look at this!" He moved right up to the display of the demonic half-mask. "The mask of Wei-Chi!"

Peter shrugged. "So what?"

"But it was not part of the Tao-Chung Exhibition!" Blythe exclaimed. "It should not be here! I have never seen it before! It's as if someone had taken the Tao-Chung exhibit and put this in its place."

"Like a Tong thing?" Peter asked. "Maybe it is an acquisition you hadn't heard about."

"I'll check the records!" Blythe muttered to himself.

We went back to the Demon Lord who was surrounded by dark shadows. "I feel your anger, Caine!"

Caine was standing in front of the ajar French doors that led to his apartment. He had an earthen bowl in his hands. He, too, was filled with rage. He was thinking about Karen Simms.

"Why did you darken my friend's chi?" he demanded. "If I am your target, come to me!"

Caine threw the wooden bowl on the floor, shattering it in his anger.

In the museum, Blythe had an errand to run and left Peter to fend for himself. He picked up the death mask and turned it over in his hands. Then he set it back. He sensed the presence of someone else in the museum. He slowly backed away from the exhibit.

In the Games Room in the old mansion, Wally set out one of the gigantic figures. "The White Prince now battles for his life!"

Rick said: "I put the Demon Warrior against the White Prince!"

We went back in the museum. A Demon Warrior had entered, clad in ceremonial robes, carrying a spear. Peter whirled. A second Demon Warrior, an exact replica of the first one, moved to the display cases, wielding a sword. Then Peter faced a third Demon Warrior. The museum was deserted at this moment. Or perhaps it was all part of the delirium that had gripped Peter as he faced these fierce Warriors. A moment later Caine was at Peter's side.

They split up.

Peter tackled one of the Warriors who lunged at him with his sword. Peter disarmed him using classic kung fu moves that sent him to the floor. Caine dealt with the second Warrior, disarming his spear which also sent him to the floor of the exhibit. Peter turned to face the third Warrior. He still had the sword he had taken from the first Warrior. The third Warrior made several passes with his sword, which Peter parried. He lashed out with his sword, deflecting the Warrior's blows, until Peter was disarmed in the fight. Then Caine was beside him. He disarmed the Warrior. Peter and Caine, fighting as a team, took out the Warrior out and him dropped him to the floor of the Exhibit Hall. Peter looked down to see that all of the Warriors had completely vanished. He turned back to his father.

"How did you know I was in trouble?" he asked. "Dumb question! You always know when I am in trouble."

"It took all of my ability to see this happening!" Caine said. He was gasping for air. "Through the web he was weaving about my chi."

"What?" Peter was taken aback. "What web are you talking about? Pop, are you hurt?"

"My senses are on fire," Caine told him. "Pain fills my being."

In the Games Room in the shadowy interior of the mansion, Rick had become frustrated. "I won maximum points on that spell! Twenty points! The White Prince should be dead!"

"Yeah, but I moved the Dragon Lord to the realm of anarchy to help the White

Prince!" Cindy said, shouting back at Rick. "Because I moved 26 points! Now he is under my spell!"

"But you can't do that!" Rick protested. "That's against the rules!"

"I am the keeper of the rules," Wally said, quietly. "I say what she did was completely correct."

"Yeah, man, you just screwed up!" Kevin said.

Rick grabbed Kevin around the throat. "Watch it, boy! I have four times the strength in this game that you do!"

"But not enough to take on the White Prince!" Kevin retorted.

"You guys are taking this game much too seriously," Wally said.

Cindy said: "Okay. Who rolls next?"

"You do!" Wally said.

Cindy rolled the dice.

We were in Cindy's house. Rachel entered her daughter's bedroom. "Cindy! Kevin? Are you here?" She got no response. She did not want to search Cindy's room, but something drew her to do so. She opened a drawer in Cindy's desk and came up with some pages of demonic drawings. She looked at them in shock, particularly at a drawing of a hooded monk.

"Oh, my God!" she murmured.

At the 101st Precinct, the usual chatter around the place was subdued. We were in Kermit's office where Captain Simms was sitting on the floor. Kermit moved over to her and sat down on the floor beside her. "I will join you! What has happened to the cops in this Precinct?"

Captain Simms shook her head helplessly. "I don't know," she said.

"You went to see Caine?" Kermit asked her.

"He said we were being controlled by a dark force."

"A Dark Force?" Kermit said. "Maybe the same force that hijacked the museum artifacts? Captain, maybe you should take some personal time, you know? See your son Todd at the Military Academy. Crime will not stop! I will see to it. Tomorrow is another day!"

Kermit lifted the Captain up into his arms. She regarded him fondly and nodded. "I might do that!" She started to leave, then she leaned back and gave him a kiss on the cheek. "Thanks, Kermit."

She left him, moving out the office door. Kermit glanced down at the scrapbook he was holding where there was a picture of Captain Simms with her son Todd at the Military Academy.

The Captain entered the squad room which was hopping today. Skalany reacted to her. She handed out some chicken legs. "Captain! Chicken!"

"Thanks, Skalany!"

"You're welcome!" Simms handed the chicken leg to a fellow cop. "Happy chicken!"

She moved through the squad room and out the door. At the police counter, Cheryl and the Ancient were waiting to leave. Chief Strenlich was also there, as well as Rachel. "Let's get out of here!" Cheryl said, but the Ancient had turned to Rachel. "You are troubled! You need assistance?"

"Yes, I need to speak to a Police Officer," Rachel said. "It is about my daughter."

"Missing persons is next door!" Strenlich said, curtly. "Take a seat and wait your turn. We are short on detectives today." He stopped Cheryl and the Ancient. "If I find you were with Peter on the night of the robbery, I'll have him dealing out parking meters at midnight!"

Strenlich stormed off.

Kermit had noticed Rachel's distress and shook her hand. "Hello! I am Detective Griffin. Actually, I am the only detective in the Precinct on this particular day you want to talk to! Would you like to step into my office?"

Once they were inside Kermit's office, Rachel Foster sat across from Kermit's desk while he looked at the demonic drawings she had given him. "Cindy, my daughter, is a fine artist, but she has never drawn anything like this before. She tried to hide these sketches from me, I'm afraid."

"She and her friends are getting involved in some kind of a cult?" Kermit asked her.

"You think it can't ever happen to your daughter or your son," Rachel said, "but just watch the 11:00 news!"

Kermit smiled. "Something I try to avoid!" He came across one of the demonic sketches and it stopped him. "Tao-Chung!"

"There is an old house in our neighborhood, the Chung House," Rachel told him. "It is supposed to be haunted by demonic spirits. They have been seen from that house with some of their friends. I'm afraid of what might have happened in that house."

Kermit went through some other demonic drawings and stopped on another familiar figure. "Wei-Chi!" Kermit murmured.

"Does the figure mean something to you?" Rachel asked him, nervously.

"I believe it belongs to a friend of mine named Blythe," Kermit said. "You say this Chung House is in your neighborhood?"

"Two blocks from our house," Rachel said.

Kermit got to his feet and opened a file cabinet. He picked up his monster gun with its laser sight. Rachel reacted to it. Kermit smiled. "Never go to spooky old Chinese houses without it!" He motioned for Rachel Foster to join him.

We were sitting outside a café where Blythe was talking with Caine and Peter. He was shaking his head in amazement. "Warriors? From another plain of existence? In my museum?"

"I believe that forces of darkness are at work here," Caine said. "They have weakened me! Altered the behavior of my friends so I cannot turn to them. They tried to murder my son."

"And you are saying these forces have something to do with the museum robbery?" Peter asked him.

"Being as powerful as they are, they could have easily removed the exhibit that you speak of by shifting time and space," Caine said.

"But why?" Blythe asked.

"It is a game," Caine said. "A game that is being played."

"By this Wei-Chi fellow?" Blythe said.

Caine suddenly reached out a hand and gripped Blythe's wrist. "What name did you say?"

"Wei-Chi. It is an exhibit of a game at the Museum of Life. It is said he was responsible for the boy Emperor's death."

"By making him play a game," Caine said and nodded. "A game of death." He turned to Peter. "Do you remember, my son, in the temple? The irrational behavior that happened when you played your board game?"

We go to a *Flashback Sequence* here to Peter at the temple. In it, Master Khan and Ping Hi were striding to confront Caine. "We are taking over this temple, Caine!" Master Khan had vowed. His manner was entirely at odds with the behavior we have seen him display at the temple, especially when Master Khan's gentle demeanor had been noted in the Dragon's Wing episode.

Caine confronted Master Khan and Ping Hi. Master Khan immediately attacked him. Caine reeled from the unexpected attack. "You would usurp my position *by force?*" Caine demanded.

"If necessary!" Old Ping Hi exclaimed.

"My son has been playing that game!" Caine suddenly realized. "I have been blinded!" He was attacked by old Ping Hi and Master Khan. Caine made quick work of Ping Hi, but Master Khan was a formidable adversary. Caine dealt with him with a mixture of strength and compassion, which sent Master Khan down to the floor. Then Caine moved away from him. He entered a room where Young Peter was playing a board game. In this episode, Young Peter was again played by Robert Bednarski, who did a great job. There were two other teenagers playing the game in Young Peter's room. The demonic figures in the game had been set out on a board. Caine strode over and kicked the board over, spilling the game pieces to the floor. Young Peter leapt to his feet as did his two friends.

"Father!"

An angry Caine faced his son. "How long have you have been playing this game?" he demanded.

"For three days!" Young Peter admitted. "We found it in the Temple library."

"You found it because it was left for you to find it!" Caine told him. "This game has a malevolent life of its own!"

Caine left his son and his friends and moved to the temple steps. We saw the Dragon Master in his black robes with the intricate engraving on it. The Demon's face was hidden by the half-mask he wore. "Lo Wei, you are no longer welcome here!" Caine said. "The game has been destroyed! Your power is gone. You will leave here!"

The Demon Master gazed at Caine, his malevolent stare chilling. "We will play the game again, you and I, Kwai Chang Caine. Away from this protected environment."

Then the Demon Lord simply vanished from the temple steps. Old Ping Hi and Master Khan approached Caine. "Kwai Chang Caine, please forgive us!" Ping Hi said.

"We were not ourselves!" Master Khan told him.

"I know," Caine said. Young Peter came over. "I am sorry to have destroyed your game," Caine said.

"That's okay," Young Peter said. "It was evil?"

"Yes! But the evil has been banished." Caine added: "For now."

We came out of this *Flashback Sequence* to Peter and Caine sitting at their table at the outdoor cafe. "I do remember!" Peter said. "So Wei-Chi is back?" Caine nodded. "Manipulating our friends at the Precinct? So why am I not infected?"

"Your chi is strong," Caine said. He looked away and saw Kermit and Rachel moving up to them. "So is Kermit's!"

"Well, if that's true, Pop," Peter said, "who is playing this game?"

"I think I can answer that!" Kermit said as he arrived with Rachel. Caine and Blythe got up from the table. Peter joined them.

Kermit made the introductions. "This is Rachel Bellows. Her friends and her daughter have been playing a special Kung Fu Dungeons and Dragons game at this very moment."

"You got a location?" Peter asked him.

"Oh, yeah," Kermit said. "And I believe that we will find your stolen museum exhibits there, Mr. Blythe."

"Right!" Blythe said.

"Rachel, stay with Blythe," Caine said. "We will find your daughter and their friends and take them from harm."

"Jolly good!" Blythe said.

He sat back down again. Caine and Peter moved through the tables in the street. Blythe glanced down at his watch. Rachel shook her head. "I can't stand this! I am going to the Chung House!"

Blythe shook his head. "No, really! I do not think that is a good idea. This must be very exciting, but I think you should leave it to the police and…"

Blythe looked around and realized that his audience had abandoned him! "Oh, good Lord!"

He jumped up to follow Rachel.

We were outside the Chung House. Inside, Peter and Kermit moved forward through the overlapping shadows. "This particular game was what my father was talking about!" Peter said. "These characters in the Dragon's Lair are the ones we were looking for, right Pop?" Peter glanced behind Kermit. "Pop?" With more conviction: "Pop?"

Inside the Chung House, Cindy had her hand on Kevin's shoulder, berating him as she stormed forward through the shadows. "We're at the first level!" she exclaimed. "We're closing in on the Dragon Lord's temple!"

From behind them, Wally said: "Okay! Just play the game! Kevin rolls next!"

The Game Players sat down at their usual table. Kevin rolled the dice.

An Ancient Warrior moved down the staircase in the house. Another Ancient Warrior moved down a corridor outside. Kermit and Peter pulled their guns.

"Welcome committee!" Kermit said.

"You guys just don't learn!" Peter said.

Peter and Kermit entered the fight. Peter made short work of the Ancient Warrior, sending him to the ground. Kermit exchanged blows with his attacker, using his fists to send his Warrior to the floor. Peter looked down at his assailant, who had mysteriously disappeared.

Kermit looked around them. "My gun's gone!"

Peter looked at the floor. "Mine too!"

Caine was in another room of the mansion where he had picked up a large book. It had a circular design on it. "I call upon my *brother Shambala* to help me face this foe!" Caine set the book on a table. "Grant me passage to his land!"

Caine felt a bright light invading his senses and then he simply vanished from the room! A moment later we picked up Caine moving down the temple stairs which was covered with an eerie, drifting mist.

Peter and Kermit ran down the long staircase that led to the first floor. Peter looked around them. "This is impossible!" he said, frustrated. "These rooms are right back where we started!"

"Unless the rooms were moving," Kermit said. "These kids are here somewhere!"

"And where is my father?" Peter asked, anxiously.

He and Kermit climbed to the first floor of the mansion. All the rooms were laid out in the same places! They came to another ornate staircase. They climbed down and found themselves back in the same hallway. Peter was beyond frustrated. "Same corridor! Back where we started!"

"Not quite," Kermit said. "See that door?" Kermit pointed to a door in the corridor. "It wasn't there before!"

Kermit whistled a spooky tune and he and Peter moved down the corridor.

In the temple room, with its drifting fog, the Dragon Lord was dressed in his black robes with his half-mask hiding most of his face. "Welcome, Kwai Chang Caine!" he intoned in his sing-song voice. "Or I should say, Dragon Lord? Welcome to my domain! It took me a long time to weave a spell that would deaden a Shambala Master's senses."

Caine turned around to face the Dragon Lord. "Release the children from the game!" Caine insisted. "The fight is between you and me! Good and evil! A fight that should have been engaged in the temple long ago!"

"It was not the right time!" The Dragon Lord said. "I had to wait until you had friends! Until your son was grown. Until you had a life that could be disrupted."

Back in the mansion, Rachel Foster walked down the long staircase to find herself on the ground floor. She was suddenly grabbed by one of the Mongolian Warriors and dragged away.

Kermit and Peter were in another room. They had flashlights which they shone around them. "There's your Tao-Chung exhibit!" Kermit told him.

Peter clutched Kermit's arm. "Kermit! I remember this game!" He picked some of the life-size figures from the Game Board. "I used to play it when I was a kid!"

Then Peter and Kermit whirled. Our four stalwart Games Players were standing in front of them. Rick and Cindy looked grotesque, as if their features had been altered. Wally and Kevin stood beside them. Cindy was carrying a spear. Their faces were barely recognizable. They projected a presence of pure evil.

"Not the way we play the game!" Rick said.

"The White Prince and his trained warrior!" Cindy said, contemptuously.

"They cannot be allowed to live!" Wally said.

"They cannot leave this place!" Kevin echoed.

In the temple, still spewing its unnerving mist, Caine faced his sworn enemy. The Dragon Lord circled around Caine, using lightning-fast kung fu moves on him. Caine was ready for him with some moves of his own. Caine and the Dragon Master clashed. The Demon kicked out at Caine, throwing him back. Caine came back at him, using his signature double-kick to drive the Dragon Master back. One of the Mongolian Warriors attacked Caine. Caine fought him off, sending him to the temple floor. A second Warrior lunged at Caine. Caine dealt with him, only to face a third Mongolian Warrior who leapt at him.

In the Games Room, Wally lunged at Kermit with a sword. Kermit avoided the blows, dancing away. Rick lunged at Kermit with a spear. He kept away from the murderous blows, trying not to hurt any of the kids. Cindy lunged at Peter with her spear. Peter deftly sidestepped the deadly weapon, but then Kevin got in the act, trying to slash at Peter.

On the temple floor the Dragon Master had hold of Rachel. But she slipped out of his grasp, running through the drifting mist that was now obscuring everything.

"Caine!" she cried out.

Caine grabbed Rachel's arm, holding out the large book we had seen him take on the temple steps. "Take the book!" he said, urgently. "As long as you hold the book, he cannot harm you!"

She backed away from him.

Caine whirled to face the Demon Master again.

In the living room Martin Blythe descended the stairs. He moved around the shadowy corridor and picked up Kermit's and Peter's guns. He straightened up with an expression that said: "Once more into the breach!" Then he moved forward. "Oh, well! Tally Ho!"

In the rooms off the first floor, Peter fought off Kevin. Cindy lunged at him with her spear. Peter fought her off with sword blows. He let Kevin go, who stumbled away from him. Kermit grabbed the spear that Rick wielded. He tried to pry it loose in his hands. Wally was also trying to stab Kermit.

In the temple room, Caine once again faced the Demon Lord. He used some major kung fu moves to send him sprawling. In the living room, Peter impaled the spear into a large basket. He grabbed the Board Game and threw it down to the floor, scattering the various game pieces around him.

"The spell is broken!" Peter said.

Kermit was fending off Wally's sword with a spear when Wally seemed to come to his senses. Rick moved over to Wally, as if trying to make sense of his murderous behavior. "What just happened?"

Blythe entered the room from another doorway. "Everyone all right?" he asked. He saw Kermit move forward. Blythe held out the firepower. "Your guns, I believe?"

Kermit actually smiled. "Talk about the cavalry!"

Peter came forward and grabbed his gun from Blythe. "I will take that!"

Kermit caught his own gun.

In the temple room, Caine finished the Demon Lord off with three kicks which sent him to the temple steps. Rachel was hugging the large book to her.

Caine turned to her. "Use the book!" he told her. "Don't be afraid!"

Rachel opened the book. A white light pulsed from it. Then it was gone and so were the Mongolian Warriors. The temple stairs just held the obscuring fog.

They were now deserted.

The Demon Lord had completed vanished.

Much later we were in Delancey's Restaurant and Bar. The place was hopping, as always. Peter moved to where Blake was sitting at one of the booths. "Did you take back the suit?"

"Yeah," Blake said. "It didn't fit!"

He laughed. Peter moved over to the bar where Chief Strenlich was pouring himself a beer. "Chief, I just got back from the museum. The Tao-Chung is back where it belongs. But now, the Tao-Chung exhibit is missing."

"Put it in your report!" Strenlich advised. "Do you think Mr. Blythe is going to worry about a missing statue? Good work, Detective." Strenlich waved a dismissive hand. "Did you think I was going to bite your head off?"

Jody moved to where Peter was standing. She had changed her clothes and was now wearing jeans and a t-shirt. "Is this more in keeping with a Detective 3rd Grade?" she asked him.

"Actually, I was getting fond of the other outfit." Peter confessed. "Particularly when it was so… close!" Jody blushed. Peter moved on to where Captain Simms was sitting at the bar looking at a magazine. "How are you doing, Captain?" he asked her.

"Better after talking to the most important people in my life!" she said.

"What makes me think I am not one of them?" Peter asked.

Captain Simms just smiled at him.

Caine was sitting on a couch across from Blythe. The Ancient and Cheryl were sitting across the table. Caine reached a hand to stop Detective Mary Margaret Skalany who was passing by. "About that picnic, Mary Margaret?" Caine asked her. "I really don't have anything to do this weekend."

"Oh, okay then!" Mary Margaret said, holding Caine's hands. "I'll pick you up at eight! I will not be late. By the way…" She leaned over and gave Caine a kiss on the cheek. "Happy Birthday!"

Skalany moved off. Caine glared at the Ancient. His smile was benevolent. "I say nothing!"

Blythe jumped into the conversation. "I knew all about it!" he said. He motioned to one of the servers who stopped. "Oh, excuse me!" He had decided to order in code! "One 'Blythe', a Stinger, a Rob Roy and a glass of Chardonnay."

"Water would be sufficient for me!" Caine said.

The server moved away.

Caine saw Rachel and Cindy enter the bar. "Ah!" Caine got to his feet to greet them with a small bow.

"I was told you would be here!" Rachel said. "I wanted to thank you for not harming my daughter!" Peter joined his father with a glass of wine in his hand. "And for rescuing me from that temple, or wherever I was taken!" she added.

"The evil has passed," Caine assured her. "You need not fear again."

"Well, that's good!" Cindy said. "Because the Chung House has been sold and a family is moving in tomorrow. I can't wait to tell them all the cool stuff that happened!"

But Caine was suddenly troubled. He moved away from Peter. Peter knew the signs.

"What's up, Pop?"

But Caine was not listening to him. He just said: "There is somewhere I need to be."

And he left Peter.

From out of the shadows, the Demon Lord waited. "Our battle is not over yet," he said, ominously.

For a moment Caine stood outside the Chung House, looking up at one of the windows in the mansion. It flared with a brilliant light, then the light died away.

Caine was filled with a foreboding of what was still coming for them out of the darkness.

Epilogue
KUNG FU: THE LEGEND CONTINUES

THERE WERE MANY MORE STORYLINES which I could have recounted for *Kung Fu: The Legend Continues*, some of them provocative, some charming and some of them harrowing. Here are a few examples:

May I Ride With You? Kwai Chang Caine got the opportunity to spend a day with his son Peter as they drove around the city solving crimes.

The Bardo was an emotional rollercoaster ride for Caine when he encountered a mind-altering drug to save a young woman's life.

The Chinatown Murder Mystery: The Case of the Poisoned Hand -- The episode was a valentine for an old-style murder mystery.

Dragon's Wing II brought back the talents of Robert Vaughn and Patrick Macnee and this time they were joined by another detective icon, "*The Saint*".

The First Temple was the site of the "First Temple" that Caine and Peter ever visited.

Illusion took place in a Magic Castle-style nightclub setting.

Shadow Assassin had Kwai Chang Caine in the shadows fighting for his life.

Chill Ride took place in a carnival setting where Caine and Peter went undercover.

Plague told the story of Caine, Peter and the Precinct gang being infected by a sinister plague. ***Circle of Light*** spotlighted a harrowing airplane crash that Caine and Peter survived.

Escape took take place in a North Korean prison camp where Caine, Peter and Kermit were incarcerated and their efforts to escape.

Blackout found Caine and Peter during a major blackout that had hit the city.

Who is Kwai Chang Caine? was an episode where it appeared that Caine had taken the role of a notorious gangster.

Obviously there were many more episodes of *Kung Fu: The Legend Continues* I could mention, but these highlights illustrated the diverse scope of the various storylines.

For me personally, this series came to represent the many ways for me to tell a story. I will always be grateful for that opportunity.

Index

Printed in the USA
CPSIA information can be obtained
at www.ICGtesting.com
LVHW012118120823
755063LV00011B/270